Data Excess in Digital Media Research

Data Excess in Digital Media Research

EDITED BY

NATALIE ANN HENDRY
The University of Melbourne, Australia

AND

INGRID RICHARDSON
RMIT University, Australia

United Kingdom – North America – Japan – India – Malaysia – China

Emerald Publishing Limited
Emerald Publishing, Floor 5, Northspring, 21-23 Wellington Street, Leeds LS1 4DL

First edition 2025

Editorial matter and selection © 2025 Natalie Ann Hendry and Ingrid Richardson.
Individual chapters © 2025 The authors.
Published under exclusive licence by Emerald Publishing Limited.

Reprints and permissions service
Contact: www.copyright.com

No part of this book may be reproduced, stored in a retrieval system, transmitted in any form or by any means electronic, mechanical, photocopying, recording or otherwise without either the prior written permission of the publisher or a licence permitting restricted copying issued in the UK by The Copyright Licensing Agency and in the USA by The Copyright Clearance Center. Any opinions expressed in the chapters are those of the authors. Whilst Emerald makes every effort to ensure the quality and accuracy of its content, Emerald makes no representation implied or otherwise, as to the chapters' suitability and application and disclaims any warranties, express or implied, to their use.

British Library Cataloguing in Publication Data
A catalogue record for this book is available from the British Library

ISBN: 978-1-80455-945-1 (Print)
ISBN: 978-1-80455-944-4 (Online)
ISBN: 978-1-80455-946-8 (Epub)

Printed and bound by CPI Group (UK) Ltd, Croydon, CR0 4YY

INVESTOR IN PEOPLE

Contents

List of Figures	vii
About the Editors	ix
About the Contributors	xi
Acknowledgements	xiii
Chapter 1 Introduction: Digital Data, Research Ethos and Haunting *Natalie Ann Hendry and Ingrid Richardson*	1
Chapter 2 Reframing Data Excess *Rowan Wilken*	13
Chapter 3 Unanticipated Excess: Inescapable Moments and Uneasy Feelings *Ben Lyall, Josie Reade and Claire Moran*	25
Chapter 4 The Digital Mess of a Digital Ethnography *Clare Southerton*	39
Chapter 5 'Digital Hoarding' and Embracing Data Excess in Digital Cultures Research *Natalie Ann Hendry*	55
Chapter 6 The Epistemic Culture of Data Minimalism: Conducting an Ethnography of Travel Influencers *Christian S. Ritter*	69

Chapter 7 Embodied Excess: Interpreting Haptic Mobile Media Practices   87
Jess Hardley and Ingrid Richardson

Chapter 8 Re-engaging With Excess Data: Newbie Researchers, Tumblr and the Evolving Research Event   105
Navid Sabet

Chapter 9 Museums, Smart Cities and Big Data: How Can We Transform Data Excess Into Data Intelligence?   123
Natalia Grincheva

Chapter 10 Evaluation, Digital Data and Excess(es) in Health Interventions   139
Benjamin Hanckel

Index   155

List of Figures

Chapter 4

Fig. 4.1.	Author's Replication of Mattel's Barbie Instagram Story, 20th March 2020.	46
Fig. 4.2.	Author's Replication of Facebook COVID-19 Information Pop-Up, 15th August 2020.	47
Fig. 4.3.	Author's Replication of Social Media Posts Captured in 2020 (Original Screenshots Not Included to Preserve Privacy and Copyright).	49

Chapter 6

Fig. 6.1.	Clusters of a YouTube Recommender Network.	79
Fig. 6.2.	Cluster of Ultra-High-Definition Vlogs About Walking Tours.	81
Fig. 6.3.	Cluster of Videos About River Cruises.	82

About the Editors

Natalie Ann Hendry is a Senior Lecturer in Youth Wellbeing in the Faculty of Education, University of Melbourne. Previously, she was a member of the Digital Ethnography Research Centre (DERC), RMIT University, and a Lecturer in Health and Wellbeing at Deakin University. Natalie's research investigates the relationships between education, health and media in young adults' lives. Her current work explores the pedagogical relationship between social media and psychotherapy and how digital finance cultures influence finance and investing practices. Her first book, *Tumblr* (Polity Press), was released in 2021 and co-authored with Katrin Tiidenberg and Crystal Abidin.

Ingrid Richardson is a Professor of Digital Media at RMIT University, Australia. She has published on a wide range of topics, including philosophy of technoscience, virtual and augmented reality, games and mobile media, social media and participatory network cultures and the phenomenology of media practices. Recent books include *Understanding Games and Game Cultures* (Sage, 2021) with Larissa Hjorth and Hugh Davies; *Bodies and Mobile Media* (Polity Press, 2023) with Rowan Wilken; and *Containment: Technologies of Holding, Filtering, Leaking* (Meson, 2024) with Marie-Luise Angerer, Hannah Schmedes and Zoë Sofoulis.

About the Contributors

Natalia Grincheva is a Programme Leader in Arts Management at LASALLE, University of Arts Singapore, and an Honorary Senior Research Fellow in the Digital Studio at the University of Melbourne. She is an internationally recognised expert on innovative forms and global trends in contemporary museology, digital diplomacy and international cultural relations. She has received many prestigious international academic awards, including Fulbright (2007–2009), Quebec Fund (2011–2013) and Australian Endeavour (2012–2013). In 2020, she was awarded Oxford Fellowship for her visiting research residency at the Digital Diplomacy Research Centre at the University of Oxford. She is the author of three monographs *Geopolitics of Digital Heritage* (Cambridge University Press, 2024), *Museum Diplomacy in the Digital Age* (Routledge, 2020) and *Global Trends in Museum Diplomacy* (Routledge, 2019).

Benjamin Hanckel (he/him) is a Sociologist at the Institute for Culture and Society at Western Sydney University. Benjamin's research explores youth health and wellbeing, social inequalities in health and social change. His work has a particular focus on the design and use of digital technologies for health and wellbeing.

Jess Hardley is a Research Fellow at Edith Cowan University in the ARC Centre of Excellence for the Digital Child. Her interdisciplinary research primarily focuses on ethnography, feminist theories of embodiment, and mobile media practices. Her research has been published in *Australian Feminist Studies, Convergence,* and *Gender and Education*. She also serves as an editorial board member of the journal *Digital Geography and Society*.

Ben Lyall is a Digital Sociologist, teaching and researching in the Faculty of Arts at Monash University. He is interested in how social lives are impacted by digital infrastructures and smart devices. Using digital mixed method approaches, his work explores education, employment, health and wellbeing and citizen relationships with public services.

Claire Moran is a Research Fellow with Action Lab at Monash University. Her research examines the use of digital technologies by marginalised and disadvantaged communities, particularly those from migrant backgrounds. Her doctoral research explored the everyday social media practices and experiences of Black

African Australian young people, the findings of which have been published in *Media, Culture & Society*, the *Journal of Youth Studies* and *Media International Australia*.

Josie Reade is a PhD candidate in the Faculty of Education at the University of Melbourne. Her research interests include the body, gender, youth and social media. Josie's doctoral research takes up a feminist new materialist approach to explore women's lived experiences and embodied practices of posting and engaging with fitspo (fitness inspiration) content on Instagram. Her work has been published in *New Media & Society*.

Christian S. Ritter is a Senior Lecturer in the Department of Geography, Media and Communication at Karlstad University, Sweden. Christian held fellowships at the Centre of Excellence in Media Innovation and Digital Culture, Tallinn University, and in the Department of Social Anthropology, Norwegian University of Science and Technology. He has conducted long-term fieldwork in Estonia, Ireland, Norway, Singapore, Turkey and the United Kingdom. He is a co-chair of the working group on Migration and Mobility, International Society of Ethnology and Folklore (SIEF). His work was published in the *Journal of Contemporary Religion*, *Qualitative Research*, *Anthropology of the Middle East* and *Tourism Geographies*. He is the author of the book *Locating the Influencer: Place and Platform in Global Tourism* (Emerald, forthcoming).

Navid Sabet is a Social Researcher with an interest in education, media, creative arts and social theory. In addition to his research, he works as a Teacher, Learning Designer and Creative Practitioner.

Clare Southerton is a Lecturer in Digital Technology and Pedagogy in the School of Education at La Trobe University. Her research explores how social media platforms and other digital technologies are used for learning and sharing knowledge. Her work has explored digital youth cultures, surveillance and privacy and digital health education. She is a co-author of *The Face Mask in COVID Times: A Sociomaterial Analysis* (De Gruyter, 2021) and a co-editor of the forthcoming book *Researching Contemporary Wellness Cultures* (Emerald, 2024). Her work has been published *in New Media & Society*, *Social Media + Society* and the *International Journal of Communication*.

Rowan Wilken is an Associate Professor in Media and Communication and an Associate Investigator in the ARC Centre of Excellence for Automated Decision-Making and Society (ADM+S), RMIT University, Melbourne, Australia. His research is focused on mobile and locative media, media and communication infrastructures and digital media platforms. His most recent books include *Bodies and Mobile Media* (Polity, 2023, with Ingrid Richardson), *Everyday Data Cultures* (Polity, 2022, with Jean Burgess, Kath Albury, and Anthony McCosker) and *Wi-Fi* (Polity, 2021, with Julian Thomas and Ellie Rennie).

Acknowledgements

Collating a book and writing chapters about the 'leftovers' of digital research often means working in our 'spare' time. We thank our contributors for enthusiastically returning to their excess data amidst the demands of life and work and for their continued interest in the project over a number of years.

Natalie and Ingrid would also like thank the team at Emerald Publishing for their patience and support and our colleagues at the Digital Ethnography Research Centre (DERC) where the idea for this book first sparked into life.

Chapter 1

Introduction: Digital Data, Research Ethos and Haunting

Natalie Ann Hendry[a] *and Ingrid Richardson*[b]

[a]The University of Melbourne, Australia
[b]RMIT University, Australia

Abstract

What do we do with the excess data from our research? 'Excess' – particularly in digital media research – is inevitable. It emerges in the research process as the 'debris' and 'leftovers' from planning, fieldwork and writing; the words cut from drafts and copied to untouched and forgotten files; and the data archived but never analysed or published. From our conversations with colleagues, to our call for contributors, we repeatedly heard researchers' stories of digital data overflow, as they shared a collective sense of excess data as *something more* than that which is simply left out of formal research outputs. Digital excess, in particular, holds discursive flexibility: it points to abundance and possibility but also to our failure to control or contain information. Excess data matter, but how and why they do is somewhat opaque and largely underexplored.

This book, *Data Excess in Digital Media Research*, is a dedicated collection that pays attention to excess data. We position 'excess' as a conceptual, methodological, ethical and pragmatic challenge and opportunity for digital media research – we examine what happens when media researchers return to their surplus archives and explore the labour and affects surrounding data overflow and excess. We suggest that data excess is – or should be – a central concern for digital media scholars because of the methodological characteristics of digital media research, the 'research ethos' around data excess and the unexpected affects and 'hauntings' of excess data. This introduction provides an overview of these concerns and outlines each chapter.

Keywords: Digital media; digital research; digital data; data excess; digital ethnography; research methodology

Introduction

What do we do with the excess data from our research? What do we do with what is left over? 'Excess' – particularly in digital media research – is inevitable. It emerges in the research process as the 'debris' and 'leftovers' from planning, fieldwork and writing; the words cut from drafts and copied to untouched and forgotten files; and the data archived but never analysed or published. Digital excess holds discursive flexibility: it points to abundance and possibility but also to our failure to control or contain information, a shared experience of never having enough time or resources to tie up all the loose ends of our theorising, thinking and writing. Sometimes, we might return to this excess and transform it into something more productive or purposeful, but often, it remains unacknowledged or cast aside in our research endeavours.

And yet our lack of attention to excess data does not mirror how intensely familiar it is to us as researchers and scholars. Excess data hold intimate impressions (and burdens) on us and symbolically mark our unfinished labour. As editors of this book, we are cognizant of the imprints of excess data in our own work and explicitly recognised excess' hold when we separately presented our work in seminars at the Digital Ethnography Research Centre at RMIT University in 2020.

From our conversations with colleagues, to our call for contributors as we compiled this book's proposal, we repeatedly heard researchers' stories of data overflow, as they shared a collective sense of excess data as *something more* than that which is simply left out of formal research outputs. What was striking to us was that grappling with this excess was common among *all* scholars of contemporary media culture, at times experienced as a lost opportunity but also as a kind of affective intensity or embodied response to its presence. The problem of 'too much' digital data or information is now mundane; the volume and overwhelm produced by the digital is not exceptional. For Clay Shirky (2010), this broader problem is 'not information overload. It's filter failure'. But for researchers, is data excess merely a filter problem? How then do we imagine and enact filters and boundaries for research to manage material, theoretical and pragmatic overload? How can and do researchers or projects embrace excess, even if only in the early brainstorming stages of project development? What opportunities might excess offer us for different methods, processes and modes of analysis or conceptual thinking? Such questions point to why this book is important – we are familiar with this excess but there has not been a collective interrogation of what it is or how it functions in our work. Excess data matter, but how and why they do is somewhat opaque and largely underexplored.

While these challenges and feelings of excess and too much data are familiar to qualitative and quantitative scholars alike, they are especially critical for digital media researchers. Media, internet and technology researchers know the possibilities and problems of 'excess' and 'TMI' – too much information – intimately. Not only does the (often unrealised) promise of big data to capture everything haunt our projects, but our media and technology interests and digital fields are expansive and perpetually being made and remade as content and data are reposted, shared and circulated through devices, apps and platforms. Our research projects and sites may end, but our research histories continue to follow us on social media through algorithmic and archival functions. This speaks to both the characteristics of digital data as much as to how we approach our research as a knowledge-making practice.

This book is a dedicated collection that pays attention to these and other dimensions of excess data. We position 'excess' as a conceptual, methodological, ethical and pragmatic challenge and opportunity for digital media research. We examine what happens when media researchers return to their surplus archives and knowledge and explore the labour and affects surrounding data overflow and excess.

We suggest that there are, at least, three reasons why data excess is – or should be – a central concern for digital media scholars. These interconnected concerns relate to the methodological characteristics of data collected through media research, the 'research ethos' around data excess and the implications of inclusion and exclusion, and the unexpected affects, productivities and 'hauntings' of excess data. Each of the chapters in the collection responds in some way to these concerns and grapples with the implications of excess data in different contexts and under different social, cultural and political conditions. Attending to these three concerns offers not only reassurance to other scholars confronting similar challenges but also provokes us to ethically reconsider what we do, or do not do, with excess data in our own research practices.

Methodologies of Excess in Digital Media Research

This book explores data that are inherently digital in form as well as data concerning the digital – digital practices, digital cultures and digital politics – that may or may not be collected as digital content. This distinction is, of course, slippery, especially as we might transform non-digital data to digital data through the research process: conversations are recorded and transcribed into digital documents; group workshop notes on poster paper are photographed, uploaded and tagged in research management software; and field notes and concept maps are scanned into laptop folders. We might do this for many reasons: work efficiency, safe care and stewardship, indexing and classifying, analysis or statistical processing.

The transformation, and often multiplication, of digital, material and bodily traces and objects happens through our actions: scanning, transcribing, copying, converting, formatting and reformatting, publishing and circulating. These activities amplify what comprises data and produce excess through transformation, often to make research work more efficiently or available 'all in one place' across screens, digital folders and archives. Likewise, much of the paradata we work with – the 'by-products' of research like letters, interviewer notes and correspondence (Goodwin et al., 2017) – are digital too. This includes emails to informants to confirm interview times, digitised lists of codes and notes, scanned ethics consent forms, notifications of new instances of keywords or hashtags on the platforms we are tracking and other mundane research processes such as saving and archiving screenshots to augment researcher memory. In her observation of health workers' use of TikTok and other social media platforms in Chapter 4, *Clare Southerton* considers the excess and seemingly 'unrelated' screenshots within her digital ethnography project during the COVID-19 pandemic. Southerton returns to these 'offcuts' alongside her recollections of her social media use during the pandemic, as a 'layering of everyday experiences'. Her work reveals the 'messy entanglement' of digital ethnography which has been intensified during pandemic lockdowns. Southerton seeks to think through the more-than-digital boundaries implicit in qualitative media and digital ethnography research, via an analysis of 'excess' screenshots.

Digital data and digital formats also pose issues related to digital data's quantitative differences (e.g. accessibility and volume of data) rather than qualitative (e.g. visual versus textual data) characteristics (Quinton & Reynolds, 2018). Yet these qualitative and quantitative characteristics of digital data are entangled. In Chapter 6, *Christian S. Ritter* addresses this problematic, drawing on ethnographic fieldwork with travel influencers to critically explore the collection of what he terms 'natively digital data', or data that is retrieved through the data infrastructures and algorithmic recommender systems of platforms such as YouTube. Such data can be analysed through computational network analysis and network visualisations, which differs from the more nuanced analysis of ethnographic material. At this methodological intersection, Ritter considers the 'boundaries' between these two forms of data, and how the integrity of the latter might be strengthened in the age of big data.

The volume of data available to us depends on different material, social and symbolic constraints. For example, what we can record from Instagram as researchers 'lurking' on a food cafe profile is different from the data available to social media managers with access to engagement metrics for that profile. Again, what data are, or could be, is very different for engineers working to modify the Instagram interface as compared to the data that researchers, managers, cafe owners and the public scroll through. The data available for this imagined food cafe is multiplied, not only through multiple posts ordered on the cafe's grid, but via posts that are reshared as Stories, reorganised on the profile's highlights or shared by loyal customers who follow the cafe and repost content to their own profiles or other platforms. Our data have materiality, whether through devices and hardware, and the metadata related to these digital traces and relationships also offer another layer of networked and aggregated data. As follower metrics and geotags become linked to photographs and comments, these likely change as data move between and through platforms, devices and servers. Digital data produce (more) digital data. This digital accessibility to a platform's digital data and content is shaped by the social and technological engagements of different people, groups and devices. This, consequently, produces different forms of digital data. Extracting data from digital platforms, software and apps is not necessarily simple, as this changes what is already an unstable context, impacting how the data are then used and understood socially, and whether the relationships that are part of the data are removed or ignored.

As Ritter's chapter highlights, big data offers a particular challenge as a source of excess digital data. The promise of big data is that we can make our boundaries expansive, make everything important and make it all matter. Being able to include everything – another part of the promise – will allow us to better calculate what is happening now and what will happen in the future. As digital researchers we are more cautious about whether the promises and claims of big data do, or could ever, become realised. As Annette Markham (2017, p. 512) suggests, the 'value... of big data is overstated, many faulty logics and premises about data, truth, and algorithmic computation can end up influencing how we make sense of the world around us'. In response, Markham frames data as both a thing and an ideology and argues that we need to focus our attention on interpretation rather than data collection or the data themselves. Here, we might add that how we understand data as excess (or not) is part of this attention to data interpretation, not only collection. What we might have once discarded as excess or leftovers may require closer attention to test any potential faulty premises about our data and how we understand our research contexts and the broader world.

Assumptions about digital data shape not only claims made about research findings but also how researchers engage across interdisciplinary divides and research domains. Writing about digital ethnography within the field of youth mental health, in Chapter 5, *Natalie Ann Hendry* explores data excess as potentially productive through the concept of 'digital hoarding'. She highlights how digital archiving practices that eschew coherent hierarchies, neat, organised digital folders or a clear sense of why data has been archived offer an approach to research that champions creativity and curiosity. Hendry shares her fieldwork processes where this excessive digital data, hoarded in chaotic folders and often multiplied many times over, is generative rather than constraining.

Ethics, Visibility and Waste

Excess data emerge through the research process. The conditions that produce excess data or designate certain research objects, products or processes as excessive are varied and exist not only because of the characteristics of the digital, as the chapters across this collection illustrate. We might also identify data as excess because they fall outside our research foci at a specific time and place, or because they are not helpful in addressing key themes and research questions. Perhaps they are discarded in the process of searching for key terms in transcript texts, or when data is 'cleansed' as irrelevant in Twitter scrapings or image files.

Rather than simply noting that excess data are only what remains outside our inclusion criteria or scope of interest, we suggest a broader take on the overlapping research practices of data identification, selection, collection and analysis. We wrap these research activities together through the notion of 'research as ethos'. By focusing on research ethos, we are engaging with Lauren Rickards, Wendy Steele, Olga Kokshagina and Oli Moraes' (2020, p. 3) work which shifts *research impact* towards *research ethos* in a way that 'does not externalise "the real world" but sees academia as part of it and researchers as partners within dynamic innovation ecosystems, willing and able to use their unique capabilities to help generate the positive transformational changes needed'. In this way, data selection and analysis are bound up in knowledge-making, dissemination and translation (now and into the future), rather than simply a discrete, post-research event, where the context of research programmes, fieldwork processes and community and stakeholder interactions take on particular importance.

Here, excess data are not represented, controlled or contained; they might be raw data, waiting for some sort of process, ritual or practice to be transformed. These data might become part of our research through automation and data scraping, or data collected, stored and not 'analysed' or engaged with. What becomes excess in research holds an implicit judgement that it does not fit our research ethos. That is, what constitutes excess data, or not, involves *ethical* decisions. We produce hierarchies and criteria and (re-)designate data as being valuable or not in line with how our research is entangled with our social, political and ethical worlds. While our methodologies shape what is and can be understood as research data, our experiences and values as researchers also shape how data are made, in any given moment, period, context or place, as excess. This is particularly the case in our decisions about how to reconcile big data sets with diversity, or how to faithfully and inclusively capture the spectrum of lived experience. As *Ingrid Richardson* and *Jess Hardley* explore in Chapter 7, everyday mobile media practices are culturally and corporeally variable and idiosyncratic, reflecting the never-settled 'multistabilities' of our human–technology relations. They point out that in ethnographic research, the documentation and interpretation of such complexity can only ever be partial, as variation can be found in every 'body' – or to put it another way, our embodiment of media interfaces is always contingent on a myriad of intersecting factors including gender, age, location, socio-economic and cultural context, media and technical literacies, bodily dis/abilities and differences and the 'mess' of feelings and affects that accompany all our communicative practices. Translating lived experience into published outcomes is inevitably an act of constraint, as we continually make ethical decisions about what aspects of that experience to include or leave out.

Data excess is a problem – or opportunity – that speaks to the boundaries and scope of our inquiries and research ethos. The work that produces and defines our fields of research often happens – materially and discursively – at the borders of inclusion and exclusion: how we continually define the parameters of what data are scraped; how we engage with sorting processes to 'clean up' data that are deemed irrelevant now or later to our research interests; and how we talk with colleagues and communities about what remains within our data sets. Our research questions do this boundary work too. We are also responsible to our informants and participants, our research fields and assemblages, our communities and contexts. Is it ethical to archive excess data without making it productive for others' or towards social change? Is it more ethical to close a data archive if we cannot control how it might be used in the future?

Boundaries of a field and what constitutes it are *produced* through research rather than being an existing pre-research phenomenon or simply what we might see within an app or browser window. For digital ethnographers and media researchers, what we notice does this boundary work: what we record, note, track and write. In his analysis of the boundary work we mobilise around what comprises *enough* data, Rowan Wilken addresses the crucial issue of data saturation within qualitative media research in Chapter 2. What does one do with data that is considered to reside outside the parameters of sufficiency, or data that never makes it into reports and publications and might otherwise be perceived as research waste? In this chapter, Wilken revisits the excess data that was gathered as part of a large collaborative research project investigating locative media and explores its contextual significance and ongoing relevance through Jacques Derrida's (1987) framing of *ergon* (work) and *parergon* (that which is outside the work) as well as reflections about methodology and *method assemblage* from John Law (2004). Wilken argues that data excess is not surplus but rather exerts 'its own "presence" prior, during, and long after papers have been presented, publications have appeared, and projects have wrapped up'.

Excess data also emerges not only in what we collect, collate, record, filter or scrape in our research endeavours but is also produced by the very technologies and media we research. Part of the promise of digital data intermediaries or platforms is that large volumes of data potentially offer more precise, intimate or predictive insights into our worlds. Digital technologies and media produce, record and archive excess data through user interactions. As noted in the section above, we can also consider interdisciplinary or transdisciplinary approaches to knowledge-making that cross the boundaries of disciplines, fields and institutions. For researchers working between fields and industries this is often a pragmatic issue, as different contexts have different values in terms of what counts as 'enough' evidence. We may need to embrace a research ethos that understands the value of different data with different characteristics, where some may be understood as excess in different contexts or methodological frames. Analysing or writing away excess, as required by different research or translation frameworks, may remove the complexity of social and digital life. *Benjamin Hanckel* explores this issue in Chapter 10 and discusses how research that aims to evaluate the efficacy of health interventions often removes data excess in the hope of transforming data into 'success measures'. Evaluation models are extractive or are imposed on (or over) data and omit research leftovers that might otherwise offer useful insights into complex systems or contexts. These top-down frameworks need to be reimagined, Hanckel argues, so that engaging with complexity includes engaging with excess data, thus better addressing health inequalities and inequities.

Further, if we understand research or knowledge translation as a process of translating academic research for a public audience or 'industry stakeholder' group, the excessiveness of academic vernacular is carved away for shorter, sharper sentences and clarity that removes nuance, complexity or authenticity. Excess then is the 'too much' or over-the-top intensity of academic doing, thinking and writing that becomes valueless and too fussy or unhelpful 'out there' in a progress-driven world. This process is not an afterthought of research. We craft our writing and work through assembling and casting off words and ideas as an ongoing practice, rewriting knowledge for different and often multiple audiences.

At the same time, excess data may also be a problem of increasing academic pressures to publish and discard data that doesn't neatly fit a project or topic, or perhaps it is an ethical problem as we actively or even unintentionally collect 'too much' data. Much of the work we do sits beyond the boundaries of academic books, journal articles and reports, as many of our contributors attest to in their chapters. Even as creative and innovative ways of doing and communicating research strive to better incorporate complex, experiential and iterative approaches; such methods also face significant challenges in addressing the complexity and excess of scholarship.

Graduate students and others new to digital media research will inevitably face these challenges of too much data: what is 'enough'? How much is too much? Of course, this challenge is not unique to digital researchers; scoping and defining research boundaries is perhaps a central problem across different research traditions, methodologies and practices. In part, this book seeks to provide early career researchers with narratives, methodological approaches and conceptual tools to manage data excess as part of a broader research ethos.

Affect, Haunting and Unexpected Discovery

In our third rationale for the importance of excess data, we argue, alongside our contributors, that excess data generates unanticipated but potentially productive outcomes and experiences. As we explored earlier in this introduction, while excess data are *produced* through research, these data are *productive or creative* themselves. This excess offers something unintended, not only the potential for data to be attended to or transformed into something different and thus becoming no longer that which is 'leftover', but the possibility of revealing emergent material, social, affective and political effects and often unanticipated implications.

For *Natalia Grincheva*, engaging with digital excess across multiple sites – for her, integrating big data in the context of galleries, museums and other cultural institutions within 'smart cities' – generates new ways to transform others' excess or superfluous data. In Chapter 9, Grincheva highlights how data excess is generative as creative data practices produce new problems, new methods of data visualisation and new opportunities. She asks how might we transform data excess into data intelligence? This chapter takes seriously the digital transformation of museums across physical and virtual realities – beyond material archives or traditional spaces of heritage preservation – and considers how museum big data can drive and enhance smart cities and urban planning across multiple sectors, including environmental protection and transportation. To these ends, Grincheva offers a three-dimensional framework for integrating digital data within smart cities and suggests data resources, data republics and data impacts as key components in the repurposing of museum data.

In part, the generative qualities of excess data emerge from the temporal instability of classifying data as excessive. Unlike other ways to categorise data, including paradata or metadata, excess data do not have any inherent qualities or characteristics. They are data with no purpose *at that time*, or they are *at present* too much or *for now* unintelligible. Excess data are transitional and hold possibilities and potentials to no longer be excess, debris or the 'leftovers' of our research practice. Because they are determined in context, they can always transform into data of significance. This returns us to our earlier discussion of how the boundaries we enact in our knowledge-making and research endeavours designate excess.

Yet this temporal instability also produces social and affective effects. This is perhaps the most familiar characteristic and concern of excess data for digital media scholars – feelings of guilt, frustration, fatigue, gloom, pressure and irritation; perhaps hope or (rarely) joy. These affects spill over and circulate alongside intensified research and institutional demands, as well as what we expect of and from our scholarship. We might, too, experience 'overwhelm' as a state of affective excess that is familiar to us while scrambling to meet research KPIs (key performance indicators) and obtain grant funding alongside the demands of academic teaching, mentorship and scholarship.

Our research haunts us long after the end of fieldwork or final publication edits. Collected data continues to wait in numerous digital folders, archives and servers, while recommendation systems, digital platforms and algorithmic processes return us back to that research. Excess data are haunting in part because they are largely amorphous, unknown and unused. But they also reside in our memories, as lingering ghosts that keep alive the possibility of revelatory analysis sometime in a less busy future. They take up material and digital 'space'. Digital excess promises it could one day *create* something: new knowledge, that uncanny sense of being known by devices and platforms, more agile information, claims of scale that encompass all possibilities. This 'unanticipated excess', as *Ben Lyall, Clare Moran* and *Josie Reade* write in Chapter 3, produces unfiltered moments and uneasy feelings. They encountered 'unfiltered moments' in each of their projects where relationships with research material and participants endured long after data collection was completed. The chapter draws on three vignettes from each author's doctoral research projects: a digital ethnography of fitness influencer content on Instagram (Reade), a social media ethnography of African young people in Australia (Moran) and interviews with people who use digital self-tracking devices (Lyall). These encounters were not neutral: watching a participant cry on their Instagram Stories (Reade), re-engaging with the BlackLivesMatter movement following the murder of George Floyd (Moran) and negotiating the 'leaky boundaries' and ambivalence towards participants' everyday uses of wearable devices (Lyall). In their chapter, Lyall, Moran and Reade hope to carry forward these excesses, between analysis rituals and formal publications, to consider how these moments fill affective spaces between writing and fieldwork. Here, data excess produces spatial encounters (between participants and researchers in the 'same space') as well as temporal experiences that endure during research but also, more troubling, after fieldwork ends.

Data ghosts take up space we might otherwise free ourselves from, to find reprieve from publication pressures, endless to-do lists or research projects with no real final end date for completion. These lists, as Sasha Su-Ling Welland (2020, p. 28) offers, 'can be tyrannical. They tell us what we are supposed to do and what we have failed to do'. The failure of not crafting the excess data, words, lists and plans into some kind of 'output' becomes that tyrannical ghost. Here is where excess data matters: as bodily flows between us and our devices, they are the unfulfilled digital ghosts of research data folders that were intended to be made into *something else*.

Excess may be digital but it can also be social, political, affective and ethical. Thus what haunts us is material as much as it is digital – notes and paragraphs and post-it notes that were 'meant to go' somewhere as if it was easy to send them on their way into the world. Is excess then the data without orientation or a pathway? Returning to a research project about Sylvia Plath poetry on Tumblr – 10 years after data collection – *Navid Sabet* explores how new knowledge can be produced when we reorient our interests in a research project. In Chapter 8, Sabet employs a 'storying approach' (Gravett & Winstone, 2019) and reflects on the institutional demands to publish, especially for emerging scholars, and how engaging with excess data from Tumblr and research interviews challenges our ideas about how and when data is usable or insightful.

Towards Excessive Thinking and Writing

Through the process of editing and writing this collection, we continually faced the challenge of finding time to return to the past and 'excavate' our excess data and project hopes and intentions. Researchers and academic life are increasingly driven by publishing and funding metrics that require new research, new data and new grant applications, disincentives for returning to one's research archives or developing new knowledge from what would otherwise be underexplored excess. This book, too, has been compiled in a context where edited collections are considered less 'valuable' than other research outputs that allow for international and local ranking, and book chapters count for less than peer-reviewed journal articles. And yet, as this collection attests, there is much to be gained – methodologically, practically, theoretically and ethically – from returning to excess and collectively reflecting on how we engage with digital data across diverse disciplines and methodologies.

In spite of these academic constraints and constant push towards the next new fundable thing, this collection explicitly engages with data that has been left behind, that which is often ignored or obscured, or even 'written out' of research publications. We hope that it offers researchers and scholars new ways to think about very familiar issues emerging from the methodological, theoretical, ethical and material implications of 'too much' data; issues that will become more critical as digital technologies and the consequences of datafication grow ever more central to our research and our lives. To inspire research towards these ends, our contributors take up the challenge and provocation to make something of their leftovers.

References

Derrida, J. (1987). *The truth in painting* (J. Bennington & I. McLeod, Trans.). University of Chicago Press.

Goodwin, J., O'Connor, H., Phoenix, A., & Edwards, R. (2017). Introduction: Working with paradata, marginalia and fieldnotes. In R. Edwards, J. Goodwin, H. O'Connor, & A. Phoenix (Eds.), *Working with paradata, marginalia and fieldnotes: The centrality of by-products of social research* (pp. 1–19). Edward Elgar.

Gravett, K., & Winstone, N. E. (2019). Storying students' becomings into and through higher education. *Studies in Higher Education, 46*(8), 1–12. https://doi.org/10.1080/03075079.2019.1695112

Law, J. (2004). *After method: Mess in social science research.* Routledge.

Markham, A. (2017). Troubling the concept of big data in qualitative digital research. In U. Flick (Ed.), *The SAGE handbook of qualitative data collection* (pp. 511–23). SAGE.

Quinton, S., & Reynolds, N. (2018). *Understanding research in the digital age.* SAGE.

Rickards, L., Steele, W., Kokshagina, O., & Moraes, O. (2020). *Research impact as ethos.* RMIT University.

Shirky, C. (2010). It's not information overload. It's filter failure. *MAS Context, 10.* https://www.mascontext.com/issues/7-information-fall-10/its-not-information-overload-its-filter-failure/

Welland, S. S.-L. (2020). List as form: Literary, ethnographic, long, short, heavy, light. In C. McGranahan (Ed.), *Writing anthropology: Essays on craft and commitment* (pp. 28–33). Duke University Press.

Chapter 2

Reframing Data Excess

Rowan Wilken

RMIT University, Australia

Abstract

There is a tendency to conceive of unpublished research material as 'excess' data, as research resources that are surplus to requirements. In this chapter, I challenge this view by rethinking and critically reframing how we might make sense of research data that, for whatever reason, does not find its way into public presentation or publication. The position I take in this chapter is that we might conceive of unpublished data as operating in dynamic relation to what is or might be presented or published from it, thus serving as vital contextual curtilage shaping 'field formation' (how one understands both the immediate context of a research project and the wider context in which the research project is situated). I develop this argument in three steps. First, I look at grounded theory approaches and ask: how do we amass qualitative research data, and how do we determine how much data is enough data? Second, I then turn to consider (less commonly considered) questions: what are the processes for converting this data into publication, and how do we conceive of data that remains unpublished? Third, I then revisit a large collaborative research project of my own that gathered more data than was ultimately reported on, using this as an opportunity for renewed critical reflection on data sets and the productive possibilities of 'unused' research data. In considering these possibilities, I draw from the philosophical ideas of Jacques Derrida and the methodological reflections of science and technology studies scholar John Law.

Keywords: Data excess; qualitative research data; grounded theory; saturation; parergon; method assemblage

Introduction

In this chapter, I seek to think through, and critically reframe, how we might make sense of research data that, for one reason or another, does not find its way into public presentation or publication. There is a tendency to conceive of this material as 'excess' data, as research resources that are surplus to requirements. In what follows, I wish to develop an alternative perspective on unused research data, suggesting that it exists not as an unused surplus. Rather, that we might conceive of it as operating in dynamic relation to what is or might be presented or published from it, and as serving as vital contextual curtilage shaping 'field formation' (how one understands the immediate context of a research project – its aims, research problems and research questions – and the wider context in which the research project is situated).

I develop this argument in three steps. First, I explore how we come to amass qualitative research data. Focusing on grounded theory approaches, I detail how the answer to the question of how much data is enough revolves around the somewhat nebulous concept of data 'saturation'. Second, I turn to consider how less attention is paid within the same literature to advising on how to convert this data (once saturation is achieved) into publication, and what to do with data that goes unpublished. Third, I then revisit a large collaborative research project I was involved in that gathered more data than was ultimately reported on, using this as an opportunity for renewed critical reflection on data sets and the productive possibilities of 'unused' research data. In considering these possibilities, I draw from, and bring into conversation, the philosophical ideas of Jacques Derrida and the methodological reflections of science and technology studies scholar John Law.

How Much Qualitative Data Is Enough Data?

Within scholarship on qualitative research methods, a great deal of critical attention has been paid to addressing questions of how much qualitative data is enough data. This is particularly evident in the methods literature documenting grounded theory approaches (Glaser & Strauss, 1967), as I examine here. Grounded theory is so named as it forms 'a general methodology for developing theory that is grounded in data systematically gathered and analyzed' (Strauss & Corbin, 1994, p. 273). Grounded theory studies are framed by 'sensitizing concepts'. These are understood as 'directions along which to look' (Blumer, 1954, p. 7), or 'initial ways of focusing on and organizing data' (Wilson, cited in Aldiabat & Le Navenec, 2018, p. 251), and serve as 'a guide for theory development' (Bowen, 2008, p. 141). This is because, in a grounded theory approach, theory is not established ex-ante, or before undertaking research. Rather, 'theory evolves during [...] research, and it does this through continuous interplay between analysis and data collection' (Strauss & Corbin, 1994, p. 273). In this sense, 'methods, their rules, and even more methods' practices, not only describe but also help to *produce* the reality that they understand' (Law, 2004, p. 5).

Within grounded theory studies, as with other forms of qualitative research, 'sampling, data collection, and analysis proceed concurrently' (Bowen, 2008, p. 139). Analysis of data collected involves the use of coding. Coding involves examining 'fragments of data – words, lines, segments, and incidents – closely for their analytic import' (Charmaz, 2006, p. 42) and then giving these fragments 'a label that simultaneously categorizes, summarizes, and accounts for each piece of data' (p. 43). Often coding procedures and protocols are established (Bowen, 2008, p. 139) in the early stages of coding (and adjusted throughout) so as to systematise the process of data capture and analysis, and ensure coding coherence, especially when this task is undertaken by multiple researchers within a team. In practice, coding might involve going back and forth between interview transcripts, for example reading them closely, and adding labels (that are continually adjusted and refined) to fragments of data that are identified by the coder's 'analytic interpretations' (Charmaz, 2006, p. 43) as being noteworthy or potentially significant. The aim is to 'establish analytic distinctions' that are applied 'at each level of analytic work' (Charmaz, 2006, p. 54). The key point here is that throughout a study, new data is constantly compared (Glaser & Strauss, 1967) with previously collected data and existing code categories; it is the coding that underpins this approach. In this way, coding drives 'theory development': it 'shapes an analytic frame' from which one 'builds the analysis' (Charmaz, 2006, p. 45).

The concept of 'saturation' is integral to this form of naturalistic inquiry (Lincoln & Guba, 1985). Data is continually brought in and coded until saturation is reached. Saturation is broadly defined as the point at which no new code categories are created, data is replicated within existing code categories and the acquisition of further data will not lead to the discovery of new information related to a project's research questions (Lowe et al., 2018). Achieving saturation is viewed as important as it 'verifies' data gathered and 'ensures comprehension and completeness' (Morse et al., 2002, p. 18), thereby contributing to 'data trustworthiness' (Denzin & Lincoln, 1994; Lincoln & Guba, 1985).

The issue, however, is that *how* saturation is determined as having been reached remains unclear. It has been noted that 'the saturation concept remains nebulous and the process lacks systematization' (Bowen, 2008, p. 139). There are 'no published guidelines or tests of adequacy for establishing the sample size required to reach saturation' (Morse, 1995, p. 147). Rather, 'the signals of saturation seem to be determined by investigator proclamation and by evaluating the adequacy and the comprehensiveness of the results' (p. 147). How is one to determine what is a sufficient number of semi-structured interviews in order to achieve data saturation (Baker & Edwards, 2012; Guest et al., 2006)?

Guest et al. (2006) conducted a review of the qualitative research methods literature, capturing recommendations around appropriate sample size. Across the publications they examined, they only found seven sources that 'provided guidelines for actual sample sizes' (Guest et al., 2006, p. 61). Between these seven sources, recommendations on desired sample size varied widely. For phenomenological studies, for example, one publication suggested 5–25 interviews to achieve saturation, while another suggested 6 interviews were sufficient (Guest et al., 2006, p. 61). For broader, qualitative ethnographic research, one article declared that 15 interviews was the 'smallest acceptable sample size in qualitative research', while another suggested that 'most ethnographic studies are based on thirty-six interviews' (p. 61). Guest, Bunce and Johnson's position, based on their own research, is that 'the full range of thematic discovery occurred almost completely within the first twelve interviews' (p. 66). Beyond this sample of seven publications, the response to achieving saturation seems to be 'it depends' (Baker & Edwards, 2012), with study design, scope, research subjects, and research questions all playing a role in determining how many participants are enough.

Published and Unpublished Data

The qualitative research methods literature – and grounded theory, in particular, as explored above – has a great deal to say about how much research is enough research. Less explicit guidance, however, is provided on (a) how to go about progressing from data collection and coding to data selection for publication and (b) what happens to the data that does not find its way into publication.

On the first question, it is striking, for instance, that the index to the 1,210 page third edition of *The Sage Handbook of Qualitative Research* (Denzin & Lincoln, 2005) lists only two single-page entries for 'publishing research findings'.[1] What guidance is offered tends to be pitched towards higher degree research students and those unfamiliar with qualitative research, and presented as sets of initial prompts (see, for example Charmaz, 2006, pp. 151–178). In an editorial for *Family Business Review* on publishing qualitative research, readers are strongly encouraged to 'go back to the research question(s) you used to guide data collection and ask yourself, "So, what is the answer to these question(s)? Is there anything surprising about what people said, or what I found in the documents?"' (Reay, 2014, p. 97). The suggestion is to use the answers to these questions to identify appropriate 'text segments' from the raw data that best connect with the research question for use in possible publication. Through this process, one's research is 'further shaped and honed' (p. 97). It is a revealing choice of metaphor in that it suggests that, while data has been gathered until saturation, publication is a process of whittling, involving reduction (selection) and a remainder (excess).

On the second question, the issue of excess data is examined in detail across a range of disciplinary and interdisciplinary research contexts, such as in critical data studies and analyses of 'big data' (e.g. Kitchin, 2014), and in discussions of information abundance (e.g. Boczkowski, 2021). One aspect of university activity that is explicitly concerned with the handling of data sets, including unused or 'excess' data, are human research ethics boards, who tend to stipulate 'best practice' data management procedures, access requirements, lengths of retention

---

[1] One contribution to the same volume, which is not captured in either of the two indexed pages, does explicitly address writing. The authors of the chapter set out to challenge 'the distinction in conventional qualitative inquiry between data collection and data analysis' by conceiving of ethnographic writing itself as a 'method of data collection ... and a method of data analysis' (Richardson & St Pierre, 2005, p. 970).

and data destruction processes (e.g. in Australia this is guided by the National Statement on Ethical Conduct in Human Research; National Health and Medical Research Council, 2007). Within the qualitative research literature, however, the issue of what one does with, and how one makes critical sense of, 'excess' data – that is, data, post coding and analysis, that does not find its way into reported findings and publications – remains largely unexplored. The presumption seems to be that such data is surplus to immediate publication requirements but is kept and viewed as a kind of informational 'standing reserve' for possible later use for presentation and publication.

Collecting Data, Generating Excess Data

Against this backdrop, here I revisit the excess data generated through a large qualitative research project of my own. I begin by describing the data that was collected, before offering some reflections on how the excess data produced from this project might be productively reframed.

The project in question was an Australian Research Council funded Discovery Early Career Researcher Award (DECRA), entitled 'The Cultural Economy of Locative Media' (DE120102114, 2012–2014). It was a three-year research fellowship that set out to examine how place-based services, or 'locative media', were transforming mobile media and communication. The premise of this project was that, although the cultural and economic implications were poorly understood at the time, these new services and technologies signalled important shifts in media institutions, policies, and businesses, and challenged then current understandings of media regulation and privacy. The project was comparative and aimed to investigate how locative media were being used in Australia and the United States, and what their cultural, political economic, and policy ramifications were in both countries. The project's programme of research consisted of three phases of work, exploring, respectively, (1) the political economy of locative media industries, (2) everyday locative media practices, and (3) the policy impacts and implications of locative media and the geocoded smartphone and social media data they generate. It should be noted at the outset that, while it involved qualitative research, this was not formally conceived of as a 'Grounded Theory' project. The first and third phases of this project involved a mix of semi-structured expert industry interviews and text-based research drawing on a range of sources, including academic scholarship, trade press sources, patent documentation, financial statements, legal rulings and so on.

The second, middle phase – and the focus of the discussion of data excess to follow – was a comparative study exploring everyday locative media use in Melbourne and New York City. Undertaken in collaboration with Professor Lee Humphreys of Cornell University, this middle phase employed two main forms of data collection. The first of these was semi-structured consumer interviews with individuals in both cities (11 in Melbourne and 20 in New York City, for a total of 31 interviews). In conducting these face-to-face interviews, we employed 'show-and-tell' approaches (Chamberlain & Lyons, 2016; Sheridan & Chamberlain, 2011), where we asked participants to lead us through certain app features (e.g. profile pages and privacy and other settings) and other aspects of everyday app use at the same time as they discussed these with us. We also employed photo elicitation techniques (Harper, 2002), with each participant providing us with five photographs associated with their own 'check-ins' to the then-popular locative social media service, Foursquare, along with short written responses to a series of questions designed to encourage them to reflect upon their motivations for recording each image.

The second form of data collection in the second project phase involved running qualitative group interviews with small business owners and operators in both Melbourne and New York City. Four groups were held, two in each city, consisting of six to eight participants per group, for a total of twenty-eight participants. A market research firm was hired to help recruit participants. The criteria for recruitment were being the manager or owner of a business, which had claimed a Foursquare venue that people could currently check into, and having personal experience using social media services, although participant discussion extended beyond Foursquare to include social media use more generally, including Facebook, Twitter, Yelp, and Instagram. We chose to conduct group interviews to encourage some interaction among the participants. Composition of interview groups can impact group dynamics (Morgan, 1997), and similarity can encourage rapport and trust building among participants. With this in mind, one group in each city was composed of highly similar businesses (i.e. bar, restaurant and nightclub managers), while the second group was composed of various small businesses. The study participants included managers of bars, restaurants, nightclubs, clothing retailers, real estate companies, community centres and auto repair garages from around New York City and Melbourne. We moderated the group interviews; in each group, we also had one of us or a research assistant observing and taking notes on the dynamics of the group. All group interviews were audio and video recorded and transcribed. Video footage was not explicitly analysed but used to ensure the accuracy of the attributions of remarks in the transcripts.

This middle, consumer-focused phase of the project generated significant quantities of qualitative data. The semi-structured interviews produced almost 2 days' worth of audio recordings, around 530 pages of interview transcriptions, 155 participant-generated photos and 31 pages of accompanying textual descriptions. The group interviews produced approximately 6 hours of video footage, 125 pages of transcribed conversations across the four groups, 38 pages of observational notes from the Melbourne focus groups alone and 31 pages of post-group demographic survey data.

In the introduction to this volume, the editors observe that 'excess data hold intimate impressions (and burdens) on us and symbolically mark our unfinished labour'. This sentiment resonates strongly with me and speaks to how I have tended to look back and reflect on the middle phase of this DECRA project. Insights from the consumer-related data we gathered were reported in two co-authored journal articles (Humphreys & Wilken, 2015; Wilken & Humphreys, 2019) and informed two sections of a sole-authored monograph (Wilken, 2019, pp. 119–154, 195–203). And yet, due to the voluminousness of the data we captured, and the detailed insights contained within it, the 'excess data' – the data that did not find its way into publication – has to me come to resemble a rich field left unharvested. This lingering sense of unfulfilled labour and of untapped research data is, I think, a direct consequence of our tendency as academics to approach data principally as source material for public presentation and publication ('outputs') and consequently of unpublished data as 'excess' data, and of academia's broader embrace of 'metric culture' (Chan et al., 2018), especially metrics oriented towards 'newness' (new work, new research, new data, etc.).

While it is fine to conceive of unused data as a kind of 'standing reserve' for possible or future publication, I think there are more productive ways of conceiving of and considering this store of information. In what follows, I seek to recast how we think about the relationship between what has been selected for publication and what was not (or is yet to be). Rather than think of excess data as forming a fallow or unharvested field, the position I take here is that this material has been cultivated in the course (and cause) of problem resolution (responding to research questions) and theory generation (in the strict 'Grounded Theory' sense of this term, and more generally). This material is also essential to *field formation* – that is, how a researcher develops an overall sense of the topography of the research area/issue under examination. All of which is to say that the relationship between what finds its way into publication, and what does not, is more complicated than appearances suggest.

'Reframing' Data Excess

To draw this point out further, this critical reframing of excess data draws together two distinct strands of thought. First, Jacques Derrida's (1987) work on frames and the permeable boundaries that separate a work from what is outside a work (extending earlier published research of mine – see Richardson & Wilken, 2012). And, second, John Law's (2004) concept of the 'method assemblage', which forms part of his efforts at prompting social science researchers to 'unmake' established 'methodological habits' (p. 9).

Parergon

In his book *The Truth in Painting*, Derrida (1987) develops a quite specific understanding of frames, which he builds from a reading of two passages in separate texts by Kant, and connects to the notion of the *parergon*. The Greek word *parergon* literally means 'outside the work' as *par* means 'past' or 'beyond' and *ergon* means 'work'. Contrary to the suggestion of clear separation, however, the implication that Derrida explores is that there is a close and mutually influencing proximity between *ergon* and *parergon* – this is in part because the prefix *par* also means 'beside'. In this way, the *parergon* 'does not fall to one side' of the *ergon*, rather 'it touches and cooperates, from a certain outside', which is 'neither simply outside nor simply inside' (Derrida, 1987, p. 54). As Derrida goes on to explain: the *parergon* 'comes to play, abut onto, brush against, rub, press against the limit itself and intervene in the inside only to the extent that the inside is lacking' (p. 56). This is the case insofar as the inside – the 'work' – 'is not complete, exhausted'; rather, 'it needs this supplement [the *parergon*] to finish it' (Mella, 2002, Para. 40).

In working through the implications of this relationship between *ergon* and *parergon*, Derrida explores three examples: the status of clothing on statuary; the role of columns on buildings; and frames for paintings. In the present context, it is the last of these that is most instructive for realising alternative ways of conceiving of 'excess' data. According to Derrida, in an art context, a painting's frame as *parergon* serves two vital yet seemingly contradictory simultaneous operations. On the one hand, its precise function is to stand out 'like a figure on a ground', both from 'the ergon (the work)' and also from 'the milieu' (which in the case of displayed art, includes both the immediate surrounding of the gallery wall, *and* a wider art context; Derrida, 1987, p. 61). This it does in order to 'delimit' the content of any given work. On the other hand, and at the same time, 'the *parergon* is a form which has as its traditional determination not that it stands out but that it disappears, buries itself, effaces itself, melts away at the moment it deploys its greatest energy' (p. 61) In this sense, then, Derrida's conception of the frame is closer in meaning to the concept of the boundary than that of the border. As Edward S. Casey (2008, p. 8) explains, 'in contrast with borders, boundaries are permeable; they are porous, full of holes; they allow, indeed often invite, movement across them', while, at the same time, remaining 'edges of a certain definite sort'. Derrida's argument, in essence, is that any attempt at drawing a neat distinction or delineation between the two (work and frame) is complicated by the fact that the two are symbiotic: a work 'is not complete, exhausted' by itself; rather, it needs the 'supplement' (the *parergon*), or what is outside of the picture frame in the case of painting, in order to 'finish it'.

The concept of *parergon*, and the relationship between *ergon* and *parergon*, as Derrida conceives of it, provides a useful way of rethinking – 'reframing' – 'excess' data. My book *Cultural Economies of Locative Data* provides a useful reference point for exploring how this is the case. This book-length work did not simply provide an opportunity to 'write up the data'. Rather, the finished work exists in a dynamic and productive tension with this data. The qualitative data gathered as part of my DECRA project, which forms the 'frame' (*parergon*) for this work, was only discussed explicitly in a few places in the book. Nevertheless, the presence and influence of this material is felt throughout. Small portions of the 530 pages of interview transcriptions were drawn from and quoted when describing how individuals interact with mobile location-based services and smartphone app settings, but this material as a whole also influenced much of the thinking that went into the rest of the book. Meanwhile, the group interview material – all 6 hours of video and close on 200 pages of written material – while not finding its way in the book, played an important role in 'framing' the book's structure, conceptual development and, in the final third, served as vital contextual curtilage, directly informing an extended examination of the concept of locational privacy. Here, project data (*parergon*) interacts with the work (*ergon*) and the immediate and wider 'milieux' informing its construction. The project data frames this work – it 'touches and cooperates' with it – in ways that are 'neither simply outside nor simply inside' the finished book (Derrida, 1987, p. 54). The *ergon/parergon* relationship is thus productive for understanding the inside/outside relation of published and unpublished ('excess') data, and the permeable relation between them.

Method Assemblage

In his book *After Method*, John Law (2004) writes, 'I would like to divest concern with method of its inheritance of hygiene' (p. 9). This statement is a reaction to what Law sees as the sanitisation and apparent neatness of much contemporary social science methods, where, in his view, complexity is 'distorted into clarity' (p. 2). Social science methods, he argues, are often ill-equipped to capture or describe 'things that are complex, diffuse and messy' (p. 2). What we need instead, he suggests, is 'a way of talking that helps us to recognise and treat with the fluidities, leakages, and entanglements that make up the hinterland of research' (p. 41), and which he regards as the 'missing seven-eighths of the iceberg of method' (p. 41). Law's response is to propose the idea of 'method assemblage', which he defines as 'the enactment of *presence, manifest absence*, and *absence as Otherness*' (p. 144). Law elaborates:

> More specifically, [method assemblage] is the crafting, bundling, or gathering of relations in three parts: (a) whatever is in-here or present (for instance a representation or an object); (b) whatever is absent but also manifest (it can be seen, is described, is manifestly relevant to presence); and (c) whatever is absent but is Other because, while necessary to presence, it is also hidden, repressed or uninteresting. (p. 144)

Law proposes method assemblage as a frame, or set of provocations, for imagining possible, alternative ways of 'crafting method' (p. 144). I would contend that Law's conception of method assemblage also provides a productive means for rethinking how we actively engage with the mess and complexity of the qualitative research data that we have already gathered. In this context, we might say that we craft accounts of what is 'in-here or *present*' in our gathered research data. Importantly, however, these accounts are always-already developed in relation to what is 'absent but also manifest' in the data (material that is 'manifestly relevant' to the 'presence' described but not captured within it), as well as to what is absent from crafted accounts because deemed 'uninteresting' or because it is 'hidden, repressed' (these last two are potentially the most challenging in that they speak to possible bias and other forms of critical lacunae).

To draw out and illustrate this point, in the sole paper we published that drew from individual interviews conducted for the DECRA project (Wilken & Humphreys, 2019), the 'in-here or *present*' that formed the impetus for that article were the five photos that each participant selected from their Foursquare app check-in history, and the captions and textual explanations that accompanied these. From among these, however, we were most concerned with those photos that captured a sense of the mundane and of everydayness, rather than photos that portrayed more overt displays of the 'spatial self' (Schwartz & Halegoua, 2015). (The spatial self is defined as 'the process of online self-presentation based on the display of off-line physical activities' (Schwartz & Halegoua, 2015, p. 1643), or what we might otherwise now refer to as 'Instagrammable moments' (Leaver et al., 2020).) Even so, those photographs that weren't examined, and our reading of the 530 pages of transcribed interview data, shaped what was 'absent but also manifest' in our crafted account of mobile location-based smartphone app use and photo-taking practices. Furthermore, given the sheer volume of insights contained within these transcripts, there was always going to be material that was absent from this specific crafted account because these insights were hidden or not revealed to us, or because we deemed them 'uninteresting', and so on. This process – involving the interplay of presence, absent presence and absence – has been repeated across all works that emerged from the project and is characteristic of the project as a whole. The twin critical approaches to reframing unpublished data described above provide a productive means of reengaging with and revealing the fuller significance of what we might refer to (after Law) as the 'missing seven-eighths' of qualitative research data.

Conclusion

In this chapter, I have sought to think through, and critically reframe, how we might make sense of research data that does not find its way into public presentation or publication. While there exists a tendency to conceive of this material as 'excess' data (research resources that are surplus to requirements), here I have presented an alternative framing for how we might conceive of unpublished research data. In developing this account, I revisit a large research project of my own, and draw on Jacques Derrida's interest in the concept of the *parergon* and John Law's notion of 'method assemblage', suggesting both provide productive conceptual tools for critically reframing how we conceive of 'unused' research data.

In their own work, their respective ideas form part of quite ambitious individual research agendas. Derrida's examination of the *parergon* is explored as part of a line of questioning that asks, 'on what conditions, if it's even possible, can one exceed, dismantle, or displace the heritage of the great philosophies of art?' (Derrida, 1987, p. 9) While Law's (2004) model of 'method assemblage' emerges from his calls for a radical shake-up of qualitative social science research methods.

My own ambition is rather more modest: to recast research data as always-already in constant, active and productive tension with what might have been (or may still be) presented from it. In this way, we can think of our qualitative research data as exerting its own 'presence' prior, during and long after papers have been presented, publications have appeared and projects have wrapped up.

References

Aldiabat, K., & Le Navenec, C. (2018). Data saturation: The mysterious step in grounded theory method. *The Qualitative Report, 23*(1), 245–261. https://doi.org/10.46743/2160-3715/2018.2994

Baker, S. E., & Edwards, R. (2012). How many qualitative interviews is enough? National Centre for Research Methods Review Paper. http://eprints.ncrm.ac.uk/2273/4/how_many_interviews.pdf

Blumer, H. (1954). What is wrong with social theory? *American Sociological Review, 19*(1), 3–10. https://doi.org/10.2307/2088165

Boczkowski, P. J. (2021). *Abundance: On the experience of living in a world of information plenty.* Oxford University Press.

Bowen, G. A. (2008). Naturalistic inquiry and the saturation concept: A research note. *Qualitative Research, 8*(1), 137–152. https://doi.org/10.1177/1468794107085301

Casey, E. S. (2008). Taking Bachelard from the instant to the edge. *Philosophy Today, 52*(Supplement), 31–37. https://doi.org/10.5840/philtoday200852Supplement51

Chamberlain, K., & Lyons, A. (2016). Using material objects and artifacts in research. In B. Smith & A. C. Sparkes (Eds.), *Routledge handbook of qualitative research in sport and exercise* (pp. 164–177). Sage.

Chan, J., Johns, F., & Bennett Moses, L. (2018). Academic metrics and positioning strategies. In B. Ajana (Ed.), *Metric culture: Ontologies of self-tracking practices* (pp. 177–195). Emerald Publishing Limited.

Charmaz, K. (2006). *Constructing grounded theory: A practical guide through qualitative analysis.* Sage.

Denzin, N. K., & Lincoln, Y. S. (1994). Introduction: Entering the field of qualitative research. In N. K. Denzin & Y. S. Lincoln (Eds.), *Handbook of qualitative research* (pp. 1–17). Sage.

Denzin, N. K. & Lincoln, Y. S. (Eds.). (2005). *The Sage handbook of qualitative research* (3rd ed.). Sage.

Derrida, J. (1987). *The truth in painting* (J. Bennington & I. McLeod, Trans.). University of Chicago Press.

Glaser, B. G., & Strauss, A. L. (1967). *The discovery of grounded theory: Strategies for qualitative research.* Aldine.

Guest, G., Bunce, A., & Johnson, L. (2006). How many interviews are enough? An experiment with data saturation and variability. *Field Methods, 18*(1), 59–82. https://doi.org/10.1177/1525822X05279903

Harper, D. (2002). Talking about pictures: A case for photo elicitation. *Visual Studies, 17*(1), 13–26. https://doi.org/10.1080/14725860220137345

Humphreys, L., & Wilken, R. (2015). Social media, small businesses, and the control of information. *Information, Communication & Society, 18*(3), 295–309. https://doi.org/10.1080/1369118X.2014.989249

Kitchin, R. (2014). Big data, new epistemologies and paradigm shifts. *Big Data & Society.* https://doi.org/10.1177/2053951714528481

Law, J. (2004). *After method: Mess in social science research.* Routledge.

Leaver, T., Highfield, T., & Abidin, C. (2020). *Instagram: Visual social media cultures.* Polity.

Lincoln, Y. S., & Guba, E. G. (1985). *Naturalistic inquiry.* Sage.

Lowe, A., Norris, A. C., Farris, J., & Babbage, D. R. (2018). Quantifying thematic saturation in qualitative data analysis. *Field Methods, 30*(3), 191–207. https://doi.org/10.1177/1525822X17749386

Mella, B. (2002). Derrida's detour. *Reconstruction: Studies in Contemporary Culture, 2*(4), Fall, https://web.archive.org/web/20130302182536/http://reconstruction.eserver.org/024/mella.htm

Morgan, D. (1997). *Focus groups as qualitative research: Planning and research design for focus groups.* Sage.

Morse, J. M. (1995). Editorial: The significance of saturation. *Qualitative Health Research, 5*(2), 147–149. https://doi.org/10.1177/104973239500500201

Morse, J. M., Barrett, M., Mayan, M., Olson, K., & Spiers, J. (2002). Verification strategies for establishing reliability and validity in qualitative research. *International Journal of Qualitative Methods, 1*(2), 13–22. https://doi.org/10.1177/160940690200100202

National Health and Medical Research Council. (2007). *National statement on ethical conduct in human research.* National Health and Medical Research Council together with the Australian Research Council and the Australian Vice Chancellors' Committee.

Reay, T. (2014). Editorial: Publishing qualitative research. *Family Business Review, 27*(2), 95–102. https://doi.org/10.1177/0894486514529209

Richardson, L., & St Pierre, E. A. (2005). Writing: A method of inquiry. In N. K. Denzin & Y. S. Lincoln (Eds.), *The Sage handbook of qualitative research* (3rd ed., pp. 959–978). Sage.

Richardson, I., & Wilken, R. (2012). Parerga of the third screen: Mobile media, place, and presence. In R. Wilken & G. Goggin (Eds.), *Mobile technology and place* (pp. 181–197). Routledge.

Schwartz, R., & Halegoua, G. (2015). The spatial self: Location-based identity performance on social media. *New Media & Society, 17*(10), 1643–1660. https://doi.org/10.1177/1461444814531364

Sheridan, J., & Chamberlain, K. (2011). The power of things. *Qualitative Research in Psychology, 8*(4), 315–332. https://psycnet.apa.org/doi/10.1080/14780880903490821

Strauss, A., & Corbin, J. (1994). Grounded theory methodology: An overview. In N. K. Denzin & Y. S. Lincoln (Eds.), *Handbook of qualitative research* (pp. 273–285). Sage.

Wilken, R. (2019). *Cultural economies of locative media.* Oxford University Press.

Wilken, R., & Humphreys, L. (2019). Constructing the check-in: Reflections on photo-taking among Foursquare users. *Communication and the Public, 4*(2), 100–117. https://doi.org/10.1177/2057047319853328

Chapter 3

Unanticipated Excess: Inescapable Moments and Uneasy Feelings

Ben Lyall[a], *Josie Reade*[b] *and Claire Moran*[a]

[a]Monash University, Australia
[b]The University of Melbourne, Australia

Abstract

In this chapter, we explore 'unanticipated excess' through the lens of our own doctoral research projects, which are presented as distinct vignettes: Reade's digital ethnography of young women's relations with 'fitspo' (fitness inspiration) content on Instagram, Moran's social media ethnography of African young people in Australia and Lyall's show-and-tell interviews with users of digital self-tracking devices. While our projects differ in many ways, we share research practices that did not fully anticipate the challenges of digitalised research fields. In coming to terms with our unanticipated excess, we reflect on inescapable moments and uneasy feelings from our fieldwork. In so doing, we argue that excess need not be considered a 'failure' – to establish boundaries, to filter data or to engage in objective analysis – but should rather be seen as an important part of reflexive research practice. Excess holds possibilities and potentials to foster care and camaraderie between digital scholars and can push us and our work – empirically, methodologically and ethically – in new directions. It also presents an opportunity to continue to champion integrity over production as we move forward in our personal and collective research journeys.

Keywords: Black Lives Matter; care; digital ethnography; fitspo; research ethics; self-tracking

Introduction

In this chapter, we take the idea of 'unanticipated excess' and use it as a provocation for thinking about the challenges and opportunities it creates for digital scholars. In three researcher vignettes, we explore how unanticipated excess produced inescapable moments and uneasy feelings that stayed with us long after our fieldwork formally concluded. Such feelings are often a feature of vulnerable conversations that take place behind closed doors, between research peers or in supervision meetings. These are experiences that, despite their importance to the research process, are often set aside in favour of other, more 'necessary', pressing stories. Researchers carry forward these excesses; they come to fill the spaces between the words of 'finished' writing and inform the work we do next.

We situate our reflections within the inherently messy process of 'doing' digital research, which is invariably marked by affective and embodied entanglements between researchers, participants and digital platforms (Jovicic, 2022; Postill & Pink, 2012). In format, we take inspiration from existing multi-author vignette-style fieldwork reflections (see Fujii, 2015; Palmer et al., 2014). Our vignettes follow a trend among digital ethnographers who offer self-reflections or 'confessions' on the 'failures' and dilemmas of their fieldwork by documenting the challenging epistemological choices and decisions they made to address them (see Abidin & de Seta, 2020; Bowles et al., 2021). We reflect on and, perhaps, apprehensively, 'confess' our fieldwork struggles, discomforts and regrets. In three vignettes, we share our experiences of navigating and coping with this overflow and excess, which appeared despite our carefully planned research designs and preparation. In writing this chapter, we satiate our cathartic need to critically reflect on and share these experiences – out in the open – with others. Moreover, we hope to encourage other researchers to take the time to dwell on, sit with, and speak about their own experiences of excess, and through communities of care, find solidarity with one another in moments of discomfort.

Contextualising Our Excess

In the first vignette, Reade draws on her ethnographic research with young women who post 'fitspo' (fitness inspiration) content on Instagram to discuss the unanticipated excess that emerged through continuing to follow participants on Instagram after the designated period of participant observation. Reade specifically attends to the embodied and cumulative effects of this excess, as well as the ethical implications it presents, by reflecting on her experience of watching a participant cry on her Instagram Stories months after data collection concluded.

In the second vignette, Moran reflects on her social media ethnography of African young people in Australia during two unanticipated global events of 2020: the resurgence of the #BlackLivesMatter (BLM) movement and the COVID-19 pandemic. She details how, while confined to her home under Melbourne's strict lockdown orders, her fieldwork was inundated with racially violent digital content as she took a front row seat to her participants' devastation, trauma, anger and grief. Moran describes the emotional and affective sensations she experienced while documenting and interpreting these experiences of racial violence amid the anxieties and isolation of the ongoing and unpredictable deadly global pandemic.

In the third vignette, Lyall draws on his experiences of interviewing users of wearable self-tracking devices. Usually linked to personal routines, physical activity and digital health, unanticipated excess appeared in the form of 'others': an othered self and, more literally, other people. Lyall describes the deep ambivalence he felt trying to reconcile the valued intimacies of these technologies with their ability to draw out shame (self) and blame (others). Participants' narratives included negative memories of weight gain, lost sleep and physical injury.

Anticipating Excess

As scholars engaging with the ephemeral flux of digital media, we anticipated extended temporalities of our projects and considered various ways to navigate our respective fields of research. These preparations weaved together long-standing ethnographic traditions as well as more recent digital media research techniques, including defining formal periods of participant observation on social media to prevent data overflow and practical measures such as cropping and blurring visual artefacts, deleting metadata and conducting reverse internet searches to ensure participant anonymity. In the lead up to our fieldwork, we also found ourselves looking beyond standardised research ethics procedures towards approaches that reimagine ethical decision-making as situational and relational. We were particularly drawn to enacting an 'ethics of care' – which prioritises relations of mutuality, kindness and respect (Swartz, 2011) – to establish and maintain care for our participants, their communities and ourselves as researchers. This commitment to care was practised through actions such as checking-in with participants after interviews, deliberating over ethical decisions with our supervisors and echoing the interactional logic of social media platforms by 'following' participants, 'liking' their posts and communicating with them via direct messages.

In the case of Reade and Moran, a deliberate choice was made to use their personal social media accounts for data collection rather than pseudonymous profiles (Ferguson, 2017; Gehl, 2016) or researcher profiles (Toffoletti et al., 2021). By opening up their extensive social media histories (for example, 10+ years on Facebook for Moran and 5+ years on Instagram for Reade), participants were able to do their own 'research' on them, mitigating power imbalances and establishing a transparent and open social media friendship. This was considered particularly important in Moran's study given she was a racial and cultural outsider (white Australian) to her participants community (Black African Australian). As we explore in the vignettes that follow, making anticipatory decisions such as these necessitated embracing an approach to research that is 'future oriented, carries an expectation of the unexpected, and demands a certain willingness to stomach uncertainty' (Tiidenberg, 2018, p. 478).

Young Women's Relations With 'fitspo' on Instagram (Reade)

Six-months after data collection concluded for my research exploring women's relations with fitspo content on Instagram, I sat in my parked car watching Instagram Stories. A story posted by one of my participants, Simone, suspended my otherwise fast swiping through Stories and gripped my attention. In it, she chatted with tears rolling down her face about the pressure she felt to post certain kinds of photos of her body on Instagram. In this vignette, I discuss the excess that emerged through continuing to follow participants on Instagram after the designated period of participant observation. I do this by providing a detailed account of my encounter with Simone's story and the ethical tensions that followed. This vignette accordingly seeks to begin a conversation – which is continued in Moran and Lyall's vignettes – about the affective and embodied labour of navigating unanticipated excess in digital research.

In 2017 and 2018, I recruited 21 Instagram users aged 20–35 years to participate in a research project exploring young women's experiences and practices of posting and engaging with fitspo content on Instagram. In addition to interviews with these participants, I followed their Instagram accounts and conducted participant observation of their profiles every day over a 3-month period. During this time, I was digitally immersed in the lives of my participants. I hid in bathrooms at social events to go on Instagram and look at participants' posts, went over my mobile phone data limit repeatedly, drove to nearby towns with internet coverage during my summer holidays and fell asleep slumped over my computer with Instagram open after midnight. Altogether, I captured an overwhelming 3,457 screenshots/screen recordings which were later compiled into numerous digital folders in the Photos application on my Mac computer.

Consistent with other social media research (e.g. Robards & Lincoln, 2020), I decided not to unfollow participants on Instagram at the end of data collection. Rather, I checked in with participants via a direct message to let them know that data collection was coming to an end and ask whether they would prefer I unfollow their account once it was over. None of the participants asked me to unfollow them and many responded with statements like 'you are most welcome to keep following me and obviously I'd love to see the outcome of your research'. While participants may have felt impolite requesting that I unfollow them, and followers are undoubtedly a currency on Instagram, I thought it was ethically important to keep a line of communication open with participants if they wanted it. In keeping with a feminist ethics of care, I also felt it could be perceived as rude or abrupt – infringing on the platform's etiquette of acting – if I was to unfollow participants once data collection finished. Continuing to follow participants on Instagram has, however, had its challenges. Given I visited participants' accounts daily throughout participant observation, Instagram's algorithmic processes returned me to their content daily for months (if not years) after data collection. Despite finding their posts and Stories interesting and strangely familiar, I found it difficult to make the transition from critically engaging with this content as 'data' to simply scrolling or swiping past it. I also found it challenging to continue viewing and reading participants' 'raw' (Reade, 2021) disclosures about mental health and body image. My encounter with Simone's Instagram Story, which I now return to, was particularly affective in provoking a range of uneasy feelings which rippled into ethical uncertainties.

While it had been 6 months since I had spoken to Simone when I watched this particular Instagram Story, I still felt a sense of closeness to her. Perhaps it was because I was in the middle of data analysis and was looking at screenshots/screen recordings of her content almost daily. Or perhaps it was because I was still viewing her Instagram Stories – which she described as sometimes 'like a therapy session' – every day due to Instagram's algorithm constantly returning me to her account. It was probably both. Nevertheless, watching Simone debrief at length and cry about her struggles with body image and the pressure she feels to post sexualised images of her body on Instagram for engagement made my heart sink. I immediately felt upset and worried about her. I certainly did not experience the 'warm and fuzzy feelings' often positively associated with participant rapport (Jovicic, 2022, p. 228). At first, I contemplated whether it was appropriate to feel upset at all. Was it a red flag that I was too close to my participants? Did I care too much? This line of questioning is unsurprising given emotion and affect have historically been neglected in (often gendered) research practices and viewed as disturbances that can contaminate scientific data (Davies & Spencer, 2010; Stodulka et al., 2019). Reassured by a feminist ethics of care, I gave myself permission to sit in the uneasy feelings of sadness and anxiety that surfaced as I watched (and rewatched) Simone's Instagram Story. As I did so, a flurry of thoughts ensued:

> Should I reply to Simone and ask if she's okay or if there's anything I can do to help? At the very least, should I reply with a love heart emoji – as is a common practice on Instagram – to let her know I am thinking of her? Maybe this would be weird though given it's been six-months since we last spoke? Simone has 45,000 followers so will probably be inundated with replies of support and may not even notice my reply. What are the temporal boundaries of participant aftercare given her story directly addresses the topics I am researching? Does 'care' always mean doing something? Simone posted similar content (albeit with slightly less intensity) during the period of participant observation, and I (regrettably) did not respond. Could it make her feel uncomfortable if I suddenly do now?

Paralysed with uncertainty, as well as a pressure to act promptly given Instagram Stories are only visible for 24 hours, I emailed one of my supervisors to ask for their guidance. They replied:

> …it all comes down to a question of boundaries and ethics […] if it were me, for someone with 45K followers, I probably wouldn't reply or comment to be honest […] if this is data you really want to use, it might be worth discussing that with them too… maybe after it has calmed down a bit, and time has passed, you can ask the person if they would mind you including this post in your analysis?

After giving it some thought and taking on my supervisor's advice, I decided not to reply to Simone's Instagram Story. This decision was influenced by Nissenbaum's (2010) concept of 'contextual integrity', which could see me replying to Simone's Story as breaching her contextual expectations of privacy given it was outside the formal period of participant observation. In other words,

Simone probably did not expect that I was watching her Stories so intently and may consider it unusual if I reached out. Given Instagram Stories are ephemeral in nature, the data inclusion question also felt inappropriate to ask after time had passed. Despite making this decision, I still – years later – feel haunted by it and question whether I failed to enact a feminist ethics of care by not reaching out to Simone. While I feel embarrassed that I was not confident enough to trust my initial impulse to reply, I recognise that navigating uncertainties such as these is an inevitable part of digital research in the making.

Ultimately, while I wish I could have explored the specifics of Simone's Instagram Story in my thesis, I had an ethical responsibility to draw boundaries – or perform 'agential cuts' (Barad, 2007) – around what social media content I would and would not include as data. Continuing to follow participants on Instagram does, however, often envelope me in their everyday lives. This has meant that I experience embodied affects that accrue over time and likely play into my understanding of participants and the phenomenon I am researching. In other words, this excess has been and continues to be difficult, if not impossible, to separate out. In the vignettes that follow, Moran and Lyall share their own unique experiences of encountering unanticipated, and often inescapable, excess in digital research.

African Australian Youth on Social Media (Moran)

Content warning: This vignette contains descriptions of racially violent content from the #BLM movement.

I acknowledge that these reflections come from a place of immense racial power and privilege. As a white Australian researching the digital practices and experiences of Black African young people during the 2020 #BLM movement, my whiteness protected me from the deadly reality of white-on-Black violence. I was able to witness and document the movement purely through my screen, never fearing that I myself would face racial violence or police brutality. I also never feared that my engagement (or lack of engagement) in BLM would prompt further retaliation, harassment, exclusion or discrimination. This starkly contrasted with the experiences of Black/Blak people and communities during this time, including African Australians (Gatwiri & Townsend-Cross, 2022; Moran & Gatwiri, 2022) and Australia's First Nations peoples (Carlson & Frazer, 2021; Newitt & Sullivan, 2022).[1]

A digital ethnographic field site crosses both online and offline worlds 'connected and constituted through the ethnographer's narrative' (Postill & Pink, 2012, p. 126). The digital field is therefore a space in which ethnographers

---

[1] In Australia, the terms 'Black' or 'Blak' are commonly used as descriptors for Australia's First Nations people, to represent their experiences and the racial divides between the Indigenous people of Australia and their settler-colonisers (see Foley, 1999; Paradies, 2006). In this chapter, I intentionally capitalise 'Black' to signify people of African descent who are raced as 'Black', acknowledging the significance of Black embodiment on their shared experiences as a racialised 'other' in white, settler-colonial Australia.

themselves must participate as they engage in a 'patchy process of discovery' (de Seta, 2020, p. 92). In this vignette, I consider the emotional and embodied experiences I encountered while conducting a social media ethnography of African young people in Australia in 2020 when two unanticipated and unprecedented global events occurred: the resurgence of the BLM movement and the COVID-19 pandemic. These two separate events – which played out in both offline and online spaces – culminated in a deep and enduring sense of hopelessness, grief and loneliness. I carried these feelings silently (and often shamefully) throughout the fieldwork and into my writing. Here, I frame these emotions as 'excess' as despite the important role they eventually played in my research, at the time they felt like a failure to detach and 'stay objective'. I hesitate to write about these feelings due to the immensely privileged position I occupied as a white researcher during the BLM movement. However, with hindsight and through engaging with other feminist research that examines the emotions of fieldwork (Biddolph, 2021), I believe that by giving voice to these deeply affective and embodied experiences (even those that feel shameful), we can demonstrate how our emotional responses to research can allow us to better represent our participants and their stories. Thus, what I initially considered as 'excess' can be embraced as a central part of the research process, shaping the stories that come to matter.

Between June 2019 and July 2020, I conducted a multi-method study – involving a social media ethnography and multiple participant interviews – that sought to understand how African young people (aged 16–25) used social media to cultivate and navigate a sense of belonging in Australia (Moran, 2022; Moran & Gatwiri, 2022; Moran & Mapedzahama, 2022a, 2022b). During a 6-month social media ethnography, I used my personal social media accounts to follow and friend my participants on Facebook, Instagram and Snapchat (see Moran & Robards, 2020). In hindsight, by using my own social media accounts in an effort to engage participants in an open and transparent research relationship, this decision, as in the case of Reade's study, resulted in deep engagement in my participants' digitally mediated lives.

For example, by using my personal social media accounts, my participants' posts were seamlessly interwoven alongside the posts of my family and friends on each of the platforms. In this way, participants' data became a normal part of my everyday scrolling and subsequently, as the study progressed it became increasingly difficult to separate my emotional responses to participants' posts from that of my friends and family. This was further intensified by what Handyside and Ringrose (2017) describe as the 'temporal fastness and ephemerality' (p. 347) of social media. Given my participants' preferences for Instagram Stories and Snapchat, I had a 'backstage pass' to their everyday lives, following them as they hung out with their friends, went to family events and shared their passions (food, travel, dance, music). I found myself congratulating participants on their graduations, voting on 'which outfit should I wear' polls and closely following their international travels. The 'sort-of' friendship that these methods established was an unanticipated part of the research design, and upon reflection, I can see how these friendships grew over the course of the fieldwork as we became more and more familiar with each other's lives through our social media posts. Subsequently, when the events of 2020 unfolded, I had become deeply invested in my participants' lives. They had become much more than research 'participants' to me, and this undoubtedly contributed to the deeply affective entanglements that I describe below.

In May 2020, I, like much of the world, was scrolling on social media, when I saw the ten-minute video documenting the murder of Black African American man George Floyd. Filmed and shared on Facebook by 17-year-old bystander Darnella Frazier, the video shows Floyd, face down on the ground, under the weight of white police officer Derek Chauvin, who slowly, in front of other white police officers and a street full of on-lookers, suffocates him to death. This video went viral on social media, and the BLM movement – which initially began in the United States in 2013 – subsequently resurfaced, with protests taking place globally. In the weeks that followed, #BLM gained momentum on social media, with new content, particularly videos, documenting other heinous and terrifying acts of white-on-Black brutality heavily documented and shared.

From May 2020 to July 2020, for hours each day, almost every day of the week, I became a front-row witness to an outpouring of rage, pain and grief as my participants – all Black African young people – used social media to engage in the BLM movement. During these 2 months (as my fieldwork concluded mid-July), I meticulously documented, analysed and notated these posts which often featured very violent and unfiltered accounts of racism and racial violence. I watched in horror as Black people were brutally attacked, restrained and murdered, often in public places and surrounded by witnesses. It was particularly confronting when participants moved from simply resharing US-based content (such as the murder of Floyd) to sharing more localised content, such as their own experiences of racial violence in Australia. Participants' personal accounts of the racism they experienced were heart breaking and I grappled with how I, as a white person, was a beneficiary of the systems causing this harm. My sadness and concern for them was underpinned by a deep shame in my complicity. My field notes at the time capture the embodied sensations I experienced as a response to these feelings: 'My hands shake' ... 'My skin feels hot' ... 'I feel so helpless'. These thoughts and feelings were all-consuming, and as the fieldwork progressed, they continuously and relentlessly occupied my waking and non-waking moments.

These feelings were, undoubtedly, exacerbated by my emotional state which had abruptly changed 2 months prior with the beginning of the first COVID-19 lockdown in Victoria, the Australian state I reside in. Overnight, our everyday lives drastically changed, as we went into what would later be known as the 'world's longest lockdown' (Miller, 2021), resulting in heightened feelings of anxiety, stress, loneliness, fear and uncertainty. During this time, confined to my home, I, like many others, turned to social media for connection, comfort and communities of care (Meier et al., 2021). And yet, as COVID-19 worsened and as BLM resurged and racially violent content intensified, I found myself feeling increasingly sad, angry and anxious when online. Social media was not a place that offered me respite from the uncertainty and loneliness of the pandemic but rather exacerbated these feelings, which continued to feel all-consuming beyond the conclusion of the fieldwork in July 2020.

When I returned to work in January 2021, BLM discourse had all but vanished from mainstream media and social media platforms, and Melbournians had spent, collectively, about 160 days in lockdown. Despite the uncertainties and anxieties of the ongoing pandemic, I felt confident returning to work, and immediately revisited the BLM data. And yet, when I rewatched the murder of George Floyd, feelings of grief, hopelessness and shame came rushing back. I found myself silently crying at my desk, feeling emotionally raw and also frustrated that these emotions had yet again surfaced. And yet, rather than be paralysed by these emotions as I had previously, I decided to try a different approach. I returned to my participants' interview transcripts (completed pre-BLM) and once again, I allowed myself to sit within their stories and to familiarise myself with a sense of who they were, beyond the racial trauma and violence that had been so overwhelming during the BLM movement. I was overcome by participants' resilience, strength and survival, emotions which allowed me to think, feel and more ethically represent their BLM stories. In this way, the unanticipated excess – all the *feelings* produced throughout my research journey – pushed the research in new directions, leading to two papers on BLM. To this end, the emotional process of this ethnographic work, while challenging, transformed my research as I embraced 'my intuition... following lines of inquiry that felt right, whether what felt right meant what felt uncomfortable, exciting and/or hopeful' (Biddolph, 2021, p. 555).

Traces of the Self in Digital Tracking Practices (Lyall)

Between 2015 and 2019, I conducted research projects exploring everyday practices of self-tracking. Like much digital media research, technosocial changes reshaped the phenomenon while I studied it. New platforms for aggregating health information (i.e. Apple Health) and sharing physical activity (i.e. Strava) rose to prominence, joining industry mainstays like Fitbit. Already specific, per the 'self' in self-tracking, practices became increasingly esoteric as the consumer marketplace for activity trackers and wearable technology exploded. Pitched as solutions to problems of contemporary life, the industry's fragmentation became fundamental to my research project: it allowed users to personalise tracking around both the passions and the problems of their lives.

In method, my research differs from Moran's and Reade's in that the approach is less ethnographic: rather than ongoing researcher observation of digital artefacts on pre-chosen platforms, my participants were asked to critically reflect on their self-tracking practices and consider what observations were possible by various audiences and via any applications they used. Essentially asking 'what does your self-tracking data say about you?' this served to pull more detailed biographic information from otherwise disparate data points: tallies of daily steps, statistics related to sleep, plots of physical activity on a map. A 'show-and-tell' approach was employed, allowing participants to explain how devices and apps were embedded in their everyday life. During interviews, participants collected screenshots and in follow-up email exchanges, sent curated examples of these.

Much of my work became centred on two possibilities: firstly, the possibility of multiple representations of experiences, in which the 'truth' might be contested. These manifested between 'objective' data (the self-tracked metrics of individuals' physical activity, diet, sleep and so on) and 'subjective' experiences (the contextualisation, clarification and contestation of datafied representations). Secondly, the communal and communicative (well articulated by Lomborg & Frandsen, 2016; Lupton, 2017) possibilities of self-tracking: despite the label, 'others' become inextricably interwoven into the data of self-tracking. These two possibilities both act in isolation to disrupt many of the designs and intentions for self-tracking applications. Each generates excesses: subjectivities are informed by entire lives that are beyond the scope of interviews, while the roles of 'others' – on platforms that refer to population-level statistics – are unknowable. But during research, these possibilities began to manifest and, in turn, generated a third possibility, one I frame here as a question: what if the tension in a participant's self-tracking metrics is tied to the absent–present 'others' they discuss in an interview? These spectres of 'otherness' were sometimes expressed as detachment from past selves and, at other times, were more literally other people.

While it was anticipated that the project would interrogate self-tracking 'going off script' in this way, the fractious aspects of participant narratives were not expected. Interviews were windows into the lifeworlds of self and other, well beyond the domain of self-tracking. A particular inflection point for this came when interviewing couples about their self-tracking (as opposed to my usual approach of individual interviews; such shifts in research approach are perhaps another form of excess). Different readings and interpretations of data were possible for this couple, and teasing out these multiple meanings became integral to how they communicated about their self-tracked activities. In subsequent interviews – and when returning to previous transcripts, recordings and screenshots – I became acutely aware of how relationships were entangled in most self-tracking practices.

An example of this was the narrative of bodily change shared by Bradley (a man in his 50s), who extensively logged his food intake using an app and tracked weight using a Wi-Fi-connected weight scale. He explained certain periods of weight gain as overindulgences, blaming his partner's cooking and meal portioning. In another example, daily steps – recorded by Daphne (a woman in her mid-forties) on her smartwatch – told stories of daily routine: revealing a home life with uneven divisions of domestic labour, ongoing illness and tense relationships to physical activity. These stories (in the moment and upon reflection) left me feeling uneasy about the specifics of relationships between partners in intimate spaces of the home and about other actors who had no right of reply. Such interpersonal interactions (and uneasy feelings) spilled over the anticipated boundaries of my research focus and interview etiquette and became excesses that I carried forward.

The same kind of excess was generated by deeper than anticipated introspection. Participants, when musing on their data, engaged with 'mediated memories' (van Dijck, 2007), stretching forward (self-tracking is after all, future orientated) and back in time. We often came across spectres of the self: negative drivers, like shame and fear, associated with self-tracking. For Adam (a man in his mid-thirties), data were a technological reminder, built on the foundation of an 'eye opening' period of inactivity where he became 'unhealthy', 'unfit' and 'tied to a desk'. For Jess (a woman in her mid-thirties), her use of technology was deeply fraught: she defined a former self – 'I don't want to go back there' – fighting against a tendency to become 'obsessed' with tracking exercise and diet. Tellingly, she arrived at our interview with her smartwatch in her backpack, rather than around her wrist. In these examples, I had to come to terms with a darker side to my chosen topic. Fun social aspects of self-tracking were stripped away, and tracking practices became actions of mitigation and expressions of fear: bodies, lifestyles and selves they wished not to regress to. I was left wondering whether the research topic reanimated or exacerbated deeper issues for these participants. Unlike Reade and Moran, my research approach had a limited window for follow-up and, regrettably, limited the enactment of a situational ethics of care.

Over time, research contemporaries and media coverage placed self-tracking in conversation with matters of morality, technology and bodies (Kent, 2020) and the transient 'heroes and villains' of diet and exercise culture. With this came an increasingly overt pathologisation of behaviour associated with self-tracking, such as diet tracking, activity monitoring and possible links to disordered eating (Berry et al., 2021; Levinson et al., 2017) and phenomena related to sleep tracking – perhaps irresponsibly – coined 'orthosomnia' (Baron et al., 2017) and 'chronorexia' (Van den Bulck, 2022). My research was not interventional, but these emerging discourses became entangled with the interpretive stages of the research project. I found that my participant's implicit and explicit disclosures of struggle tugged on the threads established in Lupton's (2017) use of 'affective atmospheres' in self-tracking. This left me worried about participants' wellbeing and, more broadly, the value of 'agnostic' research observations such as my own. If we accept the necessity of boundaries anticipated by our research designs, while recognising the inescapability of excess, what can we do to inform our work in future and 'do right' by ourselves and the people/communities that we research?

Conclusion

As the above vignettes show, we do not lack the vocabulary – rather the structures and conventions – to describe our unease and confess our uncertainty around moments of unanticipated excess. Existing structures and conventions of research can so often be technical and dehumanised, accidentally or wilfully overlooking the complex realities of conducting research on and/or with iterative and ephemeral digital platforms that generate various emotions, affects and experiences. It therefore comes as no surprise to the three of us that we found ourselves jumping at the opportunity to write about our research experiences in this book, long feeling the affective pull to channel excess into something productive. This chapter then has been both a source of comfort and camaraderie, as well a demonstration of the 'potential for excess to be attended to or transformed into something different and thus becoming no longer "excess data"' (see *Introduction*).

To return to the question posed at the end of the last vignette, we hope that through sharing our experiences of excess, other researchers can find ways to prepare for and reflect on the porous boundaries of digital research. We also hope to open up dialogue between scholars so that they can ask questions, talk through struggles and ultimately find solidarity amid discomfort and uncertainty. In learning to appreciate excess and articulate uneasy feelings as evidence of care and effort in research, the vignettes included in this chapter add to conversations in which 'non-data' and 'unplanned moments' (Fujii, 2015) are considered to have enduring value through their ongoing ability to stimulate reflexivity. As digital media places increasing demands on our attention, both as scholars and audiences, research encounters can at once become 'moments of care and carelessness' (Murray, 2020, pp. 445–446). Here, our attention as researchers can easily be co-opted and stray beyond the anticipated boundaries and scope of our inquiries, resulting in excess. Rather than remaining remnants of unease and regret, we suggest that this excess can push us and our work – empirically, methodologically and ethically – in new directions and should not be discounted.

References

Abidin, C., & de Seta, G. (2020). Doing digital ethnography: Private messages from the field. *Journal of Digital Social Research*, *2*(1), 1–97. https://doi.org/10.33621/jdsr.v2i1.35

Barad, K. (2007). *Meeting the universe halfway*. Duke University Press.

Baron, K. G., Abbott, S., Jao, N., Manalo, N., & Mullen, R. (2017). Orthosomnia: Are some patients taking the quantified self too far? *Journal of Clinical Sleep Medicine*, *13*(2), 351–354. https://doi.org/10.5664/jcsm.6472

Berry, R. A., Rodgers, R. F., & Campagna, J. (2021). Outperforming iBodies: A conceptual framework integrating body performance self-tracking technologies with body image and eating concerns. *Sex Roles*, *85*(1–2), 1–12. https://doi.org/10.1007/s11199-020-01201-6

Biddolph, C. (2021). Emotions, de/attachment, and the digital archive: Reading violence at the International Criminal Tribunal for the Former Yugoslavia (ICTY). *Millennium: Journal of International Studies*, *49*(3), 530–555. https://doi.org/10.1177/03058298211033027

Bowles, H. C. R., Fleming, S., & Parker, A. (2021). A confessional representation of ethnographic fieldwork in an academy sport setting. *Journal of Contemporary Ethnography*, *50*(5), 683–715. https://doi.org/10.1177/08912416211003152

Carlson, B., & Frazer, R. (2021). *Indigenous digital life*. Palgrave Macmillan. https://doi.org/10.1007/978-3-030-84796-8_8

Davies, J., & Spencer, D. (2010). *Emotions in the field: The psychology of anthropology of fieldwork experience*. Stanford University Press.

de Seta, G. (2020). Three lies of digital ethnography. *Journal of Digital Social Research*, *2*(1), 77–97. https://doi.org/10.33621/jdsr.v2i1.24

Ferguson, R.-H. (2017). Offline 'stranger' and online lurker: Methods for an ethnography of illicit transactions on the darknet. *Qualitative Research*, *17*(6), 683–698. https://doi.org/10.1177/1468794117718894

Foley, G. (1999). Whiteness and blackness in the Koori struggle for self-determination. *Just Policy: A Journal of Australian Social Policy, 19*(20), 74–88. https://search.informit.org/doi/abs/10.3316/ielapa.200102959

Fujii, L. A. (2015). Five stories of accidental ethnography: Turning unplanned moments in the field into data. *Qualitative Research, 15*(4), 525–539. https://doi.org/10.1177/1468794114548945

Gatwiri, K., & Townsend-Cross, M. (2022). 'Block, unfollow, delete': The impacts of the #BlackLivesMatter movement on interracial relationships in Australia. *British Journal of Social Work, 52*, 3721–3739. https://doi.org/10.1093/bjsw/bcac008

Gehl, R. W. (2016). Power/freedom on the dark web: A digital ethnography of the dark web social network. *New Media & Society, 18*(7), 1219–1235. https://doi.org/10.1177/1461444814554900

Handyside, S., & Ringrose, J. (2017). Snapchat memory and youth digital sexual cultures: Mediated temporality, duration and affect. *Journal of Gender Studies, 26*(3), 347–360. https://doi.org/10.1080/09589236.2017.1280384

Jovicic, S. (2022). The affective triad: Smartphone in the ethnographic encounter. *Media and Communication, 10*(3), 225–235. https://doi.org/10.17645/mac.v10i3.5331

Kent, R. (2020). Self-tracking and digital food cultures: Surveillance and self-representation of the moral 'healthy' body. In D. Lupton & Z. Feldman (Eds.), *Digital food cultures* (1st ed., pp. 19–34). Routledge. https://doi.org/10.4324/9780429402135

Levinson, C. A., Fewell, L., & Brosof, L. C. (2017). MyFitnessPal calorie tracker usage in eating disorders. *Eating Behaviors, 27*, 14–16. https://doi.org/10.1016/j.eatbeh.2017.08.003

Lomborg, S., & Frandsen, K. (2016). Self-tracking as communication. *Information, Communication & Society, 19*(7), 1015–1027. https://doi.org/10.1080/1369118X.2015.1067710

Lupton, D. (2017). How does health feel? Towards research on the affective atmospheres of digital health. *Digital Health, 3*, 1–11. https://doi.org/10.1177/2055207617701276

Meier, J., Noel, J. A., & Kasper, K. (2021). Alone together: Computer-mediated communication in leisure time during and after the COVID-19 pandemic. *Frontiers in Psychology, 12*, 1–13. https://doi.org/10.3389/fpsyg.2021.666655

Miller, N. (2021, October 3). Proud of mad? Melbourne's marathon lockdown becomes the world's longest. *The Age.* https://www.theage.com.au/national/victoria/proud-or-mad-melbourne-s-marathon-lockdown-becomes-the-world-s-longest-20210930-p58w9w.html

Moran, C. (2022). 'African kids can': Challenging the African gangs narrative on social media. *Media International Australia*, 1–24. https://doi.org/10.1177/1329878X221142879

Moran, C., & Gatwiri, K. (2022). #BlackLivesMatter: Exploring the digital practises of African Australian youth on social media. *Media, Culture & Society, 44*(7), 1330–1353. https://doi.org/10.1177/01634437221089246

Moran, C., & Mapedzahama, V. (2022a). Black bodies, Black queens, and the Black sisterhood on social media: Perspectives from young African women in Australia. *Journal of Youth Studies*, 1–28. https://doi.org/10.1080/13676261.2022.2098704

Moran, C., & Mapedzahama, V. (2022b). Afrocentric digital belonging: Perspectives from Black African young people in Australia. *Australasian Review of African Studies, 42*(2), 26–53.

Moran, C., & Robards, B. (2020). Researching connected African youth in Australia through social media ethnography and scroll-back interviews. *African Journalism Studies, 41*(4), 83–102. https://doi.org/10.1080/23743670.2020.1817765

Murray, S. (2020). Postdigital cultural studies. *International Journal of Cultural Studies, 23*(4), 441–450. https://doi.org/10.1177/1367877920918599

Newitt, R., & Sullivan, C. T. (2022). COVID-19, "Black lives matter" and indigenous Australians: A tale of two intersecting pandemics. In S. D. Brunn & D. Gilbreath (Eds.), *COVID-19 and a world of ad hoc geographies* (pp. 1375–1392). Springer. https://doi.org/10.1007/978-3-030-94350-9_75

Nissenbaum, H. (2010). *Privacy in context: Technology, policy, and the integrity of social life*. Stanford University Press.

Palmer, J., Fam, D., Smith, T., & Kilham, S. (2014). Ethics in fieldwork: Reflections on the unexpected. *The Qualitative Report, 19*(28), 1–13. https://doi.org/10.46743/2160-3715/2014.1136

Paradies, Y. C. (2006). Beyond black and white, essentialism, hybridity and indigeneity. *Journal of Sociology, 42*(4), 355–367. https://doi.org/10.1177/1440783306069993

Postill, J., & Pink, S. (2012). Social media ethnography: The digital researcher in a messy web. *Media International Australia, 145*(1), 123–134. https://doi.org/10.1177/1329878X1214500114

Reade, J. (2021). Keeping it raw on the 'gram: Authenticity, relatability and digital intimacy in fitness cultures on Instagram. *New Media & Society, 23*(3), 535–553. https://doi.org/10.1177/1461444819891699

Robards, B., & Lincoln, S. (2020). *Growing up on Facebook*. Peter Lang.

Stodulka, T., Dinkelaker, S., & Thajib, F. (Eds.). (2019). *Affective dimensions of fieldwork and ethnography*. Springer.

Swartz, S. (2011). 'Going deep' and 'giving back': Strategies for exceeding ethical expectations when researching amongst vulnerable youth. *Qualitative Research, 11*(1), 47–68. https://doi.org/10.1177/1468794110385885

Tiidenberg, K. (2018). Ethics in digital research. In U. Flick (Ed.), *The SAGE handbook of qualitative data collection* (pp. 466–481). SAGE. https://doi.org/10.4135/9781526416070

Toffoletti, K., Thorpe, H., Pavlidis, A., Olive, R., & Moran, C. (2021). Visibility and vulnerability on Instagram: Negotiating safety in women's online-offline fitness spaces. *Leisure Sciences*, 1–19. https://doi.org/10.1080/01490400.2021.1884628

Van den Bulck, J. (2022). Chronorexia and Orthosomnia: Towards the development of scales to measure unhealthy obsessions with sleep. *Sleep Medicine, 100*, S29. https://doi.org/10.1016/j.sleep.2022.05.091

van Dijck, J. (2007). *Mediated memories in the digital age*. Stanford University Press.

Chapter 4

The Digital Mess of a Digital Ethnography

Clare Southerton

La Trobe University, Australia

Abstract

Digital ethnographers acknowledge that online spaces are always co-produced within the social, political, material and sensory – never distinct from what we may think of as 'offline'. However, in documenting our fieldwork (e.g. fieldnotes, screenshots and recordings) and representing our findings in research outputs, scholars tend to draw more firm boundaries around our object of study. The excess, the digital life on the margins of digital ethnography often entangled with the fieldwork site, is cut away to present a neatened case study that can be analysed. In this chapter, I examine the excess and 'unrelated' screenshots I took during a digital ethnography project in 2020 to explore what these 'offcuts' can offer in contextualising my encounters with the short-form video app TikTok. Over nine months in 2020, I observed healthcare workers using the app to share health information and analyse their content. At the same time, with the pandemic unfolding across the world, I was scrolling through the news on Twitter, watching press conferences from health authorities, sharing funny TikToks with friends and receiving information in a family group chat. This layering of everyday experiences of the pandemic forms part of how I sensed and experienced TikTok content during my digital ethnography. I examine these 'excess' screenshots to think through the always more-than-digital boundaries of digital ethnographic fieldwork. I reflect on the messy entanglement of digital ethnography, where my own digital practices – intensified by COVID-19 lockdown conditions – and the broader conditions they emerged from, became inevitably enmeshed with my research practice.

Keywords: Digital ethnography; screenshots; COVID-19; fieldwork; TikTok; surplus data; qualitative research methods

Introduction

For researchers doing fieldwork online, it might appear that the COVID-19 pandemic was not disruptive to our capacity to conduct fieldwork. After all, digital communities were more central than ever as social distancing forced many to work remotely, stay indoors and avoid unnecessary travel. Digitally mediated interactions such as video calling, at times, stood in for in-person interactions even at significant social rituals like weddings and funerals for the sake of reducing the risk of spreading the virus (Southerton & Clark, 2023). However, the result was not simply that digital spaces offered a straightforward way to 'capture' the pandemic experience. Indeed, qualitative digital researchers acknowledge that online spaces are always co-produced within the social, political, material and sensory, and are never distinct from what we may think of as 'offline' (Hine, 2020; Postill & Pink, 2012). As Hjorth et al. (2022) argue, the pandemic conditions exacerbated the existing 'presence bleed' (Gregg, 2011), wherein the boundaries between work and home life have evaporated – hastened by digital practices: after work 'Zoom drinks' sitting at the same kitchen table you worked all day or doing laundry while your camera is off in a videoconference. During the pandemic, access to outside spaces and physical social interactions diminished, with care and labour entangled, and digital spaces interwoven into this mess (Hjorth et al., 2022).

I argue that the pandemic operates as a further challenge to this facade of objectivity and distance, forcing researchers to attend to the ways that fieldwork is not a 'capture' of a tangible event but rather forming and reforming in an ongoing and shifting set of affective and embodied relations. This chapter draws on the long tradition of qualitative research seeking to challenge positivist approaches to the field, in favour of acknowledging the messy and blurred boundaries that are often retrospectively stabilised by the researcher in the writing up of the research. This chapter seeks to return to these untidy boundaries, to some of the material that is carved off as to present a more coherent fieldsite, in order to draw out what this material might offer.

In 2020 from March to December I was engaged in a digital ethnography on the short video app TikTok, examining on how healthcare workers were using the app to share educational content. As the pandemic unfolded during the project, I also became interested in how they used their platforms to advocate and share information about the virus. My process involved time on the app but I also documented the process using notes, screenshotting, saving videos, etc. Alongside, this data collection, I was largely inhabiting digital spaces both for leisure and work as, with lockdowns taking place in Australia, my life outside of the digital world shrunk. I was reading the news, reading social media and then I was going to work on Zoom, doing my digital fieldwork on TikTok. More broadly, social media platforms reported significant increases in use during the pandemic with Meta, who owns WhatsApp, Instagram and Facebook, reporting a 50% increase in the use of instant messaging in March 2020 worldwide (Schultz, 2020).

The boundaries between the research and my life were messy, not only blurred by the context collapse of using social media platforms for work and leisure

(Davis & Jurgenson, 2014) but also by the pervasive affective atmospheres of the pandemic (Anderson, 2009). Affective atmosphere is a useful concept here to understand how the pandemic conditions give rise to collective emotional states. As Ben Anderson (2009, p. 78) explains, 'atmospheres are the shared ground from which subjective states and their attendant feelings and emotions emerge'. This kind of thinking has been taken up in digital scholarship, with Ian Tucker and Lewis Goodings (2017) adapting the term to 'digital atmospheres' to explore how digital spaces are experienced spatially, even if they are not constituted as physical spaces. In this chapter, I want to consider how the affective atmospheres of the coronavirus pandemic call attention to the value in the messiness of digital fieldwork. In particular, I argue that returning to these offcuts can offer insights into how affective atmospheres traverse digital platforms and, in the conditions of the pandemic, reflect the shifting emotional tone reverberating around mass global events.

In this chapter, I will first explore how the boundaries of what constitutes the empirical field have been problematised in qualitative research. I will then provide a more detailed explanation of my methodology, drawing on inspiration from Annette Markham's (2016) work on remix methodology and Tamara Kneese's (2022) work on screenshots as research tools. After outlining my methodological approach, I provide an analysis of the three major themes that emerged from my 'surplus' screenshots, using the concept of affective atmospheres, which I argue help uncover the rich edges of the research project from which digital life during the pandemic can be more deeply explored.

The Messy Boundaries of 'the Field'

The porous boundaries of the fieldsite are not a new 'problem' or indeed one unique to the challenge of doing qualitative research in digital spaces. Qualitative researchers have long argued that the research process involves a series of decisions by the researcher that work to construct the empirical, much more than it is 'uncovered' as a stable entity. Indigenous and First Nations scholars, critical race scholars, feminist scholars and queer scholars have all challenged the notion that knowledge exists 'out there' to be unearthed by the knower (Browne & Nash, 2016; Dadas, 2016; Few et al., 2003; Smith, 2021; Sundberg, 2003). As Māori scholar Linda Tuhiwai Smith (2021) argues, the positivist practice of preserving clear distinctions between the research subject and the researcher has been a weapon of colonial violence, and a way to preserve and legitimise hierarchies of knowledge.

There is much that can be gained from an orientation to the empirical that is not seeking order but instead seeking to sit within the mess. Sociologist Scott Lash (2009, p. 176) argues that rather than seeking to make the empirical coherent and ordered, the discipline might more fruitfully orient itself towards the ongoing, multiple and processual nature of empirical reality (Lash, 2009). Feminist scholar Donna Haraway (1988) similarly rejects any notion that we can analyse the empirical in any detached way – we are always embodied, partial and relational.

At the same time, Haraway compellingly acknowledges the need for some ground to hold on to and move beyond the binary of objectivity and relativism, and argues that knowledge must be understood as emerging from embodied subjectivity.

Digital ethnography, as a method in which the researcher spends an extended period of time embedded in a digital field site, involves a unique set of challenges when it comes to making decisions about the boundaries of the empirical. In digital qualitative research, scholars have taken up debates around the status of the empirical to consider how notions of objectivity and coherence shape this research practice (Baym, 2008; De Seta, 2020; Hine, 2020; Postill & Pink, 2012). Communication scholar Nancy Baym (2008, p. 176) argues that the 'research paths that offer the most novel insight are those that challenge researchers' ingrained ways of seeing things and the interpretations they build throughout the research process'. Christine Hine (2020) calls for digital ethnographers to attend to the ways the digital spaces are experienced in sensory and affective ways, and to think through the ways the digital is always more-than-digital and always experienced in embodied ways.

In reflecting on my own decisions around the boundaries of my project, I am drawn to digital anthropologist Gabriele De Seta's (2020) compelling and personal account of the 'cutting away' involved in a digital ethnography. He writes:

> Even when grounded on extensive datasets, hundreds of fieldnotes and collections of traces, the accounts produced by digital ethnographers end up including an extremely narrow selection of inscriptions, often thoroughly edited, translated, scrambled, rephrased, anonymised, cropped, selectively blurred and collated according to a constellation of ethical, argumentative and aesthetic authorial decisions. (De Seta, 2020, p. 90)

De Seta (2020) acknowledges the role that institutional pressures, including time and funding pressures, play in shaping the decisions that are made to focus on specific aspects of a project and to follow particular lines of inquiry. He also reflects on the leaky boundaries between the formal 'fieldwork' time and the time spent in digital spaces before and after, the kind of artificial boundaries imposed on the research encounter:

> Once I was formally and physically 'on fieldwork', not much changed: I was still browsing websites, scrolling through social media feeds, chatting with friends, liking their posts, commenting on news stories, watching and listening to content shared by my contacts, collecting samples of interactions and writing fieldnotes to wrap up daily observations and encounters. (De Seta, 2020, p. 85)

Indeed, these distinctions between the beginning of fieldwork or the end of the fieldwork are artificially inserted, raising questions about when a research encounter really begins or ends. When my devices retain memories of my fieldwork through search histories and invisible data doubles follow me beyond these boundaries (Haggerty & Ericson, 2000) and when presence bleed entangles my work, digital life and digital leisure (Hjorth et al., 2022), where does the digital research end and the digital researcher begin?

Remixed Methods for Pandemic Atmospheres

Building on this rich literature in which the messy boundaries of the empirical field have been explored, I am seeking to redraw and reinterpret the lines I initially drew around my digital ethnography on TikTok during the pandemic in order to examine the materials that I excluded. I take inspiration here from Annette Markham's (2016, p. 64) concept of 'remix methodology', which she offers not as a new method but as a way of thinking about methods and research. Remix methods focus on aspects of research that are often downplayed or even erased such as 'using serendipity, playing with different perspectives, generating partial renderings, moving through multiple variations' (Markham, 2016, p. 65). On the question of quality and rigour, Markham suggests that remix thinking offers some more generative modes of engagement here too. The success of remixes is based on their capacity to resonate with the audience and Markham argues that digital social research too might seek to resonate, especially with the communities we draw from. Markham argues digital research spaces are dynamic and unstable, with blurred boundaries between the self and the other and agency distributed across both individual actors, as well as platforms and other technologies. However, she encourages scholars to see this as an opportunity to think creatively – rather than as something to be conquered and overcome by ever more 'accurate' methods of capture. Like other scholars draw on here, Markham proposes a refocus of scholarship away from providing 'neat' answers, and truly shaking lingering positivist forms of inquiry, and instead focusing on the value of interrogation, retrospection and reflection. In particular, she emphasises the importance of moving away from depicting our scholarship as a linear process wherein '[v]arious stages are described as separate moments, and findings are written up at the end' (2016, p. 73).

Taking this approach to my 'excess' materials from the digital ethnography I conducted on TikTok involves refusing a neat research narrative. Exposing the false starts and errors in the process feels vulnerable. As De Seta (2020) points out, methodological choices are deployed as a way to stake a claim to legitimacy and authority in the academy. Yet, without this reflection, it is easy to smooth over important decisions that ultimately shape the project as a whole. My digital ethnography project studied health-focused content produced by healthcare workers on TikTok and was conducted from March 2020 until November 2020. The research really unfolded by accident as I initially was conducting background research for what I envisaged would be a content analysis of TikToks under a range of hashtags in a specific period of time (April 2020), which was significant because this was when much of the world was heading into significant COVID-19 related restrictions. As I became embedded in the project and more engaged with my data collection, it became clear that this approach was extremely limited. Navigating the hashtags was only really possible because I had spent hours and hours browsing other hashtags, looking at the profiles of prominent creators and getting lost down rabbit holes in my own use of TikTok. The trends only made sense because I spent my weekends on TikTok. The 'data collection' leaked at the edges into my life, and my 'sample' seemed woefully out of context without understanding the lively platform that it lived in. Eventually, I shifted my approach to conducting a months-long digital ethnography that lasted until the end of the year, taking more detailed field notes, and screenshots, saving videos, keeping untidy notes on my phone and digital traces of the project were scattered everywhere across my smartphone. I identified several case studies of healthcare workers who were prominent on the platform and spent time scrolling back through their content, tracing them across platforms.

From my digital ethnography, I was able to analyse more richly the constantly shifting atmospheres of the platform and the way that healthcare workers drew on the affordances of the platform to connect with their audiences (Southerton, 2021). However, in focusing my analysis on TikTok as an isolated platform, I felt limited in my ability to engage with the broader circulating affects surrounding the pandemic and the ways these traversed platforms. As a prolific screenshot taker of my own digital life, even beyond the boundaries of my digital ethnography, I had an abundance of digital material from the time I conducted my digital ethnography that sat just outside the boundaries of the project. I often found myself returning to these digital records as a way to access memories, a sense of a particular time and the pandemic. These screenshots reflect my digital life at the time I was in the digital field. Scrolling through the news on Twitter, watching press conferences from health authorities, sharing pandemic memes with friends and receiving information in a family group chat; this layering of everyday experiences of the pandemic forms part of how I sensed and experienced TikTok content during my digital ethnography.

I employ these screenshots not as evidence to 'prove' the existence of an objective pandemic affective atmosphere, rather I draw on these digital artefacts as a subjective record of my own sensory and affective experience. Indeed, as Kneese (2022, p. 154) argues, screenshots are a reflection of the taker's view of the digital world, '[t]hey preserve our own attention to particular moments in time and communicate our experiences to others when we share them'. Kneese argues that screenshots offer a research tool that can respond to the temporality of corporatised digital platforms, when digital content is ephemeral, and a platform's demise may erase its content – at least its lively context – and screenshots can allow digital content to live on in other ways.

The Affective Atmospheres of the Offcuts

In the section that follows, I explore the themes that emerged when I explored the screenshots I had taken throughout my digital ethnography that were 'offcuts' –

rendered peripheral to the project by the boundaries I drew around the digital ethnography project in order to present a coherent empirical object. In exploring these boundary spaces, I seek to examine the circulating emotions and affects that constituted my pandemic digital life. The screenshots presented here are fabrications of the original images to either preserve the privacy of content creators or, in some cases to preserve copyrighted materials. In doing so, I take inspiration from Markham's (2012) work on fabrication in digital research, wherein the researcher employs a bricolage-style transformation of empirical material into composite accounts or representational interactions, to preserve privacy. Some screenshots are close replications, where the material is not produced by an individual and the replication serves the purpose of avoiding copyright infringement. Others are amalgamations of multiple images to preserve individual creator privacy, and this will be indicated in the text.

In These Unprecedented Times, Barbie Is There for You

A strong theme in the captured screenshots were moments that reflected a sense of these 'unprecedented times', being acknowledged across many digital spaces in a way that was palpable as a user. While we might talk about collective moods and feelings being perceptible as we move around our everyday lives, but with our social worlds being much more limited due to travel restrictions and lockdowns, I felt these shifts in feeling increasingly through digital spaces. Screenshots captured the daily press conferences from government health officials being live-streamed on Facebook, emails sent from global brands to their customer mailing lists 'checking in' and acknowledging the pandemic and news headlines sent to friends in group chats as the pandemic unfolded.

I captured the below screenshot (Fig. 4.1, replication provided) early in the project, and early in the spread of COVID-19 in Australia, around the time the first national restrictions were introduced to limit the spread of the virus. It was an Instagram Story post, which is a temporary social media post visible for 24 hours, from the Barbie social media account – a doll brand manufactured by Mattel. The account usually posts images captioned as if from the doll, Barbie's, point of view, usually using dolls posed together in various scenes. In their analysis of Barbie's marketing, Pritchard et al. (2019, p. 344) argue that Mattel's Barbie, often depicted doing any range of high-powered jobs, is 'an embodiment of the unbounded individual choice of neoliberalism' and a postfeminist cultural icon. This image alludes to the neoliberal individualism of Barbie; however, the screenshot also captures the pervasive and all-encompassing sense of the pandemic wherein unexpected digital spaces were transformed with collective discourse about the virus reaching even the most seemingly unrelated corners. The everywhere-at-once nature of pandemic feelings speaks to both the 'presence bleed' facilitated by the entanglement of work, leisure and other activities all within the home during lockdowns (Hjorth et al., 2022), as well as the less tangible ways the pandemic created shared feelings of, as Barbie puts it, 'a lot going on'.

Fig. 4.1. Author's Replication of Mattel's Barbie Instagram Story, 20th March 2020.

Information Saturation and Responsibilisation

The most significant theme in my screenshots, especially in the earlier months of the pandemic was content I saved that provided information about the virus itself, which included symptoms, how it is transmitted, how it should be treated and other public health information being disseminated, often through official social media channels of government health organisations or global health organisations. I also screenshotted information about changes in rules and restrictions in my local area, news articles that documented the spread of the virus and a range of other related material. The screenshot below (Fig. 4.2), is a replication of an info banner I captured that was added to the social media app Facebook to give

Fig. 4.2. Author's Replication of Facebook COVID-19 Information Pop-Up, 15th August 2020.

information about the virus, including information about how to prevent spreading it, which was sourced from the World Health Organization (WHO).

This strategy to direct users towards authoritative sources of health information, such as the WHO, was a common approach to fight misinformation used by most of the mainstream social media platforms (Krishnan et al., 2021). Notable in the above image, and in many of the images I captured, was an emphasis on individual practices such as hand washing, mask wearing and social distancing. These align with broader shifts in health discourses towards risk management and prevention focused on individual risk, rather than social trends (Crawford, 1980). Health risk comes to be managed through the body, through bodily techniques such as a 'healthy diet' or exercise or in this instance hygiene practices such as handwashing. Therefore, individuals are rendered responsible for managing their risk of contracting or spreading the virus. As health sociologist Deborah Lupton (2006, p. 17) explains, '[b]eing categorized as "at risk" from a medical problem means that one is placed in a liminal category of wellness: neither actually ill (yet) nor fully well'. This atmosphere of health risk rendered me a responsible subject, tasked with seeking information about the virus and reducing my risk of contracting it.

The saturation of COVID-19 health information is also part of the phenomenon of 'doomscrolling', that is the act of obsessively engaging with upsetting news on social media (Ytre-Arne & Moe, 2021). A Norweigan qualitative study conducted early in their pandemic lockdown found that users had a complex relationship with doomscrolling, being both dependent on the news and social media for up-to-date information but simultaneously overwhelmed and emotionally drained by it (Ytre-Arne & Moe, 2021). Certainly, my screenshots of different lists of COVID-19 symptoms, locations of new cases in my city and news articles projecting negative outlooks for the months ahead align with this framing. These screenshots also speak to what Priya Vaughan et al. (2022) describe as a shared COVID-19 vocabulary, which emerged during the pandemic through greater consumption of public health education materials.

Wellness Discourses in the Crisis

When many found themselves confined within the boundaries of their homes due to lockdowns, there was a notable negative impact on mental health (Robinson et al., 2022; Serafini et al., 2020). This unprecedented period of isolation generated a collective sense of unease and uncertainty. Amidst this backdrop, there was a proliferation of social media content centred on productivity, self-care and wellness, arising from both the vacuum of other available topics for many content creators to focus on and in response to these circulating collective feelings, with digital audiences finding solidarity in shared online experiences (Levesque et al., 2023; Øvretveit, 2021; Yalın, 2021).

Among my screenshots, I found many that captured snippets of information intended to offer a kind of balm for the chaos of the time. These took the form of social media posts that featured recommendations for how to keep a daily routine, Twitter threads explaining that it is normal to find it difficult to concentrate during a global emergency, infographics on how to meditate to reduce stress and stretches to reduce the pain of sitting in improper positions for long periods of time. These speak to, I suspect, attempts I was making at the time to insert some structure and stability into my days as the months of working from home, based at the kitchen table of my small apartment had begun to take their toll. To offer an indicative example of the many different screenshots I took, and to preserve the privacy of the creators whose content I captured, I have fabricated an example post below (Fig. 4.3).

The image captures the aesthetics of the screenshots I took, a feminine 'girlboss' entrepreneurial visual reminiscent of Barbie's Instagram story that sought to 'inspire' during this time. The proliferation of this kind of content aligns with

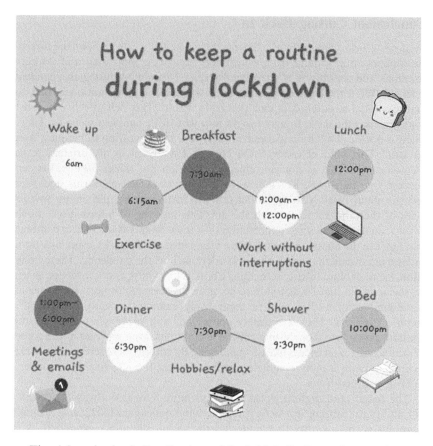

Fig. 4.3. Author's Replication of Social Media Posts Captured in 2020 (Original Screenshots Not Included to Preserve Privacy and Copyright).

findings from Rachel Wood's (2023) qualitative study where interviews with participants in the United Kingdom reported feeling that lockdown was an 'opportunity' for self-improvement and productivity, while they would not be seen daily. Wood (2023) emphasises a shift from aesthetic labour, focused on appearance, towards *affective labour* focused on producing specific affective and emotional states. We aim to be 'the "good" pandemic citizen who not only survives but thrives in crisis conditions, caring for and improving the self in ways that are both positive and productive' (Wood, 2023, p. 16).

Conclusion: Cutting Back In

By digging into these 'offcuts', these screenshots tell a story about the affective atmospheres, the ground from which the circulating individual and collective emotions and sensations of the digital spaces I inhabited during the pandemic emerged. What these screenshots revealed was the complex emotional landscape that my initial research data emerged from within. This rich affective backdrop contextualises the data. It gives insight into why, for example a video on TikTok where a doctor playfully criticises common poor mask wearing techniques, would go viral. This kind of content, the content I analysed in my original project focused on TikTok, is not consumed in isolation but rather *only* makes sense because the audiences, like me, were living lives across platforms and seeing content about mask wearing, about how the virus spreads and about how particles of the virus move through the air. This layering of information, moving *through* digital spaces gives opportunities for these moments of collective intimacy that tap into the dominant feeling like a viral video about masks, especially during widespread events that reach across borders such as the pandemic. These images allow me to explore further something about information and knowledge sharing on social media that I was trying to get at in my research project. Platforms and the digital content that renders them lively cannot be neatly carved off as empirical objects. They are deeply connected, and make sense through their relationships to broader shifting collective emotions, even more so in the context of significant global events like the pandemic. By cutting these screenshots back in I can help paint a more complete picture of where the affective atmospheres of TikTok emerged from.

The social (and digital) world is always more-than and always in excess of our ability to 'capture' it. As Orit Halpern and colleagues (2022, p. 210) put it, '[s]urplus is the quantity that underlies the social, the affect generated by the sheer volume of circulating and acting data converted into the quality of quantity itself'. When we talk about the more-than-digital of digital research, we are talking about the emotional and material landscapes that digital worlds are forming and reforming within. As many scholars have argued, the process of research involves an inevitable carving off of the field site in order to present a kind of tangible project. However, this process always constructs a partial empirical object, organised and constituted by our editorial choices. For those of us involved in digital qualitative research, we sometimes find ourselves facing the temptation, or even feel the necessity, to draw the line of the project at the platform's boundary. At other times, we might create an artificial divide, separating the digital realm from the so-called offline world. As this chapter has explored, the conditions of the COVID-19 pandemic rendered such cutting perhaps even more messy and incomplete, as context collapse and blurred boundaries allowed the affective atmospheres of the pandemic to filter from research contexts to personal lives and everywhere in between.

References

Anderson, B. (2009). Affective atmospheres. *Emotion, Space and Society*, 2(2), 77–81. https://doi.org/10.1016/j.emospa.2009.08.005

Baym, N. K. (2008). Question 6 - What constitutes quality in qualitative internet research? In A. Markham & N. K. Baym (Eds.), *Internet inquiry: Conversations about method* (pp. 173–190). SAGE Publications.

Browne, K., & Nash, C. J. (2016). Queer methods and methodologies: An introduction. In K. Browne & C. J. Nash (Eds.), *Queer methods and methodologies* (pp. 1–24). Routledge.

Crawford, R. (1980). Healthism and the medicalization of everyday life. *International Journal of Health Services: Planning, Administration, Evaluation*, 10(3), 365–388. https://doi.org/10.2190/3H2H-3XJN-3KAY-G9NY

Dadas, C. (2016). Messy methods: Queer methodological approaches to researching social media. *Computers and Composition*, 40, 60–72. https://doi.org/10.1016/j.compcom.2016.03.007

Davis, J. L., & Jurgenson, N. (2014). Context collapse: Theorizing context collusions and collisions. *Information, Communication & Society*, 17(4), 476–485. https://doi.org/10.1080/1369118x.2014.888458

De Seta, G. (2020). Three lies of digital ethnography. *Journal of Digital Social Research*, 2(1), 77–97. https://doi.org/10.33621/jdsr.v2i1.24

Few, A. L., Stephens, D. P., & Rouse-Arnett, M. (2003). Sister-to-sister talk: Transcending boundaries and challenges in qualitative research with black women. *Family Relations*, 52(3), 205–215. https://doi.org/10.1111/j.1741-3729.2003.00205.x

Gregg, M. (2011). *Work's intimacy*. Polity Press.

Haggerty, K., & Ericson, R. (2000). The surveillant assemblage. *British Journal of Sociology*, 51(4), 605–622. https://doi.org/10.1080/00071310020015280

Halpern, O., Jagoda, P., Kirkwood, J. W., & Weatherby, L. (2022). Surplus data: An introduction. *Critical Inquiry*, 48(2), 197–210. https://doi.org/10.1086/717320

Haraway, D. J. (1988). Situated knowledges: The science question in feminism and the privilege of partial perspective. *Feminist Studies*, 14(3), 575–599. https://doi.org/10.2307/3178066

Hine, C. (2020). *Ethnography for the internet: Embedded, embodied and everyday*. Routledge.

Hjorth, L., Coombs, G., Hussey-Smith, K., & van Loon, J. (2022). Work, care and creativity in a time of COVID-19: Creatively mapping presence bleed in the home. *Digital Creativity*, 33(3), 219–233. https://doi.org/10.1080/14626268.2022.2082487

Kneese, T. (2022). Breakdown as method: Screenshots for dying worlds. *Media Theory*, 5(2), 142–166.

Krishnan, N., Gu, J., Tromble, R., & Abroms, L. C. (2021). Research note: Examining how various social media platforms have responded to COVID-19 misinformation. *Harvard Kennedy School Misinformation Review*. https://doi.org/10.37016/mr-2020-85

Lash, S. (2009). Afterword: In praise of the a posteriori. *European Journal of Social Theory*, 12(1), 175–187. https://doi.org/10.1177/1368431008099646

Levesque, N., Hachey, A., & Pergelova, A. (2023). No filter: Navigating well-being in troubled times as social media influencers. *Journal of Marketing Management*, 39(11–12), 1–34.

Lupton, D. (2006). Sociology and risk. In G. Mythen & S. Walklate (Eds.), *Beyond the risk society: Critical reflections on risk and human security* (pp. 11–24). Open University Press.

Markham, A. (2012). Fabrication as ethical practice. *Information, Communication & Society, 15*(3), 334–353. https://doi.org/10.1080/1369118x.2011.641993

Markham, A. (2016). Remix cultures, remix methods: Reframing qualitative inquiry for social media contexts. In N. K. Denzin & M. D. Giardina (Eds.), *Global dimensions of qualitative inquiry* (pp. 63–82). Routledge.

Øvretveit, J. (2021). Innovations in self care and close care made during COVID 19 pandemic: A narrative review. *International Journal of Health Governance, 26*(2), 88–99. https://doi.org/10.1108/ijhg-02-2021-0007

Postill, J., & Pink, S. (2012). Social media ethnography: The digital researcher in a messy web. *Media International Australia, 145*(1), 123–134. https://doi.org/10.1177/1329878x1214500114

Pritchard, K., Mackenzie Davey, K., & Cooper, H. (2019). Aesthetic labouring and the female entrepreneur: 'Entrepreneurship that wouldn't chip your nails'. *International Small Business Journal, 37*(4), 343–364. https://doi.org/10.1177/0266242618823408

Robinson, E., Sutin, A. R., Daly, M., & Jones, A. (2022). A systematic review and meta-analysis of longitudinal cohort studies comparing mental health before versus during the COVID-19 pandemic in 2020. *Journal of Affective Disorders, 296*, 567–576. https://doi.org/10.1016/j.jad.2021.09.098

Schultz, A. (2020, March 24). Keeping our services stable and reliable during the COVID-19 outbreak. *Meta Newsroom.* https://about.fb.com/news/2020/03/keeping-our-apps-stable-during-covid-19/

Serafini, G., Parmigiani, B., Amerio, A., Aguglia, A., Sher, L., & Amore, M. (2020). The psychological impact of COVID-19 on the mental health in the general population. *QJM: Monthly Journal of the Association of Physicians, 113*(8), 531–537. https://doi.org/10.1093/qjmed/hcaa201

Smith, L. T. (2021). *Decolonizing methodologies: Indigenous peoples and research* (3rd ed.). Zed Books.

Southerton, C. (2021). Research perspectives on TikTok & its legacy apps|Lip-syncing and saving lives: Healthcare workers on TikTok. *International Journal of Communication, 15*, 3248–3268.

Southerton, C., & Clark, M. (2023). Imagining intimacy after COVID. In R. W. Paul & F. Kristen (Eds.), *The Emerald handbook of the sociology of emotions for a post-pandemic world* (pp. 161–176). Emerald Publishing Limited.

Sundberg, J. (2003). Masculinist epistemologies and the politics of fieldwork in Latin Americanist geography. *The Professional Geographer: The Journal of the Association of American Geographers, 55*(2), 180–190. https://doi.org/10.1111/0033-0124.5502006

Tucker, I. M., & Goodings, L. (2017). Digital atmospheres: Affective practices of care in Elefriends. *Sociology of Health & Illness, 39*(4), 629–642. https://doi.org/10.1111/1467-9566.12545

Vaughan, P., Lenette, C., & Boydell, K. (2022). "This bloody rona!": Using the digital story completion method and thematic analysis to explore the mental health impacts of COVID-19 in Australia. *BMJ Open, 12*(1), e057393. https://doi.org/10.1136/bmjopen-2021-057393

Wood, R. (2023). From aesthetic labour to affective labour: Feminine beauty and body work as self-care in UK 'lockdown'. *Gender, Place & Culture: A Journal of Feminist Geography*, 1–20. https://doi.org/10.1080/0966369x.2023.2192892

Yalın, A. (2021). Quarantine vlogs: Digital affective labor and self-governance during COVID-19. *AoIR Selected Papers of Internet Research, 2021*. https://doi.org/10.5210/spir.v2021i0.12076

Ytre-Arne, B., & Moe, H. (2021). Doomscrolling, monitoring and avoiding: News use in COVID-19 pandemic Lockdown. *Journalism Studies*, *22*(13), 1739–1755. https://doi.org/10.1080/1461670x.2021.1952475

Chapter 5

'Digital Hoarding' and Embracing Data Excess in Digital Cultures Research

Natalie Ann Hendry

The University of Melbourne, Australia

Abstract

When I think about the relative abundance of data in digital media research, I often recall a remark I overheard – *it's just like digital hoarding?* – while presenting digital ethnographic research at a youth mental health conference. I study youth mental health and social media and often interact with scholars who privilege more systematic, empiricist ways of understanding young people's lives, in contrast to my own iterative approaches to collecting, archiving and creating with what feels like endless digital and non-digital data. In this chapter, I return to the remark and explore digital hoarding as a productive and generative concept for exploring excess digital data in digital ethnography research and fieldwork. I argue for interpreting excess data as inevitable in digital fieldwork and something that is potentially, but not necessarily always, generative for digital media researchers. By sharing research on how people talk about hoarding possessions and reviewing hoarding in digital contexts, I discuss how digital media research may mirror, or at least attempt to mirror, the complex yet everyday quotidian digital practices, including digital hoarding, of people and the digital cultures they create and participate in. This chapter considers the implications of digital hoarding in fieldwork and how embracing digital excess and hoarding may disrupt systematic approaches to digital organisation or attempts to predetermine hierarchical relationships between data. In doing so, I do not attempt to formalise my methods as a digital ethnographer but instead aim to focus on creativity, curiosity and fluidity as guiding principles in digital fieldwork.

Keywords: Digital hoarding; digital archives; digital ethnography; health research; ethnography; digital fieldwork

Introduction

When I think about data excess and digital media research, my thoughts often return to a comment someone made several years ago. It was a quick, half-whispered remark, in a small room at a youth mental health research conference. I had been on a panel, speaking with other mental health researchers about social media and young people's lives. At one point in the session, I briefly noted my research approach as a digital ethnographer, sharing that my fieldwork rituals included collecting, curating and archiving what felt like endless digital and non-digital data, sometimes without a precise idea of why but hopefully with a sense of how mental health cultures circulate through social media, digital platforms and beyond. Someone remarked quickly – *it's just like digital hoarding?* – perhaps to me, perhaps to one of the other panel members or a colleague beside them. I doubt the comment was pejorative or accusatory, that it claimed that I was not a 'real' researcher, or that there was no value to what I shared with the panel and audience. I also doubt the commenter could ever realise how that little remark had grabbed me and that I would recall it years later.

Adding a disclaimer to my research is now common for me in those youth health, mixed-up-but-mostly-clinical research spaces. My work is critical, interdisciplinary and informed by media studies, cultural studies and sociologies of health and education, as well as my training in digital ethnography, an approach unfamiliar to many mental health practitioners and scholars. It attempts to move away from the typical epistemological and methodological standards of clinical, public or even some social health scholarship. Yet I want to speak to and with others who are not from my same research world about mental health, wellbeing and digital cultures; this is a task of translation, to remake my research practices and processes into something coherent to public health and mental health colleagues and audiences. At times, doing this can feel like bluffing a cohesive, linear map of my methods out of my fieldwork, out of my hoarded digital data, sanitising my research into something orderly for others who tell different, more systematic stories of our social worlds.

Speaking with others from dissimilar disciplines and fields often requires me to offer more formal details of methodologies and methods – and those expectations sprawl out into the world of social research too. I can recall reviewer comments asking for more precise descriptions of methods of analysis or to *exactly* quantify the pieces of 'data' that inform my journal articles. But how would this work? How do I count screenshots of posts from social media accounts I still follow via my research accounts? Do comments to posts or images count as separate data or part of a post? What of field notes tracking my movement between accounts and platforms? How do I break apart digital data into pieces when I experience it as some sort of partial insight into a whole – a post, an account, a forum, a platform, a browser, a culture?

In this chapter, I return to the remark – *it's just like digital hoarding?* – as a productive concept to explore digital data excess in digital ethnography research and discuss research that moves away from certainty as a guiding value. Here, I argue for interpreting excess data as inevitable in digital fieldwork and something that is potentially, but not necessarily always, generative for digital media researchers. Hoarding as a playful metaphor and digital hoarding as a concept describing personal archiving and research practices both seem to be organic to my digital fieldwork. By sharing research on how people talk about hoarding possessions and reviewing hoarding in digital contexts, I discuss how digital media research may mirror, or at least attempt to mirror, the complex and everyday quotidian digital practices, including digital hoarding, of the people and digital cultures we study. This chapter considers what the implications of digital hoarding in fieldwork might be and how embracing digital hoarding may disrupt systematic approaches to digital organisation or attempts to predetermine hierarchical relationships between data. In doing so, I do not attempt to formalise my methods as a digital ethnographer but instead aim to focus on creativity, curiosity and fluidity as guiding principles in digital fieldwork.

Hoarding Possessions and Personal Digital Archiving

> Value embedded but not declared. (Anderson et al., 2008, p. 187)

While reading public health, nursing and social work scholarship on hoarding, I came upon Elizabeth Andersen and colleagues' (2008, p. 187) nursing study of older people in Canada who collected, did not discard and thus hoarded their possessions. I was struck by how they described why older people hoarded material items, that these 'possessions had value embedded but not declared' (p. 187). Hoarding was not some cognitive disorder or disruption, nor merely an individual obsession; among other comforts and rewards, hoarding offered these older adults social connection to other people and the world through newspapers and books, reassurance that they could remember information if an item was kept, a feeling of being needed by others as they could pass on useful items and a sense of control as they could organise and arrange possessions within their sight. The article included photographs from the team's fieldwork – images chosen by the participants for the researchers to keep – of their homes, their living conditions and examples of the possessions they lived among. Some of the images were captioned with interview quotes that could otherwise mirror my own research notes: 'I am in the middle of things' (Alice), 'How the hell did I get that?' (Raymond), 'Don't touch anything on the kitchen table' (Leona) and 'Stuff I have got that doesn't go anywhere' (William; Andersen et al., 2008).

I begin here, thinking about hoarding, not to appropriate what might otherwise (and debatably) be identified as psychiatric language (given hoarding is labelled as a disorder in the DSM-5; American Psychiatric Association, 2013) nor to explore hoarding as psychopathology or interrogate alternative social or cultural possibilities of the term. Instead, these insights into hoarding echo much of my practice as a digital ethnographer and media scholar. *Stuff I have got that doesn't go anywhere* could be the motto of my fieldwork process to collect, collate, engage with and encounter digital data – digital data that doesn't go anywhere (yet) but is archived, driven by a sense of some sort of scholarly value that is embedded but cannot yet be declared.

Writing about the digital context, curator and English scholar Anna Chen (2014, p. 117) turns to the language of hoarding and suggests that 'the image of the "digital hoarder", buried under the disorganized turmoil created by the volume of his digital possessions' is now positioned within everyday vernacular to convey 'everyday digital collecting habits'. While some in the archival trade shy away from any claims of being professionally obsessed hoarders, people are using the concept of hoarding popularly to describe their personal digital collections. For the professional curators and archivists Chen reviews, such vernacular digital collecting is positioned as less significant, less valuable and less than rational, often a failure in organisation. While specialist archivists might call for the public to more strategically organise their files and folders, Chen (2014) disagrees with these appeals for organisation over disorder, as:

> ...encouraging individuals to apply analog filing and organizational structures in a digital environment may have limited utility and success: not only do the different behaviours of digital and analog records impede users from following these instructions, but accumulating and organizing one's personal documents can also, like hoarding, *be an idiosyncratic, complex, and emotionally significant act that serves many purposes beyond expediting access and retrieval*. (my emphasis, p. 133)

Retelling insights from studies about personal digital archiving including Marshall (2011) and Kim (2013), Chen (2014) highlights how the vernacular practice of digital hoarding extends and exceeds physical hoarding. Both physical and digital hoarding are often disorganised, but not indiscriminate, and offer people emotional reassurance through collecting possessions. People too may prioritise aesthetic over practical value through their physical *and* digital hoarding or archiving. Yet digital hoarding offers an abundance that physical hoarding can only dream of. Digital hoarding is relatively unlimited, and the capacity for digital storage to be seemingly endless – especially as storage options continue to proliferate beyond one's own hardware into cloud options across multiple devices and platforms – removes the limits of space that constrain physical hoarding practices (Chen, 2014; Kim, 2013). While personal digital archiving and digital hoarding practices are characterised by poor naming conventions and unsystematic file organisation, individuals are increasingly reliant on digital search functions rather than folders for finding files and data; 'retention, rather than destruction, is now the norm' (Chen, 2014, p. 127). Given this practical context, there is a complex relationship between people and their digital data in these studies. Data holds memories, may be saved in duplicate to preserve the embeddedness of data or preserve how it is networked to other memories or relationships (e.g. a photo may be saved in a digital album but may also still be attached to the original message so the context of the photo persists) and moves in response to what tasks are active and what are inactive (e.g. organising files that are actively being used at one time, while inactive files are unsystematically saved; Chen, 2014; Kim, 2013; Marshall, 2011). Chen (2014) stresses that:

> Creators who are increasingly engaging in "digital pack-rattery" are not accumulating without thought or intellect, but rather indulging, like hoarders, in a multiplicity of values – emotional, psychological, and practical – that can be assigned *without hierarchical privilege* to a much wider array of objects and actions. Records can be saved because they represent nuanced social relationships, arranged as an expression of self-identity or deleted simply because doing so is "fun." (my emphasis, p. 132)

The Inevitability of Data Excess and Digital Hoarding in Research

Such digital hoarding is inevitable given the nature of digital data and people's complex relationships to data, archiving and (re-)organising their digital lives. Digital data are increasingly abundant (Boczkowski, 2021); more and more, the process of datafication produces intentional and unintentional datasets as users' digital and non-digital 'actions and behaviours are translated into [digital] data that can be recorded, sorted or indeed commodified by governments and private companies' (Pangrazio & Sefton-Green, 2022, p. 1). Through datafication, everyday life is transformed into vast volumes of digital data as 'more and more aspects of social life are rendered machine-readable, quantifiable by virtue of the fact that more of social life plays out in digital spaces' (Southerton & Taylor, 2021, p. 250). The dynamic outcomes of this process to turn everyday life into data are frequently automated and, in turn, shape the algorithmic decisions that organise users' interfaces and interactions (Burgess et al., 2022). When individuals and groups participate in digital cultures and data cultures (Burgess et al., 2022), their interactions contribute to the proliferation of data creation and circulation. In this way, personal digital hoarding becomes increasingly inevitable as people's relationships with data grow more complex and intertwined with their lives – they engage with an expanding array of digital data or datafied processes, expanding the possibilities of their personal digital archives.

Likewise, I propose that excess data, and thus digital hoarding, are inherent to digital media research. As researchers, our digital interactions and encounters across diverse devices, platforms, sites and digital and non-digital contexts intrinsically give rise to an abundance of data. Here, Chen's (2014) argument translates almost too easily to the research context and runs parallel to my practices as a digital ethnographer. Digital hoarding as a *research practice*, rather than a personal archival practice, is part of the organic work of digital media research, just as it is organic to an individual's everyday digital life as they save and archive content and data. For researchers too, attempts to characterise disorganised digital data as merely indiscriminately accumulated or in need of hierarchical or systematic organisation potentially ignore the messy and elaborate relationships between data and cultures – the very relationships that are often central to the questions that guide fieldwork inquiries.

In my youth mental health and social media research, my digital fieldwork processes emphasise the 'excessive' nature of digital data, digital cultures and processes of datafication. Illustrating this messy excess, my data is often regularly and immediately replicated during fieldwork as I navigate through platforms, apps and sites, both a function of using those platforms and my practices as a researcher to 'capture' data. Most of the time, I employ non-automated approaches to my fieldwork. These practices do not involve automatically scraping or extracting data from devices, platforms or sites. Instead, I manually scroll through, collate, save, collect and note how social media platforms and profiles operate and circulate; however, this approach does engage with automated processes in other ways. For example, I might save a video meme from a particular mental health advocate's Instagram account within my research account on the Instagram app. It then becomes listed in my series of saved posts on the platform. Or I may video screen record how I move through my For You home screen on the TikTok app via my phone, tracking how self-help and therapy content is merged between videos of cute dogs or viral cooking recipes. This video is then synchronised and automatically uploaded to my cloud-based research folder, even before I write field notes or go through individual TikTok videos or creator accounts. In both examples, what may be included in my research data is multiplied as I move between taking notes during fieldwork, screen, video or audio recording content in the moment, saving or collating content, posts or profiles through the platforms and then accessing different content, profiles or accounts through device, platform or app functions that duplicate and re-circulate data – as a user of those platforms (thus producing metadata for the platform about me as a user) but also as a researcher duplicating data and content across my research datasets both within and beyond platforms and sites.

Understanding digital research practices as digital hoarding also reminds us of the temporal dimensions of digital data. Like other digital ethnographers, my fieldwork experiences illustrate that digital data is unstable and often ephemeral (Møller & Robards, 2019); it changes over time, appearing and disappearing, reappearing and disappearing. As digital scholars Møller and Robards (2019) note, following and mapping digital traces – the recorded media inscriptions of people's digital practices (Howison et al., 2011) – cannot be achieved only through automated or algorithmic processes but 'requires often-disparate elements across different temporal and spatial planes to be combined in ways that achieve internal structural cohesion by virtue of their internal relations and not by externally given logics' (p. 98). In my own work, I not only follow and track data within and across platforms but also return later in my fieldwork to digital platforms, sites and profiles to update or reengage with content or data that may have moved, refreshed or has shifted (e.g. reviewing changes to comments on a post, following how a news article has circulated across multiple platforms). At times, this includes discovering 'lost' data as content has been removed from an account or website or my access has been revoked; this shifts how the data emerges in my digital archives, perhaps only as a screenshot saved or written into my field notes, rather than also embedded in different profiles or accounts within social media platforms.

Given the potential volume, complexity and instability of digital data and data processes in research – due to datafication, digital cultures and fieldwork contexts and practices – the crux of digital media research, as I see it, lies in *organising* data rather than *collecting* data. While collecting data is not always simple or straightforward, I suggest that because digital data is relatively abundant or at least that digital cultures offer us multiple modes of data collection, our challenge is in exploring the potential value for creating ethnographic knowledge through our digital archiving, organising and 'hoarding'. Of course, there are constraints and limits for researchers when collecting data, including those related to institutional concerns (e.g. what practices are 'permitted' within ethical guidelines with or without some sort of consent process; see Hokke et al., 2020), commercial or proprietary concerns (e.g. what activities are within terms of service of a site or app, what access to Application Programming Interfaces or metadata is permitted to researchers or users, what digital processes remain 'black-boxed'; see Tromble, 2021) and practical concerns (e.g. what time commitment is available for fieldwork, what digital traces may be accessed or tracked by researchers, if researchers are using manual or automated collection processes or other digital tools), among others. Although these are important concerns to consider, here I am interested in how we might make sense of the messiness of creating knowledge through digital hoarding. If digital hoarding is an inevitable researcher data archiving practice, how might we engage with the potential value of hoarding as researchers?

This question recalls the personal digital archival practices discussed by Chen (2014) that I outlined earlier in the chapter, where *how* data is stored is guided by multiple emotional, psychological and practical values where there is no overarching hierarchical order to personal digital organisation. Akin to these everyday personal archivists, saving and storing their lives and data across multiple platforms and devices, as a researcher, I too attempt to privilege multiple, non-hierarchical relationships between data, contexts, people and my analysis. By multiplying my data and archives, I attempt to maintain relationships between data and context (e.g. saving a post within my research accounts so I can return to where it was first posted or reshared), as well as track other emerging relationships (e.g. follow how others have shared posts or content, archive how content might recirculate in memes or other forums). I move and rearrange digital data by recreating and changing my digital folders and relationships between data (e.g. duplicate files in different folders) and reorganise non-digital data over and over. This includes printing visual data to map out relationships between data spread out across a table, or rewriting and reorganising data and field notes over and over. By incorporating my (somewhat chaotic) digital archives, live-in-the-moment digital fieldwork and field notes and other writing, this approach attempts to 'integrate analyses of media objects and media environments reflexively, with traces of use, observation of participant media practice and media narration' (Møller & Robards, 2019, p. 98). Organisation and reorganisation is key to the meaning-making process here. I do not try to cull down my archives or notes because saving and hoarding such digital excess is relatively possible for my (mostly) manual process.

Through my research, I am reminded again and again that what is potentially insightful or of value for a researcher cannot be easily determined in advance of fieldwork or data collection or curation. Holding my research questions loosely through my fieldwork offers room to embrace what emerges from organising and reorganising data throughout my research. What is valuable, useful or generative, months or years later, is created through reorganisation and remaking of relationships between data and various configurations of fields or networks. This eschews empiricist demands for pre-establishing neat boundaries of research fields (see later in this chapter), systematic thematic codes or other organisational hierarchies to curate digital data collection. Again, we circle back to digital hoarding where the value of accumulated data is not declared (yet!).

However, the value of this data abundance is *not* because of any possible quantity or volume of digital data we may encounter, nor that a massive dataset could point us closer to some sort of truth. If we adopted that approach and aimed for the largest dataset possible, we would move closer to quantitative or positivist claims where the sheer *size* of a data set is (typically) positively associated with its *value* – to be able to enact calculations and predictions based on 'big' data, find patterns where one would not be looking for them or know the 'correct' statistical analysis to be undertaken to predict and increasingly *produce* reality (see discussions in boyd & Crawford, 2012; Elish & boyd, 2018). These assertions – that data volume is valuable in and of itself – contribute to positivist critique regarding youth mental health research, which devalues research that moves away from systematic methodologies to understand and know young people's lives in the context of digital cultures.

These assertions drive the queries and demands for more *precise* detail or that I offer large datasets to justify my research claims, as I discussed in the introduction to this chapter. For example, we can see how this logic is replicated in public health research to understand mental health-related content on social media platforms. Methodologically, these studies typically define what is relevant to their dataset at the start of their research (such as social media images that demonstrate explicit representations of depression or self-injury) and then collect data that meet predetermined inclusion criteria through hashtag or other tagging functions of platforms, in order to make claims about the potential harms (or benefits) of this content (for example, Fulcher et al., 2020; see also discussion in Hendry, 2024). In my own digital ethnography research and interviewing participants on multiple occasions, the meanings and practices associated with what might be seen as distressing social media content shifted and changed over time, duplicating interpretations about my data; at one point, an image might reassure a participant that they are not alone in their mental health struggles, at other times an image may be a marker of their mental health progress (Hendry, 2018). In a different approach, digital scholars Anthony McCosker and Ysabel Gerrard (2020) explored *hashtag practices* related to depression on Instagram, rather than the hashtag depression itself. In their dataset following #depressed on Instagram, they found 'seemingly irrelevant content' – content and posts that would otherwise be cut out from a dataset that only included images that met strict inclusion criteria – but that this 'noise in our data set showed us that only a minority of posts tagged with #depressed seem to explicitly convey aspects of the actual embodied experience of depression' (p. 1901). Seemingly excessive, irrelevant and indiscriminate data had a central role in their study and complicated too-simple assumptions about mental health themes on social media.

Unlike empiricist perspectives that emphasise 'big data' or large datasets as inherently valuable, my digital hoarding approach to digital ethnography views the value of abundant digital data as emergent. The 'excessiveness' of digital data is interpretative, not calculative; it invites questions of value throughout the research process rather than pre-determining value before fieldwork begins. In some of my research studying health, wellbeing and wellness cultures, it was only through regular, years-long fieldwork in multiple platforms and sites that I came to refine my research questions or notice what was of value within my hoarded data. By repeatedly noticing funny animal videos or mundane images of flowers again and again in my data related to young people and mental health, I started to ask: how might endless scrolling of posts on the social media platform Tumblr offer comfort for someone even as they circulate through the most mundane or non-spectacular photos, images or memes when they feel distressed or disillusioned (for example, Hendry, 2020)?

Data volume and quantity here are aligned to the rhythm of fieldwork: to be curious about how and why social media cultures emerge and circulate or to interpret patterns (or lack of patterns) in what is mundane in people's posting and sharing, to pay attention to what tropes and genres of communication appear again and again. This brings us to a central challenge through the history of (digital) ethnography: how then might we understand our research fields or sites if we embrace digital abundance and hoarding?

Digital Ethnography, Relations as Fields and an Ethnographic Sensibility

Reflecting on years of ethnographic discussion and debate, sociologist Matthew Desmond (2014) holds that the vital task for ethnographers – one that he believes is often ignored or under-acknowledged – is to define or create their object of analysis, their ethnographic object. He observes that while 'Ethnographers have proven to be as critical and careful about *how* to study something', such as the ethical dimensions of their fieldwork or the validity of ethnography, 'they have been cavalier about *what* to study' (p. 549). Desmond argues that ethnographers typically establish *groups* (e.g. practices of people with some shared attribute) or *places* (e.g. location-based structures or organisations of activity) as their objects. Yet these ethnographic objects fall short in accounting for the dynamic relationships and processes of social life and instead presuppose groups or places as fixed entities with clear boundaries. In contrast to these static ethnographic objects, Desmond offers 'relational ethnography' to instead attend to 'processes involving configurations of relations among different actors or institutions' (p. 547). Here, fieldwork is guided by a relational object – 'fields rather than places, boundaries rather than bounded groups, processes rather than processed people, and cultural conflict rather than group culture' (p. 547) – that follows people across different social contexts and settings.

In this account of research as relational ethnography, *relationships* are central to establishing the boundaries or scope of fieldwork. While Desmond argues that the object of analysis for ethnographers has received less attention, my own experience as a digital ethnographer suggests otherwise. My entry to ethnography was through *digital* ethnography – a digital orientation to ethnography as an iterative and inductive approach – where the nature of the ethnographic 'field' has been, and remains, challenging to neatly define and bound. The often blurred boundaries of digital fields and the edges of digital projects continue to motivate and confront ethnographers and other digital scholars (for example, see Markham & Baym, 2009).

Indeed, as technology sociologist Christine Hine (2015, p. 14) carefully outlines, understanding *what* we are studying is a central responsibility for ethnographers of the digital. As the internet (and what we might designate as 'the digital') blends into the background of everyday life, we need to 'capture and make visible such aspects of the Internet as have become unremarkable'. Digital cultures, social media, digital technologies and digital platforms are, just as Hine writes about the internet, not 'singular object[s] contained within one site' (p. 62). Here, we can also recall George E. Marcus' (1995) 'multi-sited' approach to ethnography and to track and follow traces of people, activities and other interests instead of studying a bounded, single-site location. Building on Marcus' work, digital technology scholar Jenna Burrell (2016, p. 181) offers that we can understand our fields as *networks* that include 'physical, virtual and imagined spaces' where the field is created through the researcher themselves tracing participants and phenomena and creating a network as a field site. Burrell's approach emphasises the 'potential for empirical surprises and novel insights' (p. 196).

Given the inherent excess of digital research, we might be guided by our research questions to narrow how we produce our networked fields or we may also be guided by an amorphous, emergent or relational sense of the 'field'. This in turn creates never-static relations between data, people and practices – data is produced through research practices where data is always changing, multiplying and transforming. One's dataset, as I see it, can never be predicted or even coded without the capacity to move, rearrange, reorganise data and relationships between data and writing. Hine (2015, p. 87) urges that ethnography for the internet, as a holistic approach, requires an 'ethnographer's openness to unanticipated aspects of meaning-making, and to the emergence of forms of connection and boundary not anticipated at the outset of the study'. Uncertainty is standard; field sites, fields and boundaries are 'fluid and emergent construct[s]' as the internet, digital platforms or other digital media

> ...can be taken as multiply embedded in diverse frames of activity and meaning-making. Taking this multiple embedding seriously encourages an open approach to the identification of field sites,

focused on exploring connections and discontinuities as they emerge rather than assuming the existence of boundaries, and adopting various means of visualising and moving through the field. (2015, p. 87)

The work of digital, internet or virtual ethnography is to establish a 'sensitivity to various possibilities of connection that different modes of presence and interaction offer' (Hine, 2015, p. 15). We might call this an 'ethnographic sensibility' alongside other scholars who point to ethnography requiring an ever-evolving 'attunement to worlds shared via participant-observation that extend beyond the parameters of a narrowly defined research question [... and that] its unique contribution is in that space of excess, of telling us more than we knew to ask' (McGranahan, 2018, p. 7). Part of this research work is being open to creating research insights that do offer us more than we knew to ask but also knowing that sometimes digital excess may not (yet) be meaningful to our projects. To return to Chen's (2014, p. 134) discussion of digital hoarding, I share her perspective that not 'all disorganization is deeply meaningful'. Digital disorganisation and excess can have meaning or produce new insights, but this is not always what happens in research; value may still remain undeclared. Abundant data do not guarantee research insights but provide a possibility for new knowledge to be created.

In the last few years, I have been using ethnographic writing as my primary practice for analysis and creating and declaring value from my digital excess and hoarding. I write alongside moving around, curating and retracing my data or digital fields. This involves opening files across multiple devices, revisiting or rewatching data or profiles, rearranging, printing and annotating data or representations of data (e.g. screenshots of videos), relistening to interviews or other recordings and then writing 'into' the data. I forgo thematic coding or organising hierarchies of themes and instead write and rewrite field notes and analytic notes. My writing often has no clear ending, nor a central identified theme that guides my writing before I start, but I am open to creating themes or foci through writing.

This writing process points towards what Australian education scholars Coles and Thomson (2016) call 'inbetween writing', the taken-for-granted writing that occurs between original field notes and reflective writing that incorporates data, theory and analysis. They suggest that ethnographic writing emerges between rewriting (description, redescription and reflection) and intertextuality (how the writing incorporates fieldwork records, memory and other documents, as well as different descriptions and/or other theoretical or ethnographic texts). In my writing practice, I move back and forth between these modes of in-between writing: writing descriptions of digital data, then redescriptions incorporating other field notes, then reflecting on my analysis, then back to description again as I reorganise data and notes. This feels like writing in spirals, rather than trying to hierarchically organise data and analysis, narrow down my focus, return strictly to my research questions or attempt to write as a linear process that starts with description and moves slowly towards reflection and 'final' analysis. Similarly, digital hoarding denotes a research practice with no clear conclusion. It requires re-working, recasting and recreating – where to put things, what goes next to something, and is there more room to think about something else? Each writing excerpt or section becomes part of the digital hoarding of data; as I return to data and write, I produce more data, and in turn, this motivates new data, returning to data (even if it has shifted as I have noted earlier in this chapter) or reorganising data to produce new insights or directions from the excess – the very value I aim to produce as a digital researcher.

Conclusion

Digital hoarding as a research practice embraces digital data excess. Like physical hoarding or personal digital archiving, digital hoarding for digital media researchers points to the potential value or hope of a valuable future: value is embedded in our data or datasets but may not yet be declared at the start of, or even throughout, our research processes. This value of digital hoarding, excessive digital data or 'too much' data – screenshots, liked posts, downloaded videos, written notes about digital encounters and so on – cannot be determined a priori. While a research question may guide digital ethnographers, my approach is to attempt to map or engage with the mundane and routine in digital cultures, hold my questions loosely and be guided by feelings, uncertainties or curiosities.

At the same time, I acknowledge that the urge to try to record, capture or curate seemingly 'everything' also comes from the challenges that I shared in the introduction to this chapter. Making visible research processes or accounting for what is in a dataset to other audiences and researchers, especially those demanding clear and logical methodological decisions, feels like sanitising and reorganising my digital hoarding into something quite distanced from my fieldwork practices and 'inbetween writing' (Coles & Thomson, 2016).

I am reassured though when I read American sociologist Howard S. Becker (2007) who reminds us that 'there is no best way to tell a story about society' (p. 285) and that he is:

> ...convinced that contemporary social science has crippled itself by imposing strict limits on the permissible ways of telling that researchers find out about the things they study. The formulaic nature of journal articles leaves no room for "extraneous" detail or multiple interpretive possibilities that other modes of presenting what we know allow, encourage, or even require. (2007, p. 286)

This reminds me of how demands for formalising our methods and methodologies resemble what sociologist John Law (2004, p. 9) calls a 'desire for certainty' or 'the expectations of generality' that are typically enacted through activities towards replicability or reliability. I am reassured too when I discover Dutch media scholars Michael Stevenson and Tamara Witschge (2020, p. 117) writing about the 'methods we live by' and finding my disciplinary challenges on their pages. Like Stevenson and Witschge, I am interested in how we might move methods away from 'a social purpose of legitimation or distinction' (p. 118) towards research guided by uncertainty, curiosity or another value, one perhaps unstated or yet to be determined in the early stages of fieldwork.

Encouraged by these conversations about embracing uncertainty in the research process, I have offered digital hoarding as one generative concept to describe ways of doing digital research that champion the potential value of digital excess for knowledge creation and production. By embracing digital hoarding and disorder as a valued digital process and experience – even if it might distance me at times from more clinical approaches to studying youth mental health or wellbeing – this may allow more space for curiosity, fluidity and other ways to tell stories about digital cultures.

References

American Psychiatric Association. (2013). *Diagnostic and statistical manual of mental disorders* (5th ed.). American Psychiatric Association.

Andersen, E., Raffin-Bouchal, S., & Marcy-Edwards, D. (2008). Reasons to accumulate excess: Older adults who hoard possessions. *Home Health Care Services Quarterly*, *27*(3), 187–216. https://doi.org/10.1080/01621420802319993

Becker, H. S. (2007). *Telling about society*. University of Chicago Press.

Boczkowski, P. J. (2021). *Abundance: On the experience of living in a world of information plenty*. Oxford University Press.

boyd, d., & Crawford, K. (2012). Critical questions for big data: Provocations for a cultural, technological, and scholarly phenomenon. *Information, Communication & Society*, *15*(5), 662–679. https://doi.org/10.1080/1369118X.2012.678878

Burgess, J., Albury, K., McCosker, A., & Wilken, R. (2022). *Everyday data cultures*. Polity Press.

Burrell, J. (2016). How the machine 'thinks': Understanding opacity in machine learning algorithms. *Big Data & Society*, *3*(1), https://doi.org/10.1177/2053951715622512

Chen, A. (2014). Disorder: Vocabularies of hoarding in personal digital archiving practices. *Archivaria*, *78*(Fall), 115–134.

Coles, R., & Thomson, P. (2016). Beyond records and representations: Inbetween writing in educational ethnography. *Ethnography and Education*, *11*(3), 253–266. https://doi.org/10.1080/17457823.2015.1085324

Desmond, M. (2014). Relational ethnography. *Theory and Society*, *43*(5), 547–579. https://doi.org/10.1007/s11186-014-9232-5

Elish, M. C., & boyd, d. (2018). Situating methods in the magic of big data and AI. *Communication Monographs*, *85*(1), 57–80. https://doi.org/10.1080/03637751.2017.1375130

Fulcher, J. A., Dunbar, S., Orlando, E., Woodruff, S. J., & Santarossa, S. (2020). #selfharn on Instagram: Understanding online communities surrounding non-suicidal self-injury through conversations and common properties among authors. *Digital Health*, *6*. https://doi.org/10.1177/2055207620922389

Hendry, N. A. (2018). *Everyday anxieties: Young women, mental illness and social media practices of visibility and connection*. Doctoral dissertation, RMIT University.

Hendry, N. A. (2020). Young women's mental illness and (in-)visible social media practices of control and emotional recognition. *Social Media + Society*, *6*(4), 1–10. https://doi.org/10.1177/2056305120963832

Hendry, N. A. (2024). Youth health and wellbeing in digital cultures. In H. Cahill & H. Cuervo (Eds.), *Handbook of children and youth studies* (pp. 1–14). Springer.

Hine, C. (2015). *Ethnography for the internet: Embedded, embodied and everyday*. Bloomsbury Publishing.

Hokke, S., Hackworth, N. J., Bennetts, S. K., Nicholson, J. M., Keyzer, P., Lucke, J., Zion, L., & Crawford, S. B. (2020). Ethical considerations in using social media to engage research participants: Perspectives of Australian researchers and ethics committee members. *Journal of Empirical Research on Human Research Ethics*, *15*(1–2), 12–27. https://doi.org/10.1177/1556264619854629

Howison, J., Wiggins, A., & Crowston, K. (2011). Validity issues in the use of social network analysis with digital trace data. *Journal of the Association for Information Systems*, *12*(12), 767–797. https://doi.org/10.17705/1jais.00282

Kim, S. (2013). *Personal digital archives: Preservation of documents, preservation of self*. PhD dissertation, University of Texas.

Law, J. (2004). *After method: Mess in social science research*. Routledge.

Marcus, G. E. (1995). Ethnography in/of the world system: The emergence of multi-sited ethnography. *Annual Review of Anthropology*, *24*, 95–117.

Markham, A. N., & Baym, N. K. (2009). *Internet inquiry: Conversations about method*. Sage Publications.

Marshall, C. C. (2011). Challenges and opportunities for personal digital archiving. In C. Lee (Ed.), *I, digital. Personal collections in the digital era* (pp. 90–114). Society of American Archivists.

McCosker, A., & Gerrard, Y. (2020). Hashtagging depression on Instagram: Towards a more inclusive mental health research methodology. *New Media & Society*, *23*(7), 1899–1919. https://doi.org/10.1177/1461444820921349

McGranahan, C. (2018). Ethnography beyond method: The importance of an ethnographic sensibility. *Sites: A Journal of Social Anthropology and Cultural Studies*, *15*(1), 1–10. https://doi.org/10.11157/sites-id373

Møller, K., & Robards, B. (2019). Walking through, going along and scrolling back: Ephemeral mobilities in digital ethnography. *Nordicom Review*, *40*(s1), 95–109.

Pangrazio, L., & Sefton-Green, J. (2022). Learning to live well with data: Concepts and challenges. In L. Pangrazio & J. Sefton-Green (Eds.), *Learning to live with datafication: Educational case studies and initiatives from across the world* (pp. 1–16). Routledge. https://doi.org/10.4324/9781003136842

Southerton, C., & Taylor, E. (2021). Dataveillance and the dividuated self: The everyday digital surveillance of young people. In B. A. Arrigo & B. G. Sellers (Eds.), *The pre-crime society: Crime, culture and control in the ultramodern age* (pp. 249–268). Bristol University Press.

Stevenson, M., & Witschge, T. (2020). Methods we live by: Proceduralism, process, and pedagogy. *NECSUS European Journal of Media Studies*, *9*, 117–138. https://doi.org/10.25969/MEDIAREP/15344

Tromble, R. (2021). Where have all the data gone? A critical reflection on academic digital research in the post-API age. *Social Media + Society*, *7*(1). https://doi.org/10.1177/2056305121988929

Chapter 6

The Epistemic Culture of Data Minimalism: Conducting an Ethnography of Travel Influencers

Christian S. Ritter

Karlstad University, Sweden

Abstract

This chapter assesses the possibilities of integrating computational network analysis into ethnographic fieldwork. Grounded in examples from an ethnographic case of travel vlogging in Singapore, I discuss how participant observation in urban areas can be combined with network cluster analysis. The huge variety of data collection tools available to present-day media researchers has prompted a plethora of disparate data points and a multitude of ethical dilemmas. Computational network analysis provides manifold avenues for combining interpretations of localised meaning-making with visual evidence about networks of recommended videos on the popular video-sharing platform YouTube. The dissemination of video content is largely shaped by the platform's recommender system. Exploring how the YouTube recommender algorithm drives the circulation of vlogs about Singapore's touristic Clark Quay area, this chapter brings to light that the act of recommending a video is based on semantic similarities among video titles and video keywords. Furthermore, the methodological reflections presented in this chapter demonstrate that the combination of computational network analysis and ethnographic fieldwork provides holistic understandings of how highly mediated tourist places are unbound from their physical settings and drawn into platform ecologies, consisting of local areas of production, algorithmic technologies, disseminated place images and platform audiences. As algorithmic mediation plays an important part in accessing platform content about politics, health, culture and entertainment, a myriad of everyday practices is affected by recommender systems. Such algorithmic technologies raise multiple ethical concerns about the accountability of platform owners for a fair and balanced distribution of content on the internet.

Data Excess in Digital Media Research, 69–85
Copyright © 2025 Christian S. Ritter
Published under exclusive licence by Emerald Publishing Limited
doi:10.1108/978-1-80455-944-420241006

Keywords: Ethnography; travel vlog; algorithm; network analysis; query design; YouTube

Introduction

Shamal[1] exits the MRT station Clarke Quay and strolls over to the Boat Quay. Night has fallen, and the streets of Singapore are filled with an exuberant ambiance. Small passenger boats float on the Singapore river; many are out to have dinner in one of the numerous restaurants near the riverbanks. Shamal brought his Canon EOS R camera to the Clarke Quay area as he wishes to complete his vlog about this fine-grained urban landscape. A few days ago, he recorded scenes of urban life here during daylight, but he still needs footage of the busy area at night-time for his travel video. Shamal attaches his camera to a portable tripod and walks past a Chinese restaurant, a Turkish ice-cream parlour and the art boutique café *The Connoisseur Concerto*. A nearby outdoor restaurant offers Brazilian dishes, and buskers congregate at the embankment. Shamal captures the vivid scenery of escaping impressions. The Malaysian travel influencer is creating a new vlog about Singapore. He has already portrayed numerous tourist attractions of Singapore on his YouTube channel *Sleepy Tourist* and hopes that a further vlog about another spectacular area will be endorsed by his followers and help him grow his channel. Very recently, his channel surpassed the 100,000-subscriber mark, and he remains ambitious to travel the world and upload more content.

Shamal's story relates to a wider phenomenon in global tourism. Urban areas popular with tourists are increasingly mediated on digital platforms. The ever-growing circulation of vlogs portraying tourist places on digital platforms transformed the techno-social relationships among local stakeholders, tourists and professional content creators. Drawing on a digital ethnography of travel influencers in Singapore, I discuss the methodological prospects of complementing ethnographic fieldwork with computational network analysis. Ethnographic research into vlogging about Singapore's Clarke Quay area raises a number of questions about the socio-technical life of algorithms: In what ways do the localised videomaking practices of travel vloggers expand the interpretive repertoire inscribed in the Clarke Quay area? What kind of content does YouTube's video recommendation algorithm suggest to viewers who watch videos about Singapore's Clarke Quay area? And, finally, how do answers to these empirical questions provide insights into the enhancement of digital ethnography through computational network analysis? Singapore's urban areas feature in numerous TV series and movies and are widely displayed on digital platforms, such as YouTube and Instagram. Platformisation processes transformed the ways in which tourist places are portrayed and experienced (Capineri & Romano, 2021). Platforms act as mediators between guests and hosts, making possible an unprecedented circulation of content about tourist places.

---

[1] A pseudonym is used for the vlogger and his YouTube channel to protect his personal identity.

The circulation of touristic content is crucially shaped by algorithms, which has substantial ramifications for both local tourism stakeholders and content creators. Since travel influencers continuously blur the boundaries between the online world of their platform audiences and the offline world of tourist attractions, ethnographic research can greatly benefit from computational methods illuminating the dissemination of place images.

Amplifying methodological debates around the integration of computational tools in ethnographic research (e.g. Born & Haworth, 2017; Knox & Nafus, 2018), this chapter proposes an approach that strengthens place-based fieldwork with computational network analysis. Locating the multiplicities and particularities of digital data in diverse local worlds (Douglas-Jones et al., 2021, p. 10), this chapter seeks to assess the possibilities and limitations inherent in digital ethnography of platformed videomaking by combining participant observation in urban areas with cluster analysis of a YouTube recommender network. Computational research techniques harness an excessive abundance of data, providing ample data for location-based inquiries. Combining place-based fieldwork and computational tools, this chapter outlines ethnographic tactics in the increasingly datafied worlds of cultural production. Based on a case of travel vlogging in Singapore, I suggest that the combination of computational network analysis and ethnographic fieldwork provides holistic understandings of how highly mediated tourist places are unbound from their physical settings and drawn into platform ecologies, including local areas of production, algorithmic technologies, disseminated place images, and platform audiences. The following part of the chapter addresses the role of algorithms in the circulation of platform content. In the second part, I discuss how ethnographers can research the production of travel vlogs. Finally, I assess the potential of network analysis for assessing YouTube's recommender algorithm.

Algorithmic Mediation on YouTube

Recommender algorithms are omnipresent features of the contemporary internet. Such technologies increasingly shape which music people enjoy, which TV series they watch and how they access their daily news. In her pioneering work on algorithmic mediation on Facebook, Bucher (2012) assessed how Facebook's EdgeRank algorithm shapes the distribution of Facebook posts in users' newsfeeds. Recommender algorithms also affect everyday choice-making, including decisions on financial investments or healthy lifestyles (Kotliar, 2020). Numerous media scholars have examined the techno-social dynamics of widespread recommender systems, such as Spotify and Netflix. The distribution of Spotify's music content through the interfaces 'related artists', 'discover' and 'browse' is widely governed by its recommender algorithm, which re-organises music tastes through similarities in genre and gender (Werner, 2020). Furthermore, Netflix's recommender algorithm regulates its content by classifying videos into genres (Hallinan & Striphas, 2016). Pajkovic (2022) describes Netflix's recommender system as an instrument of taste-making in the film and television industry. In the last few years, the algorithmic mediation on the video-sharing platform YouTube also came under scrutiny. YouTube's recommender algorithm heightens precarious labour conditions and reinforces inequalities in the influencer industry (Glatt, 2022). To secure financial consistency and visibility, professional vloggers share practical knowledge on algorithmic systems (Bishop, 2019).

Founded by former employees of the transaction website PayPal, YouTube was launched in June 2005. The start-up evolved as a repository for amateur videos, competing with many other free video-sharing services. Google acquired YouTube in October 2006. In recent years, the platform has become one of the most-watched video-sharing platforms on the planet. An estimated 2.7 billion people worldwide use YouTube per month (Global Media Insight, 2024). The platform's affordances are organised by three interlocking interfaces: channels, playlists and videos. Channels consist of playlists, and playlists consist of videos. The uploads playlist is a default feature of all channels. However, vloggers can also create playlists and organise their videos in themes. Users can leave comments after watching YouTube clips. A list of related videos can be found next to or below each video, enticing audiences into binge-watching. Lists are a persistent cultural form of structuring everyday routines as they reflect underlying ways of ordering and organisational principles (Welland, 2020, p. 28). Lists are recurring affordances of YouTube, providing glimpses at its organisation of video content.

The platform YouTube incentivises its content creators to develop popular channels and grow large audiences. Vloggers who manage to amass a high number of subscribers and reach a high level of watch time for their videos can monetise their channels and make a living from their craft. In order to launch a successful career as YouTubers, vloggers need to adjust their videomaking practices to the constraints of algorithmic mediation. Professional content creators can receive detailed advice on YouTube's recommendation algorithm in videos uploaded by the official YouTube channel *YouTube Creators*. Its content is mainly earmarked for emerging vloggers:

> In this one, we are taking a look at suggested videos. These are videos YouTube recommends based on what viewers were watching beforehand, related topics, and past watch history. You can find them on the right side of the watch page, below the video you're watching on the mobile app, and as the next video to auto-play. Suggested videos can be from any channel including from the one you're watching. What can you do to get your videos suggested to more viewers? Consider the following: Make a strong call to action. Suggest they watch another video in your series, and really sell them on why. Be mindful of long endings as they might delay viewers from watching more. Use playlists, links, cards, and end screens to suggest the next video. (YouTube Creators, 2017)

While the commentary voice of this official channel does not provide lengthy explanations of technical features of the recommender algorithm, the narrative contains clear advice on how aspiring vloggers should act on the platform. The official YouTube channel seeks to increase overall video consumption and regulate the platform practices of vloggers, encouraging them to make use of all the channel features. The video indirectly suggests that vloggers who implement links, cards and end screens in their videos will be rewarded by the algorithmic mediation in the long run.

Observing the Production of Place Images

Foregrounding epistemological opportunities for integrating computational network analysis with ethnographic fieldwork, this chapter demonstrates how such a methodological fusion can elucidate the role of YouTube's recommender algorithm in the circulation of its video content. The context for this endeavour is given by an ethnographic investigation I began in the summer of 2018 in Estonia. During the initial phase of fieldwork, I encountered travel influencers from various countries who had been invited to fly into Tallinn for the creation of content for digital platforms. As the production of their travel vlogs was intrinsically connected with their mobile lifestyles, I decided to follow them on their journeys. By using the ethnographic research tool travel-along (Howard, 2017), I could actively explore the travel influencers' experiences and the localised meaning-making within their travel destinations. Between summer 2018 and spring 2020, I studied the videomaking practices of several travel influencers, while following them to various tourism destinations, including Angkor Wat, Bangkok, Berlin, Chiang Mai, Chiang Rai, Hanoi, Helsinki, Kyiv, Kuala Lumpur, Riga, Singapore, Sofia, Stockholm, Tallinn and Vilnius. Participant observation was conducted in numerous tourist places. I travelled three times to Singapore for the exploration of tourist places in January 2019, January 2020, July and August 2023. The ethnographic immersion in mobile communities of travel influencers was complemented by 35 in-depth interviews. The research materials of the investigation included fieldnotes, interview transcripts, photographs, as well as screengrabs and archived videos from Instagram and YouTube. The qualitative data was analysed in accordance with the procedures of grounded theory (Jinghong et al., 2019). Sensitising concepts served as starting points for the coding process (Bowen, 2006, p. 14). Categories occurring frequently in the qualitative data were identified through open, axial and selective coding.

Although platform corporations hide the design of their algorithms through black-boxing strategies (Bonini & Gandini, 2020), media scholars have developed robust tactics for researching algorithmic systems. The algorithms of recommender systems, such as Spotify and YouTube, can be studied as a culture, namely a collection of human choices and practices enfolded in local worlds of reference (Seaver, 2018, p. 379). By uploading video content at specific times and in specific intervals or by strategically choosing titles and keywords, the researched travel influencers contributed to the algorithmic culture surrounding YouTube travel vlogs. Following several travel influencers to their travel destinations enabled me to closely study their platform practices and the localised meaning-making in which the production of travel vlogs is embedded. The mobile practices of travel influencers are constitutive of their videomaking practices. Travel vlogs are an influencer genre that depends on 'authentic' imagery of tourist places. The researched vloggers spent the better part of the year on the move, travelling to and through tourism destinations. Often, they only stayed for a few days in a given destination and planned the recording of footage well in advance. After I travelled with Shamal from Kuala Lumpur to Singapore, I took part in one of his video shoots in the Clarke Quay area. This event epitomises how the localised videomaking practices of the researched travel influencers shape meaning-making processes in the platformised, global tourism industry.

I meet Shamal on the promenade of Clarke Quay on a sunny day in mid-January. He has brought his backpack to carry his comprehensive video equipment. Finalising his camera preparations, he routinely adjusts the camera's zoom and shutter speed. His plan is to capture a panoramic view of the river and the busy square in the morning hours before the midday heat arrives. He evaluates the sunlight and different angles from which he aims to film the area. After 20 minutes of scenery planning, he starts recording himself on an edge of the square and walks slowly towards the embankment. Speaking to the camera attached to a portable tripod, Shamal intends to build a personal relationship with his subscribers in the first sequence of the video. Committed to a first-person style of storytelling, he says:

> Fabulous people. Welcome to the channel. Today, I'm in Singapore and checking out the local food. Today's video is perfect for everyone who plans on traveling to Singapore. Especially if it is your first time...

The opening statement is important for connecting with existing viewers and encouraging new viewers to subscribe to the channel. Many travel vloggers record themselves directly in the tourist places, hoping to enhance the authentic feel of the video. The video shoot ends with a backward walking sequence, which Jamal plans to use in a reverse video. In the following interview passage, Shamal compares his platform practices on Instagram and YouTube:

> I think the community of YouTube is slightly different to the community on Instagram. Also, the way in which the videos are discovered and shared on YouTube is quite different. I feel like with Instagram... [w]hen you post something, it's seen for one or two days and then never seen again. Whereas with YouTube, sometimes, you know, after three years suddenly you will see a huge spike on a video. Seemingly out of nowhere. I guess that is just the recommendation engine on YouTube. Just working differently.

The interview passage indicates Shamal's perspective on the circulation of video content on YouTube. While he recognises the platform's power for video discovery, he experiences its 'recommendation engine' as a rather obscure and unpredictable force.

During the above-described event, Shamal recorded representations of local places and events within the Clarke Quay area. By spending time with the travel influencer in urban spaces of Singapore, I was able to observe how he chose urban sceneries for his videos. The first-person perspective of travel vlogs requires that the creator recounts being-in-the-place experiences. In the video about the Clarke Quay area, he presents among other things the local market, restaurants and the surrounding architecture to his viewers. In the narratives of the video, he attributes meanings to the different artefacts and events of the quay area. In video editing sessions, which took place in further travel destinations, he used the best footage for a 9-minute-long video. The uploaded vlog, which he titled *Things to see and do in Clarke Quay – Singapore*, is filled with manifold representations of local artefacts, events and places.

The urban space of Singapore is composed of different types of places with different local textures. Many tourist places in Singapore are highly mediated. Their urban textures are symbolically represented in still and moving images on various digital platforms, including Instagram and YouTube. While personal attendance at video shoots provides ethnographers with crucial insights into video production practices, the circulation of a vlog on platforms is equally important for ethnographic inquiries into travel influencers. The travel vlogs that Shamal uploaded on YouTube contain a myriad of place images about tourism destinations. Such place images are embodied through direct experience of urban landscapes, but also through mediated experiences induced by TV shows, magazines, newspapers, movies and platform content. Place images are shaped by an endless cycle of capture and representation, allowing content creators to express ways of seeing which are subsequently embodied by their audiences (Adams, 2009, p. 139). A place image consists of four main elements: the media; the place being portrayed; the audience and the creator of the image (Zonn, 1990, p. 3). The platform dynamics of YouTube complicate present-day phenomenologies of tourist places by multiplying the interpretations of a given physical place. The interpretations of research participants and researchers are expanded through the interpretations of place images shared on YouTube. The ways in which vloggers interpret a tourist place are archived in YouTube videos and their audiences can express their views on tourist places in comment threads. Ethnographic tactics should not only involve the observation of places and production practices in situ, but also the following of place images on YouTube. A video of a walking tour in Singapore's Clarke Quay area contains place images that shape the touristic experience of YouTube audiences. Furthermore, ethnographic researchers can trace the algorithmic circulation of videos by visualising the structures of video networks connected through recommendation. In doing so, they can understand how the circulation of place images is organised on the platform.

Ethnography is well suited for studying the meaning-making processes unfolding within tourist places. The case of travel vloggers traces transformations in how meanings are assigned to local sites. Participant observation onsite reveals the meanings that travel influencers ascribe to urban landscapes of Singapore. However, the distribution of place images about the Clarke Quay area on YouTube transforms the ways in which meaning is assigned to this local area. The experiences of travel influencers and other tourists are pre-shaped by YouTube content. The flows of place images through YouTube's infrastructures expand the ways in which tourist sites can be experienced and may affect decisions on which sites are worth a visit. Platform content is an integral part of the cycle of meaning-making in which Singapore's tourist places are entangled. Localised meaning-making is also accompanied by the assigning of meaning to the area in video commentaries and comments viewers leave under videos. Place images which are disseminated in travel vlogs on YouTube guide the experience of actual local places among tourists. The videomaking of travel influencers epitomises the role of platforms in the phenomenology of highly mediated tourist places, which are entangled in a multi-layered circulation process of signifiers and signified entities. Such processes increasingly involve the techno-social dynamics of recommender systems. The localised videomaking practices of the researched travel vloggers accelerate the circulation of places images portraying the Clarke Quay area on YouTube, expanding the repertoire of meanings associated with the urban area.

Locating Place Images on YouTube

The videomaking practices of travel influencers are directed to both local places where footage is recorded and digital platforms where their videos are circulated. Place-bound fieldwork can make transparent emic perspectives on videomaking and localised meaning-making processes. The hallmark of such perspectives is an interpretation of practices and events from within a given community. Meanings are ascribed to practices and events in terms that are meaningful to insiders of the community. As travel vloggers enter the world of platforms, they constantly leave digital traces which can be harvested for computational network analysis. Computational methods pose a substantial challenge for ethnographic research that focuses on internet technologies as a major object of concern. This conundrum 'takes the form of an opposition between physical embodiment and informational modes' (Beaulieu, 2017, p. 30). To fruitfully combine participant observation with computational network analysis, media researchers should align the data collection goals for both methods. A clearly circumscribed locale can be a solid anchor point for the integration of both methods. For this reason, I make a case for location-based query design in researching the everyday practices of travel influencers.

Query design is characterised by the search-as-research approach, allowing researchers to study influential voices, positioning, commitment, concern and alignment (Rogers, 2019, p. 38). Choosing locations as search terms for an assessment of platform data can enhance ethnographic research in urban areas as it makes transparent how recommender systems such as YouTube curate place images. Urban locations such as the Clarke Quay area are adequate for a comprehensive immersion and are widely portrayed in YouTube videos about which natively digital data can be gathered. In contrast to digitised data, such as Google Books and the Wikimedia Commons Painting Collection, natively digital data derives directly from the web and contains for instance information about hyperlinks, URLs, retweets or comments (Rogers, 2015). By combining ethnographic observations in local places with computational network analysis, media researchers initiate a dialectical spiral of media-centric and non-media-centric methods. This tension creates a dynamic interplay that yields different angles on the phenomenon of travel vlogging on YouTube. The media-centric method illuminates the circulation and consumption of videos, whereas the non-media-centric method sheds light on localised production practices. As digital platforms proliferate in everyday life, datafication processes render into data an increasing number of activities and things. Although the mining of such data is widely considered a clear pathway to objective truth about human behaviour, data sets retrieved from digital platforms are interpreted in situated contexts where subjectivities shape how they are stored, packaged and analysed. The increasing variety of data collection tools available to media researchers has generated data abundances and filtering challenges. Ethical dilemmas often revolve around questions of how to handle leftover data containing personal information. To sensibly balance the boundaries between ethnographic and network data, media researchers should ground their decisions and choices in a virtue-based ethos. Given the messiness of ethnographic fieldwork and the uncertainties of digital data collection, researchers should be primarily committed to empathy and loyalty towards their research participants.

Instead of focusing on the opaque production processes of recommender algorithms within wider data assemblages, media researchers can assess how algorithms are deployed to perform tasks in local contexts of everyday life or examine how algorithms unfold in the world (Kitchin, 2017, p. 25). The concept of data assemblage relates to all technological, political, social and economic apparatuses and elements that constitute and frame the generation, circulation and deployment of data (Kitchin & Lauriault, 2014). For the investigation into travel vlogs about Singapore's Clarke Quay area, a major task of YouTube's recommender algorithm is the circulation of content through video suggestions for its viewers. In such contexts of video consumption, the role of YouTube's recommender system can be examined. YouTube's back-end databases are repositories in which the algorithmically mediated circulation of vlogs is materialised. The platform allows academic researchers to retrieve natively digital data from its application programming interface (API). The analysis of such data provides insights into the operating of YouTube's recommender system.

For the investigation into travel vlogs about Singapore's Clarke Quay area, I gathered natively digital data for a YouTube recommender network. The search query used for the data set was entered in mid-January 2023, and included the terms 'Clarke Quay' to retrieve a data set from YouTube's API v3. These words were entered in NodeXL Pro's data collection interface for YouTube videos. The set of videos assembled with this query contained a variety of place images about Clarke Quay, including audiovisual views on a small stretch of the Singapore river, the quay promenade, restaurants and shops. The collected data set comprised 4,763 edges and 2,898 nodes. The YouTube videos included in the data set were published on the platform between 22/01/2007 and 11/01/2023. While the nodes of the recommender network refer to specific YouTube videos, the edges relate to the act of video recommendation. To assemble this recommender network, the edge type 'recommended video' was selected as a parameter of the data collection in NodeXL Pro's interface for YouTube videos. The digital trace 'recommended video' which is stored in YouTube's back-end databases corresponds with a list of suggested videos displayed in the front-end of YouTube, either next to the watched video for desktop-based usage or below the clip for smartphone users.

A hallmark of ethnographic methodologies is their commitment to 'open-ended, non-linear methods of data collection' (Strathern, 2004, p. 5), and, indeed, location-based query design involves numerous iterative movements between data collection in local places and through APIs. In addition, this research design type is, to a large extent, dependent on the accessibility of local places and the availability of natively digital data. For this reason, the grounding of data collection strategies in phenomena that are accessible in ethnographic field sites is of paramount importance. The data collection interfaces of the software program NodeXL Pro allowed me to retrieve relevant relational data from YouTube. The network data for the investigation into travel vlogging in Singapore was filtered for locations that were represented in YouTube videos and contained relevant place images. Although platform corporations restrict access to specific data from their APIs and the data collection with NodeXL Pro is subject to daily limits, huge amounts of data can be amassed about highly mediated tourism destinations such as Singapore.

API-based research involves the collection of large amounts of data, and such data excess generates plentiful data for location-based inquiries. The data sets were retrieved as CSV and GRAPHML files. They stored a lot of unused data, such as 'thumb up' counts for specific videos or subscriber counts for YouTube channels. In particular, digital data collection tools generate more data than investigators are aware of at the time of data collection. Location-based query design allows media researchers to unerringly navigate through the maze of digital data, by searching for data that is aligned with phenomena observed during fieldwork. This form of data minimalism revolves around the study of urban areas, local places or picturesque landscapes which are represented in platform content, i. e. YouTube videos. The minimalistic approach to digital data collection practices is committed to an appropriation of data for iterative qualitative research, creating a common ground and shared research foci for differing methods. The observed everyday practices and localised meaning-making can inform the search query for collecting network data. Despite the vast amount of data available through APIs, merely relational data for network nodes and edges is used for the visualisation. Location-based query design enables ethnographic researchers to interweave their direct observations and personal experiences of field sites with an exploration of often-obscured data assemblages. This approach allows for an immersion in the thick semantic layers of tourist places while following the circulation of the representations of those places on platforms. In the context of the highly mediated tourist sites of Singapore, tourist attractions come into being in conjunction with their place images distributed on digital platforms.

Classifying Tourism Destinations on YouTube

The researched travel influencers frequently engaged in 'algospeak' while meeting in tourism destinations or at creator events. They shared expressions that they successfully used to bypass word filters that may downrank their content. Such code words were used for content that was perceived as 'problematic'. For example, the research participants replaced the word 'pandemic' with the word 'panini' and used the word 'oui'd' instead of 'weed'. Many of them regularly followed the advice of algorithmic experts on popular platforms, such as Instagram and YouTube, seeking to enhance their content dissemination strategies. The fieldnotes and interview transcripts gathered during the investigation entailed ample evidence for the perceived effects of algorithms on the working conditions of travel influencers. Although such voices of experienced content creators illuminate the algorithmic mediation of travel videos on YouTube, computational network analysis enables media researchers to trace actual clusters of suggested videos on the platform. Travel influencers are constantly intertwined with datafied practices that shape their lifeworlds. The travel vlogs that they post on YouTube leave digital traces in the data infrastructures of the platform. Based on the collected network data, network graphs were generated which make visible clusters among YouTube videos that are connected through the act of video suggestion. The network visualisation software Gephi provides media researchers with tools for a network cluster analysis (Jacomy et al., 2014). This type of network analysis involves a modularity measure that helps identify clusters within a given network through the visualisation of a network graph. The set of network nodes is displayed as a structure that is divided into various clusters. In this investigation, clusters consist of a set of YouTube videos which are directly connected through the act of recommending. By organising nodes into clusters, Gephi detects particular cluster structures which researchers can interpret. Fig. 6.1 presents visual evidence of how YouTube's recommender algorithm distributes video content. The network nodes are displayed as clusters.

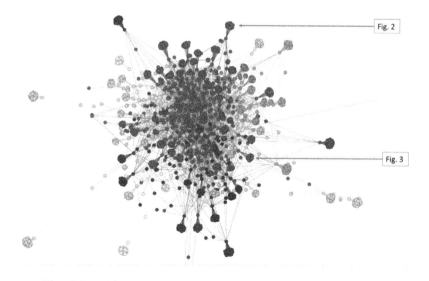

Fig. 6.1.   Clusters of a YouTube Recommender Network.

Gephi's layout algorithm ForceAtlas 2 was employed to create the visualisation of the giant component, which is the largest connected fraction of the network (Fig. 6.1). The graph shows 26 clusters that consist of connected nodes. The shapes of the visualised clusters resemble the geometric form of a cone. In the middle part of the graph, many smaller clusters can be found. Larger clusters are drawn away from the giant component and are connected only to a few other clusters. The video clusters of the YouTube recommender network mainly contain a single node representing a video portraying the Clarke Quay area. For example, the edges of a video about restaurants in this area indicate that the group of videos at the other end of the cluster was recommended while a YouTube user watched this video about restaurants. Single videos, which portray Singapore's Clarke Quay area, are linked to the other nodes through the edge type 'recommended video'. In the following extracts from the network graph (Figs. 6.2 and 6.3), two clusters will be analysed in greater detail.

The first example of a video cluster is conveyed in Fig. 6.2. The video *Singapore Clarke Quay Walking Tour (4K UHD) – Travel Guide Video,* which can be seen in the left top corner, recommends 24 videos, which are displayed in the right part of the visualisation. The video about Clarke Quay contains place images from the area. For instance, the Ellenborough Market Café and the Read Bridge feature in the clip. The vast majority of the videos that are recommended in conjunction with the video about the walking tour in the Clarke Quay area contain the words 'walking' and 'ultra-high-definition' in their video titles. A detailed examination of the visual evidence shows that – in addition to other tourist places of Singapore – numerous popular travel destinations outside of Singapore are represented in the video cluster, including walking tours in Budapest, Dublin, Hong Kong, London, Paris and Split. Tourism destinations compete over visibility on YouTube. The analysis of the circulation of YouTube content through suggested videos indicates that travel destinations that were recorded with high-end video equipment seem to be more frequently recommended by YouTube's recommendation algorithm. In doing so, the YouTube recommender algorithm appears to cement global inequalities in tourism. Furthermore, a textual analysis of the video titles reveals that the formation of the video cluster is based on semantic similarity such as 'walking tour' (see Fig. 6.2) and 'river cruise' (see Fig. 6.3). Geographical proximity did not play a part in the curation of the video content.

Fig. 6.3 shows a video cluster revolving around a vlog produced by the Indian travel influencer Latika. The vlog, which is titled *River cruise at Clarke Quay, Singapore, Latikas World*, depicts an eventful cruise on the Singapore river while passing through the Clarke Quay area. Themes like cruise, river and nature frequently appear in the titles of the 28 videos which are recommended with the video on the river cruise in the Clarke Quay area. Furthermore, vlogs about 12 further tourist attractions of Singapore are recommended. This second video cluster is also formed through semantic similarity revolving around certain thematic aspects of the video content. The content is not curated in terms of channels. Only two other vlogs by the content creator Latika are recommended.

When content creators upload new videos on YouTube, they are prompted to enter keywords related to the themes of the content. Media researchers can find the specific keywords of a YouTube video in the source code of the video page

The Epistemic Culture of Data Minimalism 81

Fig. 6.2. Cluster of Ultra-High-Definition Vlogs About Walking Tours.

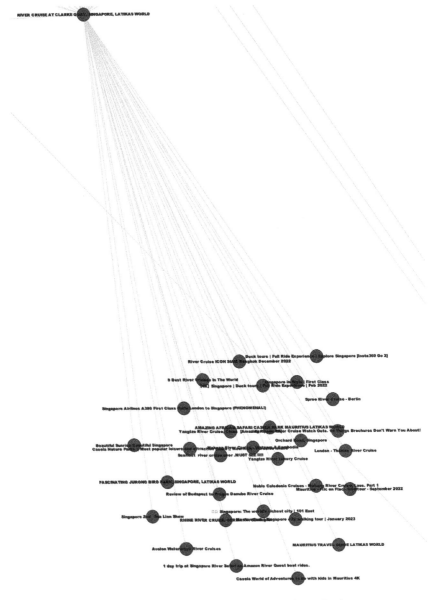

Fig. 6.3. Cluster of Videos About River Cruises.

which can be displayed by pressing the view-page-source button in the browser Google Chrome. Such additional information complements the visual evidence of the video clusters generated in Gephi. The keywords for all videos of the video clusters discussed above were looked up in the source code, indicating that the videos in a given video cluster widely shared numerous central keywords. The classification of cultural content within YouTube's techno-social recommender system is based on the identification of shared characteristics among videos. Based on an analysis of the 26 clusters in the network graph assembled with the query 'Clarke Quay', semantic similarity among video titles could be identified as a major driving force of video recommendation. The circulated videos were mainly classified into groups with semantically similar content. The cluster analysis of a YouTube recommender network reveals that the video suggestions for viewers of the Clarke Quay content were based on semantic similarities among the titles of videos and their keywords. As the algorithmic mediation is based on semantic similarities, YouTube audiences who watch travel vlogs about Clarke Quay are inclined to experience similarly themed place images. YouTube's affordances encourage the watching of 'related videos' listed next to a video or on the 'end screen' of a video. Such recommendations undermine the curative practices of content creators who compile 'watch lists' for their channels. The relationship between creators and their audiences is substantially shaped by chains of recommended videos, allowing viewers to discover new content based on semantic connections. This type of content dissemination serves the interests of platform corporations rather than those of the creators.

Conclusion

Travel influencers aspire to make a living from both content creation and sponsorship deals with local tourism stakeholders. The production of travel vlogs is bound to local tourist places while travel vlogs circulating on YouTube are entangled in the algorithmic system of the platform. Hence, travel influencers constantly blur the boundaries between online and offline worlds, seeking to deliver authentic imagery of tourist attractions to large platform audiences. The network visualisations discussed above demonstrate how YouTube's recommender system stitches together webs of significance independently from the curative practices of content creators. YouTube's official videos for creators encourage a false sense of agency by motivating vloggers to actively curate themed playlists for their channels. Instead, the platform's recommender system orders content to incite continuous video creation and consumption while disregarding more adequate classification principles, such as geographical affinity of travel content or channel affiliation of videos.

Grounded in an empirical investigation into travel vlogging in Singapore, I suggest that the combination of computational network analysis and ethnographic fieldwork provides holistic understandings of how highly mediated tourist places are unbound from their physical settings and drawn into platform ecologies, including local areas of production, algorithmic technologies, disseminated place images and platform audiences. Location-based query design serves as an auspicious tactic for dealing with data excess and can make visible the relations between data assemblages of platforms and localised creative practices. However, API-based methods are constantly vulnerable to data collection restrictions imposed by platform corporations and can only provide partial data. This investigation into YouTube's recommender system was based on data that merely allows for an analysis of video titles and keywords. Data about further central metrics, such as watch time and returning viewer counts, could not be accessed. Given that travel vlogs represent sites of cultural heritage, architecture, food cultures, performances or even complete guided tours, more transparency is needed for algorithmic systems circulating cultural content. Local stakeholders and creators should have more agency in content curation and circulation. YouTube's recommendation algorithm can make or break creator careers, but it can also make or break a tourism destination. Since algorithmic mediation increasingly pervades datafied life-worlds, a huge variety of everyday practices is affected by recommender systems, raising ethical concerns about the accountability of platform owners for a fair and balanced distribution of cultural content on the internet. The implementation of algorithmic technologies in the data infrastructures of platform corporations thus necessitates more transparency and the involvement of multiple stakeholders.

References

Adams, P. (2009). *Geographies of media and communication*. Wiley.
Beaulieu, A. (2017). Vectors for fieldwork: Computational thinking and new modes of ethnography. In L. Hjorth, H. Horst, & A. Galloway (Eds.), *The Routledge companion to digital ethnography* (pp. 29–39). Routledge.
Bishop, S. (2019). Managing visibility on YouTube through algorithmic gossip. *New Media & Society*, *21*(11–12), 2589–2606.
Bonini, T., & Gandini, A. (2020). The field as a black box: Ethnographic research in the age of platforms. *Social Media + Society*, *6*(4), 1–10. https://doi.org/10.1177/2056305120984477
Born, G., & Haworth, C. (2017). Mixing it: Digital ethnography and online research methods — A tale of two global digital music genres. In L. Hjorth, H. Horst, & A. Galloway (Eds.), *The Routledge companion to digital ethnography* (pp. 96–112). Routledge.
Bowen, G. (2006). Grounded theory and sensitizing concepts. *International Journal of Qualitative Methods*, *5*(3), 12–23. https://doi.org/10.1177/160940690600500304
Bucher, T. (2012). Want to be on the top? Algorithmic power and the threat of invisibility on Facebook. *New Media & Society*, *14*(7), 1164–1180. https://doi.org/10.1177/1461444812440159
Capineri, C., & Romano, A. (2021). The platformization of tourism: From accommodation to experiences. *Digital Geography and Society*, (2), 1–7. https://doi.org/10.1016/j.diggeo.2021.100012
Douglas-Jones, R., Walford, A., & Seaver, N. (2021). Introduction: Towards an anthropology of data. *Journal of the Royal Anthropological Institute*, *27*(S1), 9–25. https://doi.org/10.1111/1467-9655.13477
Glatt, Z. (2022). Precarity, discrimination and (in)visibility: An ethnography of 'the algorithm' in the YouTube influencer industry. In E. Costa, P. Lange, N. Haynes, & J. Sinanan (Eds.), *The Routledge companion to media anthropology* (pp. 546–559). Routledge.

Global Media Insight. (2024, February 6). Interesting YouTube statistics 2024. https://www.globalmediainsight.com/blog/youtube-users-statistics/#stat

Hallinan, B., & Striphas, T. (2016). Recommended for you: The Netflix Prize and the production of algorithmic culture. *New Media & Society, 18*(1), 117–137. https://doi.org/10.1177/1461444814538646

Howard, C. (2017). *Mobile lifeworlds: An ethnography of tourism and pilgrimage in the Himalayas*. Routledge.

Jacomy, M., Venturini, T., Heymann, S., & Bastian, M. (2014). ForceAtlas2, a continuous graph layout algorithm for handy network visualization designed for the Gephi software. *PLoS One, 9*(6), e98679. https://doi.org/10.1371/journal.pone.0098679

Jinghong, X., Xinyang, Y., Shiming, H., & Wenbing, C. (2019). Grounded theory in journalism and communication studies in the Chinese mainland (2004–2017): Status quo and problems. *Global Media and China, 4*(1), 138–152. https://doi.org/10.1177/2059436418821043

Kitchin, R. (2017). Thinking critically about and researching algorithms. *Information, Communication & Society, 20*(1), 14–29. https://doi.org/10.1080/1369118X.2016.1154087

Kitchin, R., & Lauriault, T. (2014). Towards critical data studies: Charting and unpacking data assemblages and their work. In J. Eckert, A. Shears, & J. Thatcher (Eds.), *Geoweb and big data* (pp. 1–19). University of Nebraska Press.

Knox, H., & Nafus, D. (2018). Introduction: Ethnography for a data-saturated world. In H. Knox & N. Dawn (Eds.), *Ethnography for a data-saturated world* (pp. 1–29). Manchester University Press.

Kotliar, D. (2020). Who gets to choose? On the socio-algorithmic construction of choice. *Science, Technology, & Human Values*, 1–30. https://doi.org/10.1177/0162243920925147

Pajkovic, N. (2022). Algorithms and taste-making: Exposing the Netflix recommender system's operational logics. *Convergence, 28*(1), 214–235. https://doi.org/10.1177/13548565211014464

Rogers, R. (2015). Digital methods for web research. In R. Scott & S. Kosslyn (Eds.), *Emerging trends in the behavioral and social sciences* (pp. 1–22). Wiley.

Rogers, R. (2019). *Doing digital methods*. Sage.

Seaver, N. (2018). What should an anthropology of algorithms do? *Cultural Anthropology, 33*(3), 375–385.

Strathern, M. (2004). *Commons and borderlands: Working papers on interdisciplinarity, accountability, and the flow of knowledge*. Sean Kingston Publishing.

Welland, S. S.-L. (2020). List as form: Literary, ethnographic, long, short, heavy, light. In C. McGranahan (Ed.), *Writing anthropology: Essays on craft and commitment* (pp. 28–33). Duke University Press.

Werner, A. (2020). Organizing music, organizing gender: Algorithmic culture and Spotify recommendations. *Popular Communication, 18*(1), 78–90. https://doi.org/10.1080/15405702.2020.1715980

YouTube Creators. (2017, August 30). How YouTube's suggested videos work [Video]. YouTube. https://www.youtube.com/watch?v=E6pC6iql5xM

Zonn, E. (1990). Tusayan, the traveler, and the IMAX theatre: An introduction to place images in media. In E. Zonn (Ed.), *Place images in media portrayal, experience, and meaning* (pp. 1–5). Rowman & Littlefield Publishers.

Chapter 7

Embodied Excess: Interpreting Haptic Mobile Media Practices

Jess Hardley[a] *and Ingrid Richardson*[b]

[a]Edith Cowan University, Australia
[b]RMIT University, Australia

Abstract

This chapter considers how phenomenology and ethnography can be combined as an interpretive strategy for studying mobile media practices in everyday life. We argue that haptic methodologies in mobile media research generate an overflow of data that are often difficult to capture in written form. The dilemma of data excess is discussed in the context of a 4-year research project on gendered mobile media practices, exploring how mobile devices are often intertwined with the experience of bodily safety in urban environments. Our primary aim was to investigate the relationship between networked connectivity, mobile media and perceptions of risk in terms of bodily experience, including affective or emotional feelings. This chapter focuses on the haptic methods and techniques used during home visits with participants and the various ways that the volume and density of data are subsequently thinned out to become manageable and publishable. We first situate our research within haptic and mobile media studies, followed by an explanation of phenomenology and how it can be used to inform ethnographic methods in ways that are particularly useful for researching haptic media practices. This chapter then provides some examples of how the data are always in excess, an overflow resulting from the variability and individuality of participant experience and the difficulty of describing and accounting for personal histories and feelings. Finally, we show how the data can be strategically 'contained' in the process of writing for the purposes of publication, thematic framing and knowledge translation.

Keywords: Phenomenology; ethnography; mobile phone; mobile media; haptic media; haptic methods

Introduction

The mobile device is simultaneously – and often equally – an aural, visual, haptic and peripatetic interface, requiring an evolving sensibility and a cross-modal literacy of which our bodies, in their perceptual flexibility, are inherently and essentially capable. Mobile media usage is quite literally a way of 'having a body' that demands complex adaptation to new material and technological conditions of communication. Indeed, our use of mobile media can be described in Leder's (1990) terms as an ongoing incorporation by which we reshape the 'ability structure' of our bodies. In these terms, then, how does this portability, along with the prosthetic and orthotic capacities of mobile media, impact upon our experience of the world? How can we (as researchers) capture a holistic sense of collective practices, while also critically interpreting the complex and individualised contextures of mobile media practices?

This chapter describes how our combined use of phenomenology and ethnography as an interpretive strategy allowed insights into how users incorporate mobile media into their sensory experiences of urban space, and how mobile media practices are habituated as embodied knowledge. Haptic methodologies in mobile media research inevitably generate an overflow of data that are often difficult to capture in written form or reveal idiosyncratic sensory and affective experiences that elude representation in digestible research outputs.

We consider the conundrum of data excess in the context of a 4-year research project on gendered mobile media practices. The project combined phenomenology, feminist phenomenology, post-phenomenology and ethnography and was primarily about exploring how mobile devices impact experiences of bodily safety in urban environments. It sought to understand how people use mobile media affordances to stay safe in urban spaces and how networked connectivity often generates a perceived sense of security. Such practices include using mobile devices to create a telecocoon or shield while in public, using smartphones as a prop to discourage strangers from engaging or using social networking apps and digital maps to quickly or ambiently alert known and trusted contacts if something goes wrong. Our primary aim was to investigate the relationship between networked connectivity and perceptions of risk in terms of bodily experience, including affective or emotional feelings, with a particular interest in gendered mobile media practices.

The research took place in Perth and Melbourne from 2016 to 2020 and included a total of 79 participants across both cities with ages ranging from 19 to 70 years old. Over this 4-year period, the project deployed a number of techniques, including interviews in situ, haptic experiments and observations. In this chapter, we will focus on the first two of these techniques conducted during home visits and explore the volume and density of data that are subsequently thinned out to become manageable and publishable. We first situate our research in mobile media studies and the 'sensory turn' in media research and explore the entangled significance of touch, vision and movement in mobile media practices. We then explain phenomenology and how it can be used to inform ethnographic methods in ways that are particularly useful for understanding and revealing mobile and haptic media practices. In the final sections, we provide some examples of how the data are always in excess, an overflow resulting from the variability and multistabilities of participant experience and the difficulty of describing situated practices in ways that account for personal histories and feelings. We show how the data are deliberately and strategically 'contained' by writing for the purposes of publication and knowledge translation.

Mobile Media and the Haptic Turn

The mobile phone is an object of corporeal intimacy. As Fortunati (2005) argued in the early phase of mobile phone uptake, the mobile interface requires a complex range of hermeneutic visual, aural and haptic skills on the part of the user and is also highly mutable because 'it is held very close to the body or stays on the body surface' (p. 153). Even when on silent or vibrate mode, the mobile phone is almost always in close proximity. The way people hold and 'handle' their phones even when not in use reveals how mobile touchscreens are not only 'ready-to-hand' in a Heideggerian sense but perpetually in the hand and close to the body. The evolution of haptic screens over the past decade has further strengthened this sensory bond (Parisi et al., 2017; Richardson & Hjorth, 2017). This intimacy – together with the communicative reach afforded by mobile media – is fundamental to our reliance on the mobile phone as a provider and conduit of connection, safety, familiarity and comfort.

Over the past decade, mobile media studies has enthusiastically engaged with the corporeal and embodied aspects of mobile media practices (Farman, 2012, 2015; Moores, 2012, 2013; Richardson & Wilken, 2012, 2017, 2023) and more recently in the context of mobile games (Hjorth & Richardson, 2020; Keogh, 2018). Concurrently, haptic media studies have emerged in tandem with developments in touchscreen and gestural devices (Parisi, 2018; Parisi et al., 2017; Richardson & Hjorth, 2017). All media, in these analyses, are at the same time material, experiential and affective in culturally specific ways. In the context of mobile touchscreens, it is not that such devices demand a more embodied or sensory mode of interaction, but that they have 'alerted us to the sensoriality of our embodied and affective engagement with media in new ways' (Pink, 2015, p. 6).

In his text *The Senses of Touch: Haptics, Affects and Technologies*, Paterson (2007) explores both the historical and contemporary theorisations and dimensions of touch. He argues that touch cannot simply be defined in physiological terms; it is also always 'a sense of communication' (p. 1), and more significantly, it is *manifold*. Touch is a sense ensemble that incorporates cutaneous, kinaesthetic, proprioceptive, somatic, metaphoric and affective modes of perception. Earlier work, such as that by McCullough (1996), suggests that our deepest human engagement with the world is through touch.

In tandem with new materialist approaches and the emergence of sensory studies and as exemplified by the sensory ethnography of Pink (2009) and others, there has also been a return to the analysis of everyday life practices in media studies, which has attended to the corporeal and sensory aspects of our engagement with personal, domestic and public media screens. As Wiley et al. (2012) argue:

> The increasing complexity of social relations, mobility and mediated connectivity in late modernity requires a new approach to the study of social space – one which does not start with a sweeping, metahistorical narrative about the transformation of space and place ... but begins, instead, with what is happening on the ground: with empirical fieldwork that will allow us to *discover* the realities of spatial transformation that people are (or *may* be) actually experiencing. (p. 184, our emphasis)

Within this ethnographic work on the mundane and habitual, researchers acknowledge that perception is intrinsically variable, subject to collective perceptual histories and habit.

Consequently, if our quotidian modes of being in the world are situated, contingent and enacted, for those of us who seek 'deep' interpretations of such experience, analysis must be ethnographically and contextually informed if we are to capture shifts in the relational ontology of media and sensoria. In other words, the unintentional, creative and ad hoc usage of media can only be gleaned from the critical observation of *actual* and *individual* practices. Through careful observation and critical interpretation of body habits, gestures, micro-movements and practices, we aim to 'reveal' how mobile media are woven into our experience of place and being with others.

As an extension of the human hand, mobile phones also reconfigure both touch and the 'presence' of others accessible through the touchscreen as users literally tap, swipe and pinch on profiles, photos and personal information. In this way, 'haptic mobile media have changed the way we understand and experience the relationship between intimacy, proximity and touch' (Hjorth & Richardson, 2020, p. 33). 'Mediated social touch' (Paterson, 2007) or 'ambient touch' (Hjorth & Richardson, 2020) refers to the ways in which users connect and communicate with others via networks and devices. As smartphones are *held* – cradled in, and touched by, the hand – the sensory complexity of haptic intimacy becomes of key interest to the researcher.

Several scholars have explored the significance of the hand in both research of mobile media (Pink et al., 2016) and in terms of our being in the world (Richardson & Hjorth, 2017), while books such as *Figures of Touch: Sense, Technics, Body* (Elo & Luoto, 2018) and *Interdisciplinary Insights for Digital Touch Communication* (Jewitt et al., 2020) investigate the importance of touch and the hand in the use of technology and digital media. Especially in the work of Pink et al. (2016), researching the hand is linked with haptic methods and sensory ethnography. Pink et al. (2016) explore the importance of the hand in their research through 'tactile digital ethnography' (p. 238), which attends to the micro-movements of the hand as a way of furthering our understanding of the relation between mobile media and everyday intimacy and privacy.

Cooley (2014) argues that when designers and developers showcase the supposedly intuitive 'feel' and sensory familiarity of mobile interfaces, they engage in a rhetorical practice that 'collapses a plurality of human hands into the abstract ideal of a universal "human hand"', which overrides the myriad other factors of skill, (dis)ability, literacy, age and gender with a biomechanical, ergonomic abstraction (pp. 28, 32). Similarly, Parisi (2022, np) posits that beyond the 'mundane' haptics that we experience today in mobile phones, wearables and games, future interfaces will at best be built on normative models that posit an impossibly universal body, and that '[g]iven touch's impossible complexity, any attempt to digitally remake it will be necessarily incomplete and fragmentary'. As Wilson (1998) states:

> The problem of understanding what the hand *is* becomes infinitely more complicated, and the inquiry far more difficult to contain, if we try to account for the differences in the way people use their hands, or if we try to understand how individuals acquire skill in the use of their hands. When we connect the hands to real life, in other words, we confront the open-ended and overlapping worlds of sensorimotor and cognitive function and the endless combination of speed, strength, and dexterity seen in individual human skill and performance. We also confront the vagaries of human learning. (p. 9, emphasis in original)

Moreover, the lived experience of touch is not uniform but nuanced, shaped by the intersecting effects of culture, environment, gender, past experiences or physiological conditions and disabilities. As mobile touchscreens have become increasingly ubiquitous, we have similarly acquired a new repertoire of sensory awareness that expansively accommodates ambient proprioception and the telepresent intimacy of mediated social touch. As Powers and Parisi (2020) note, while we tend to think about touch as 'a fundamentally biological sense, its meaning is continually renegotiated in response to shifting cultural conditions and new technologies' (n.p.). Through the research process, an attempt to capture such minute yet expansive experiences with, and engagement through, touch generates an enormous amount of data.

Capturing this relationship between personal difference and social habitudes is perhaps one of the key challenges for researchers of media use in everyday life; as Paterson et al. (2012) argue, the 'cultural chronology of the formulation of a "sensorium" necessitates that the senses are ineluctably social: felt individually, but also always shared intersubjectively' (p. 2). Mobile media research thus presents many conundrums for analysis, from the inadequacy of techniques and methods in their (in)capacity to faithfully capture the nuances of personal experience to the overwhelming surplus of data in the form of numerous pages of transcripts, observational notes and hundreds of photographs and video files.

Phenomenology, Post-phenomenology and Ethnography

Phenomenology is a branch of philosophy that directly challenged Descartes' famous adage 'I think therefore I am', which positioned the mind and the intellect as that which grants us our awareness and defines the essence of what it means to be human. In phenomenology – particularly through the work of Merleau-Ponty – knowing and being are primordially grounded in sensory perception, in the fact that we have the kind of bodies that we do: bodies that see, hear, smell, taste and touch in synaesthetic ways and move about in a world of gravity and matter. Sensory perception is also always contextual and situated, intertwined with the objects around us, including not least our own tools and technologies. For Merleau-Ponty (1964, 2004 [1962]), tools and technologies are continually and dynamically incorporated as 'fresh instruments' into our ways of perceiving the world. In this view, our media interfaces and corresponding user-habits work to 'dilate' our being in the world. Within the phenomenological tradition, the coupling of tools and bodies is a process of *intercorporeality*, a word that describes the fundamental perceptual and material interconnection between technology, bodies and ways of being and knowing.

Subsequent theorists such as Ihde (1993) and Morris (2004) have further complexified this socio-material relation by including the nuances of personal practices and cultural specificity. Morris (2004) argues that the dynamics of perception 'are not anchored in a fixed, objective framework, they are intrinsic to the situation of perception, and can differ across individuals, habits, and social setting' (p. 23). Post-phenomenology – a contemporary approach to phenomenology developed by Ihde – moves away from the idea that the 'body' is or has some universal standard, to consider how embodiment is partially determined by sociocultural context, including gender and ethnicity, and how this inflects collective and individual sensory memories and experiences. The term multistability – as one of the central overarching concepts of post-phenomenology – conveys the inherent adaptability and mutability of both bodies and technology use, always depending on the *contexts* or *situatedness* of praxis.

Importantly, within corporeal feminist scholarship, Ihde's approach is further extended to account for the way situated and habitual experience is anchored in the gendered body. Corporeal feminism is associated with a diverse group of theorists including Elizabeth Grosz (2018), Moira Gatens (2013) and Iris Marion Young (1990). The confluence of corporeal feminism and phenomenology highlights the immediate, specific, local and concrete conditions of our embodiment. Simply centralising the role of the body is in itself problematic for feminism, as it seeks to avoid the essentialist reduction of women to their bodies, or universalising the notion of what a body is. Rather, corporeal feminists focus on how embodiment is lived out in its *specificity*, that is, in its inescapably cultural, social, historical, gendered and technological *situatedness*. As Weiss (2008) notes, the complexities of race, gender, class and geography, together with individual habits, environments and abilities, form the horizons or everyday experience. Our research weaves together post-phenomenological, corporeal feminist *and* ethnographic approaches to understand the role of mobile media in urban experience, including at night, providing us with conceptual and methodological tools to interpret gendered experiences and perceptions of urban space, darkness and risk.

Richardson and Hjorth (2017) argue that the integration of phenomenology into haptic media studies and the ethnographic collection of data is needed to effectively document the significance of touchscreens. The special issue of *New*

Media and Society titled 'Haptic Media Studies' (Parisi et al., 2017) emerged from the recognition that we are in a 'haptic moment' and introduced haptic media studies as a sub-field.

Both ethnography and post-phenomenology – as approaches that are deeply entwined in socio-somatic specificity and variability – also remind us of the significance of self-reflexivity in qualitative research. Since the 1980s, there has been a strong feminist tradition of calling for accountable scientific and academic inquiry alongside self-reflexivity. Scholars such as Haraway (1991) call this 'partial perspective' or 'situated knowledge' and insist on the responsibility of the researcher to acknowledge their own positionality and bias. As researchers, our own experience as embodied beings and the way we engage meaningfully with others (both human and nonhuman) and enact collective habits of being in the world mean that we bring these ways of knowing to bear on our interpretive work. As Pink (2007) writes:

> Ethnography is a process of creating and representing knowledge (about society, culture and individuals) that is based on ethnographers' own experiences. It does not claim to produce an objective or truthful account of reality, but should aim to offer versions of ethnographers' experiences of reality that are as loyal as possible to the context, negotiations and intersubjectivities through which the knowledge was produced. (p. 22)

In this sense, all ethnography is at least implicitly autoethnographic to some extent, and it is important that we are reflexive about the sedimented perceptual biases we embed seamlessly into our studies of everyday media practices. Self-reflexivity is a necessary ethical consideration in the research process, from methodological design through to epistemological claims. As such, we considered our perspective as researchers and interviewers to be partial and sedimented. One of the benefits of researching and writing together was that it involved an ongoing process of conversation and provocation, with a continuing discussion around knowledge production, and an explicit awareness of our situated research practices. For instance, when analysing interviews with participants reflecting on their perceptual experience of being alone in public at night, our own memories were often revisited in colloquial ways that invoked a kind of autoethnographic element. We shared the felt sense of fear when discussing recent violent attacks on women in Australian cities at night – an empathic and vicarious horror as we agreed 'it could have been me' – and reflected on how such high profile cases altered the way we moved through city spaces after dark. We also spoke of the dismay we shared at the lack of reporting when Aboriginal and Torres Strait Islander women are the victims of such violence, with the recognition that the sentiment of 'it could have been me' frequently exists within a complex stratification of privilege that exists across Australia.

As Koskela (1997) revealed in her influential ethnographic research, women's fear of urban violence is strategically counteracted by performing the action of 'walking boldly'. Koskela (1997) describes this as an 'appearance [that] constantly projects the message that they are not afraid, [as they] walk determinedly with confident steps and keep their head up' (p. 309). Here, women enact a different kind of self-conscious variant of 'environmental knowing' (McCullough, 2003) that is recognisable to those around them. As a digital iteration of the 'bold walk', women in our research told us about their experiences of pretending to make a phone call while walking alone at night as a means of managing their fear of potential risk from unknown men. When listening to these stories, we both 'knew' and 'felt' this vulnerability in our bodies; we too 'walked boldly' and used our mobile phones to bolster that bravado. Self-reflexivity adds to the complex layering of data and creates an additional 'excess' of data in the form of one's own media histories and literacies.

Like phenomenology, ethnography is primarily a mode of discovery through description, in that the data collected are represented and interpreted in predominantly text-based narrative form. They are always-partial translations of the human–technology relation that rely on the inducement of 'vicarious experience' in the reader. In the following section, we describe the data collection process in more detail and show some of the ways that data were selected and contained to tell stories of partial translation by invoking a sense of 'me too' familiarity.

Haptic Methods

Interviews and Observations In Situ

Home visits were conducted between November 2016 and March 2017, and each visit included a range of qualitative methods, including interviews, our own observations of participants' embodied interaction with media and several 'haptic experiments'. After each visit, we transcribed the recording while the visit was fresh in our minds. We combined the recording and our notes into one document and linked corresponding visual data (photos and video) that we could refer back to throughout the analytical process.

The start of each interview was geared towards getting to know participants and their personal media histories, building a rapport with them and establishing a relaxed atmosphere in the hope that they would feel comfortable talking about their experiences. We asked them questions about themselves, such as who they live with, where they work, how they travel within their city and what their daily and night-time activities generally entailed. We also asked participants to walk us through their most frequently used apps and smartphone functions and to re-enact their use of the device in the home, where and how they would usually do so, while responding to questions and providing ongoing commentary of their activity. We were also interested in how participants used their smartphone before bed and first thing in the morning, to gain insights into smartphone usage in such liminal times. We did this to explore mobile devices and intimacy, both in terms of their haptic affordances and communicative reach, and to gather data on the intersecting experience of touch and intimacy. Each session was recorded on an iPhone using the Voice Record app.

In *Crafting Phenomenological Research,* Vagle (2014) recommends that researchers 'write down everything. Be a constant note-taker' (p. 85). Our observational notes included where we sat during the interview, facial expressions when pausing to think about a question, posture, hand gestures, facial expressions, pauses or silences and the location of participants' phones during the interview (e.g. in their pocket, being carried or held in their hand during the walk-through, whether it was face up or face down, on silent or being charged in a designated location within their house). Observation, as a method, is a 'strategic and technical aspect of crafting phenomenological research' (Vagle, 2014, p. 77). Vagle (2014) proposes that when deciding to explicitly engage in phenomenological methods, one must consider:

> the phenomenon under investigation, the contexts in which it is being studied, how many research participants are involved, what fields of study you are trying to speak to – but most importantly, one needs to pay very careful attention and remain open, to the phenomenon. One must be willing to make a data-gathering and analysis plan and then, once carrying out that plan, be willing to make adjustments and explore new ways to open up the phenomenon. (p. 77)

Notes and photographs were also taken throughout the home visits, especially during the enacted parts of the haptic experiments (see below), to later pair with the recorded interviews. In a later phase of the project, online interviews aimed to capture experiences of mobile media and the urban night, and women in particular spoke of their habitual and pre-reflective use of mobile phones when walking alone. A post-phenomenological approach is useful here because, as Ihde (2002) suggests, human–technology relations are contextually variable and multistable, and feminist phenomenology provides a conceptual framework to analyse gendered human-world connections.

From a haptic media perspective, interviews alone are not sufficient to capture nuance and detail of embodied use, as it is often difficult to observe and record mobile media use as it happens (e.g. reaching for a device when bored) – because so much of the interview process is about remembering and describing instances from the past. Interviewing can thus only reveal so much about behaviour as it happens. To overcome this limitation, walk-throughs and haptic experiments (discussed below) were conducted with participants in situ and often involved asking participants to enact an immediately observable micro-movement (handling their phone or placing it away from the body, as described below). Participants employ what Moores (2014) describes as tacit performative motions (he gives the example of his own practice of automatically checking social media or news apps upon waking). That is, they enact a 'going through the motions' of media use. To go beyond verbal representations and enacted simulations of previous experience, we became particularly interested in exploring experimental and in-the-moment haptic techniques as part of our qualitative research repertoire.

Haptic Experiments

The haptic experiments conducted during the home visits revealed the importance of understanding the intimate body–technology relation people have with their phones, which emerged as a key thematic focus. Our approach to these haptic experiments was explicitly phenomenological and informed by Moores' adaptation of Merleau-Ponty's knowledge in the hands to 'ways of the hand'. Moores' (2014) reworking of the concept points to how ordinary and habitual movement functions 'in an unreflective, taken for granted manner' (p. 197), such as the selection of keys on a keyboard or pinching two fingers on a touchpad to minimise an app. Moores (2014) describes this unreflective and habitual movement as 'an embodied and sensuous knowledge' (p. 197) that typifies many of our medium-body relations. We applied this insight to the haptic experiments conducted during home visits, by observing how participants handled their mobile device in ordinary and habitual ways in the organic setting of their home.

The experiments were also guided by haptic ethnographic methods, as demonstrated by Richardson and Hjorth's (2017) study of everyday gaming in Australian households and Paterson's (2007, 2009) research into embodied knowledge, proximity, intimacy and technologies of touch. Richardson and Hjorth (2017), for instance, describe their participants' in situ usage and handling of their smartphones as follows:

> We have frequently observed the way participants manage their mobile device as a changeable material interface, such as habitually placing their phone face down, in between showing us what is on their screens and how they use it. When questioned about this 'handling' of their device, participants reveal how this seemingly trivial gesture actually embodied a wealth of 'deep' attitudes about privacy, boundaries between work and play, social etiquette and care for the device. It is clear that the bodily methods of interfacing with the materiality of the screen are of paramount importance to participants' engagement. (p. 1654)

Building on this observation and analysis of in-the-moment actions, in the first haptic experiment, participants were invited to hold their mobile device in their hand for about one minute and describe what their smartphone means to them, and how it makes them feel and what it feels like to be without it. In one instance, a participant kept his eyes closed while he spoke about how his smartphone makes him feel, and as he explained how most of the time it was an annoying component of his everyday life, he also gestured outwards in a circular motion with the phone in hand and said, 'it connects me to everything in my life'. Another participant spoke about a time they left their smartphone at home:

> I was once half-way to work and realised I'd left my phone at home. I seriously considered turning to get it but decided not to because I wanted to prove a point to myself. That I'm not

dependent on my phone. But being without it was really intense! When I got bored at work, I kept reaching for my phone to scroll through Facebook or check my dating apps for new matches. Like, I would literally reach towards my backpack to get my phone, and then remember it was at home. I felt like I was missing out.

While our analytic focus is on the way mobile phones have become 'fresh instruments' and habitualised aspects of our embodiment, always within reach, the quote might just as well be used as anecdotal support for a different research paper, e.g. what does it reveal about the attention economy and role of mobile phones and apps to fill the numerous in-between moments of everyday life? That is, the quote might be considered a form of 'worlding' that holds entire cultural contexts that are both local and global. Ethnographically informed research and analysis is always partial, always a matter of choice and selection.

When asking participants to reflect on what their mobile phone means to them, especially for women participants, the conversation often organically led to stories about safety and risk. What does it feel like to be out of the house with little or no phone battery? What does it feel like to be without one's mobile phone? One participant told us of her experience visiting an unfamiliar city:

I started to panic because I realised I had no idea where I was... like literally, I did not know how to get back to the hotel. I closed all my apps and stopped listening to music. I even got lost a few times because I was too worried to use Google Maps. Eventually, I turned my phone off to preserve battery so I'd still be able to get an Uber once it got dark. What would I have done otherwise?

As noted above, media ethnography relies on capturing tacit everyday practices that are then analysed through an interpretive process that is 'revelatory' – i.e. using the data to 'surface' invisible or opaque yet significant aspects of human–technology relations. The first participant quote above, one that we deliberately selected for analysis, is a good example of how collective embodiment and tacit knowledge are relied upon to induce a vicarious 'me too' moment in the reader that does not need to be explained – from reluctant dependency on one's mobile phone to the use of mobile media to manage workplace boredom. Much of the descriptive or analytic work is also underlain by much deeper sedimented tacit knowledges and cultural habitudes, collective understandings of media use and common feelings about digital technologies that we share with both scholarly and more generalist readers. Part of our interpretation of data into publishable form involved making careful decisions about what can be assumed (e.g. with reference to the second quote: Google Maps, Uber, the feeling of being lost) and what is specific to certain users and situations (e.g. women in urban spaces, the extent of – and different reasons for – reliance on one's mobile phone), in order to show how mobile media practices are now embedded in a broader 'politics' of the everyday (e.g. how mobile phones are used to manage the risk that bodies are unequally exposed to in urban environments, especially after dark). At every point of this interpretative process, there is excess to be managed and cut away from the final text, both in terms of selective choices about what participant stories to use and in terms of the collective knowledges that can be assumed.

A final experiment involved asking participants if we could hold their phone. This question was often met by laughter and surprise, and responses ranged from an immediate willingness to hesitation, suspicion and reluctance. At no point did we reach for participants' phones unless they offered, and we only asked the question once. No participant declined to be involved in this haptic experiment. We were interested in using this experiment as a provocation to explore perceptions of haptic and affective intimacy. In this handling-as-haptic method, the relationship between the mobile device, participants and ourselves as the researchers came to the fore as an important component of the study. As suggested by Pink, this relationship can offer 'a means of reflexively understanding the processes through which ethnographic knowledge is produced' (Pink, 2007). In this way, phenomenological and ethnographic techniques became part of a creative, experimental and reflexive process in the co-production of knowledge.

The methods above were adopted to explore participants' embodied relations to their mobile devices, both as intimate physical objects and as networked conduits of perceptual reach. If we had, for instance, only visited participants in their homes and asked them to tell us about their mobile device, we would most likely have received discursive accounts of what they use their mobile device for throughout the day. Instead, deploying a haptic method yielded insights into participants' reflective knowledge of their use of their mobile device, as well as their affective embodiment. We gathered deep and granular data about how participants' devices, as fresh instruments, have been incorporated into their bodily schema and being in the world. In this way, we would argue that methodological choices, both in terms of the conceptual frameworks chosen and the specific techniques used to gather data, result in different stories, stories that are already inflected by participant idiosyncrasies, recent and past experiences and even how they are feeling on the day.

Our aim in this section has been to convey the inevitable overflow of data that characterises ethnographic and phenomenological research and how this excess must be critically and reflexively managed by the researcher to inform partial translations of everyday media practices. In the final section, we discuss another interpretive technique that can be used to 'contain' the data.

Fabrication and Partial Translation

A key aspect of our research concerned the practicalities of 'how' (in an active sense) to weave participants' stories into our conceptual and phenomenological inquiry. From the overwhelming surplus of data generated by our haptic methodology – in the form of transcripts, observational notes, records of brainstorming sessions and conversations, thematic clustering, photographs and audiovisual content – how could we provide 'thick' descriptions that were reflective of the rich diversity of practices, yet for the more utilitarian purposes of publication, 'left room' for broader critical analysis and disciplinary concerns? Our approach to this conundrum emerged from amalgamating various innovative techniques from qualitative research, such as the use of vignettes in addition to anecdotes. Ely et al. (2005) suggest that:

> Vignettes, much in the same way as anecdotes, are narrative investigations that carry with them an interpretation of the person, experience or situation that the writer describes. Yet, we see an important difference in intent; while anecdotes tend to be a written representation of a meaningful event, a vignette restructures the complexities of its subject for the purpose of capturing, in a brief portrayal, what has been learned over a period of time. (p. 70)

Our use of vignettes is a means to explore, assemble and map observations from the ethnographic data, which are then used to illustrate the broader implications of mobile media use in urban spaces. Vignettes can be used as an extended form of anecdotal storytelling, a fusion of observations drawn from multiple participants. This method has been a widely, and successfully, used strategy deployed by prominent qualitative researchers in the fields of digital ethnography and mobile media (Humphreys & Watson, 2009; Pink & Leder Mackley, 2013). While no parts of a vignette or 'story amalgam' are fictionalised, they are at times a composite construction of several participants' experiences. Markham (2012) calls this style of presenting data *fabrication* – a provocative name for an innovative method that is increasingly used in research involving 'Internet-mediated social contexts' (p. 334), and particularly useful in cases where anonymising data is not sufficient to protect the privacy of research participants. We provide two examples below.

> Dane is an Indigenous bisexual man in his early 40s. He lives alone in inner-city Naarm (Melbourne), and works in community development. He lived in Sydney for a few years in his 20s, but apart from that he's spent his whole life in Melbourne. Dane is a proud late adopter of smartphones. His main reason for buying a smartphone was the camera function, and he playfully refers to his smartphone as "a camera that rings". As someone who has suffered from insomnia most of his life, Dane spends many hours walking in his neighbourhood at night, capturing shadows and uploading the images to his public Instagram account. Most of his followers are from Australia and the United States, and a few in Europe. He sometimes chats to them via Instagram Messenger, and especially likes connecting with other people who are also into photography. He particularly enjoys taking photos at night, during which time the familiar streets become "moody and strange". Referring to his dark skin and shaved head, he jokes, "I'd look great in a line-up" and adds "sometimes I feel a

bit self-conscious on the bus or train, particularly late at night, I think maybe I could seem like a threat or something. So, I'll play a game or chat to friends about my photos via Instagram. I figure it works both ways – I don't notice anyone, and people don't notice me".

Sara is in her late 20s and grew up in the western suburbs of Sydney. She knows Western Sydney well, and despite its "bad" reputation she has never felt unsafe there herself. She likes that it has a strong multicultural atmosphere, and described it as the kind of place where you know your neighbours and you look out for one another. When she started studying at university, she became friends with other students from all over Sydney, and she observed that Western Sydney was seen by others as a really unsafe place to live. She expressed, "That was so weird to me! When my new friends would come to visit me, they were always so nervous. They didn't want me catching the train home alone, so they would always drive me even though it was totally out of their way. They had this thing about me being unsafe because I'm a five-foot girl. But I grew up out there – it was my home, and I knew which areas to avoid". She recently moved to Melbourne and often feels on guard because she's in an unfamiliar city. She works late in sport retail in the CBD, and when possible, her boyfriend will meet her at work to travel home with her on the tram. When her boyfriend is unavailable, she makes sure to wear a big coat in an attempt to disguise her small build and to "cover up" because she's often wearing a short sporty uniform. She keeps her phone in hand and has it set up to respond to voice-activated calling, and always uses her headphones with the listen-through function. In this way, she aware of what's happening around her, while at the same time presenting to strangers that she is not "available" for conversation.

Vignettes such as these can then be used to engage with multiple themes, depending on the specific focus or interests of the researcher or the intended venue for publication. For our purposes, across a number of publications (Hardley, 2021; Hardley & Richardson, 2019, 2021a, 2021b), these or similar composite stories were used or adapted to narratively frame thematic analysis. For example: we explored the gendered experience of urban darkness and the way mobile phones become co-opted into the management of risk (for Dane, as a way to minimise what he perceives as his 'threatening' appearance, for Sara, as a way to feel safer); examined the dominant cultural narratives surrounding violence against women in Australia and the problematic reliance on mobile phones by women alone at night; considered how mobile media and visual literacies are integral to both the creative and safety affordances of smartphones; looked at the gendered nature of bodily comportment and how mobile phones are strategic tools used for negotiating proximal encounters with strangers; and discussed the way mobile phones are conduits of ambient presence (presence at-a-distance) or 'social proprioception' in Farman's (2015) terms, whether via speed dial or social media apps. In this mode of interpretation, it is understood that the stories themselves 'exceed' holistic analysis, and that they also rely on tacit collective knowledges within and about Western cultures, but they can nevertheless provide a loosely contained framing or anchor point.

Of most interest to our analysis is the way mobile phones work to modify women's geospatial and proprioceptive awareness of both co-located and networked others, and how this has emerged as a new form of perceptual vigilance (Hardley & Richardson, 2021a). The notion of perceptual vigilance describes the situated and networked hyper-awareness that frequently accompanies women's experience of urban darkness. Mobile phones provide us with an 'as-if' sense of safety – that is, they connect us to our intimate others, and we perceive ourselves safer simply because other people are aware of our location – yet it is also well understood that in actuality, they offer no real protection in the face of immediate and present danger. While mobile media may reconfigure our relation to actual and virtual space, such that we reside in net-local space, in the dark, we are returned to brute actuality. The connectivity afforded by network functionality provides comforting and familiar feelings of ambient presence or co-presence (Hjorth & Richardson, 2020), even while we are concurrently aware of the inadequacies of online communicative reach in situations of bodily risk. It is this strange incongruity, coupled with users' knowledge that mobile phones and networks are unforeseeably unreliable, that describes the safety paradox – a contradiction that sits uneasily in the body, and particularly women's bodies, as part of our sensorial incorporation of mobile media. Throughout our research and conversations with women, we often reflected on the difficulty of faithfully describing their experience of fear when alone at night and the vital role of mobile phones in providing some (small) sense of protection and safety. In the broadest sense, this is a problem of language, of words and text-based analysis, which can only imperfectly communicate what bodies feel and perceive.

Conclusion

By the start of 2020, some participants had been involved in our research project for almost 5 years. One woman, for instance, had participated in our initial survey in 2016, home visits in 2017 and again for an online interview in 2020. In that time, she had become a mother and in the final interview reflected on how her everyday use of her smartphone had changed after childbirth, especially as her baby developed into a toddler and was frequently reaching and grabbing for household items, including smartphones. Longitudinal research presents its own 'excess', further layers to add to the palimpsest of data that we have discussed in this chapter, as it demands a more assiduous incorporation of, and rigorous attention to, both individual and sociotechnical trajectories of change.

In *Phenomenology of Practice,* van Manen (2014) comments that analysing lived experience 'is a complex and creative process of insightful invention, discovery, and disclosure. Grasping and formulating a thematic understanding is not a rule-bound process but a free act of "seeing" meaning' (p. 320). A similar statement might be made about ethnographic approaches, which are also not prescribed but rather 'follow the data'. Throughout our collaborative research, we have combined these methodologies and employed creative or experimental modes of discovery, remaining open to the variability of the lifeworld in terms of perceptual and experiential difference. It is important for us to remember, as media researchers, that our modes of embodiment and perception are not uniform or neutral but saturated with conceptual and perceptual histories, individual variation, collective habitudes and sedimented ways of being in the world and being with others. Much of our work, particularly for the task of publication and partial translation, involves deliberate and ethical decisions about what gets included and what is relegated to our ever-expanding data archives. In this process, the conundrum of excess data is not something that can be avoided or a problem to be solved; it is the inevitable consequence of studying everyday life.

References

Cooley, H. R. (2014). *Finding Augusta: Habits of mobility and governance in the digital era*. University Press of New England.

Elo, M., & Luoto, M. (Eds.). (2018). *Figures of touch: Sense, technics, body*. The Academy of Fine Arts at the University of the Arts Helsinki.

Ely, M., Vinz, R., Anzul, M., & Downing, M. (2005). *On writing qualitative research: Living by words*. The Falmer Press.

Farman, J. (2012). *Mobile interface theory: Embodied space and locative media*. Routledge.

Farman, J. (2015). Stories, spaces, and bodies: The production of embodied space through mobile media storytelling. *Communication Research and Practice, 1*(2), 101–116. https://doi.org/10.1080/22041451.2015.1047941

Fortunati, L. (2005). The mobile phone as technological artefact. In P. Glotz, S. Bertschi, & C. Locke (Eds.), *Thumb culture: The meaning of mobile phones for society* (pp. 149–160). Transcript Verlag.

Gatens, M. (2013). *Imaginary bodies: Ethics, power and corporeality*. Routledge.

Grosz, E. (2018). *The incorporeal: Ontology, ethics, and the limits of materialism*. Columbia University Press.

Haraway, D. J. (1991). *Simians, cyborgs and women: The reinvention of nature*. Routledge.

Hardley, J. (2021). Embodied perceptions of darkness: Multistable experiences of mobile media in the urban night. *M/C Journal, 24*(2). https://doi.org/10.5204/mcj.2756

Hardley, J., & Richardson, I. (2019). Mobile media and the embodiment of risk and safety in the urban night. In *Paper Presented at Association of Internet Researchers Conference*, Brisbane, Australia, October 2–5. https://doi.org/10.5210/spir.v2019i0.11051

Hardley, J., & Richardson, I. (2021a). Mistrust of the city at night: Networked connectivity and embodied perceptions of risk and safety. *Australian Feminist Studies*, *36*(107), 65–81. https://doi.org/10.1080/08164649.2021.1934815

Hardley, J., & Richardson, I. (2021b). Digital placemaking and networked corporeality: Embodied mobile media practices in domestic space during Covid-19. *Convergence*, *27*(3), 625–636. https://doi.org/10.1177/1354856520979963

Hjorth, L., & Richardson, I. (2020). *Ambient play*. MIT Press.

Humphreys, M., & Watson, T. (2009). Ethnographic practices: From 'writing-up ethnographic research' to 'writing ethnography'. In S. Ybema, D. Yanow, H. Wels, & F. Kamstegg (Eds.), *Organizational ethnography: Studying the complexity of everyday life* (pp. 40–55). Sage.

Ihde, D. (1993). *Postphenomenology: Essays in the postmodern context*. Northwestern University Press.

Ihde, D. (2002). *Bodies in technology*. University of Minnesota Press.

Jewitt, C., Price, S., Leder Mackley, K., Yiannoutsou, N., & Atkinson, D. (2020). *Interdisciplinary insights for digital touch communication*. Springer International Publishing. https://doi.org/10.1007/978-3-030-24564-1

Keogh, B. (2018). *A play of bodies*. MIT Press.

Koskela, H. (1997). 'Bold walk and breakings': Women's spatial confidence versus fear of violence. *Gender, Place & Culture*, *4*(3), 301–320. https://doi.org/10.1080/09663699725369

Leder, D. (1990). *The absent body*. University of Chicago Press.

Markham, A. (2012). Fabrication as ethical practice: Qualitative inquiry in ambiguous internet contexts. *Information, Communication & Society*, *15*(3), 334–353. https://doi.org/10.1080/1369118x.2011.641993

McCullough, M. (1996). *Abstracting craft: The practiced digital hand*. MIT Press.

McCullough, M. (2003). *On digital ground: Architecture, pervasive computing, and environmental knowing*. MIT Press.

Merleau-Ponty, M. (1964). *The primacy of perception, and other essays on phenomenological psychology, the philosophy of art, history and politics*. Northwestern University Press.

Merleau-Ponty, M. (2004 [1962]). *Phenomenology of perception*. Routledge & Kegan Paul.

Moores, S. (2012). *Media, place and mobility*. Palgrave Macmillan.

Moores, S. (2013). We find our way about: Everyday media use and 'inhabitant knowledge. *Mobilities*, *10*(1), 17–35. https://doi.org/10.1080/17450101.2013.819624

Moores, S. (2014). Digital orientations: "Ways of the hand" and practical knowing in media uses and other manual activities. *Mobile Media and Communication*, *2*(2), 196–208. https://doi.org/10.1177/2050157914521091

Morris, D. (2004). *The sense of space*. University of New York Press.

Parisi, D. (2018). *Archaeologies of touch: Interfacing with haptics from electricity to computing*. University of Minnesota Press.

Parisi, D. (2022, March 3). Can't touch this. Haptic devices probably won't ever live up to their promise to replicate physical contact. *Real Life*. https://reallifemag.com/cant-touch-this

Parisi, D., Paterson, M., & Archer, J. E. (2017). Haptic media studies. *New Media & Society*, *19*(10), 1513–1522. https://doi.org/10.1177/1461444817717518

Paterson, M. (2007). *Senses of touch: Haptics, affects and technologies*. Berg.

Paterson, M. (2009). Haptic geographies: Ethnography, haptic knowledges and sensuous dispositions. *Progress in Human Geography, 33*(6), 766–788. https://doi.org/10.1080/1369118x.2011.641993

Paterson, M., Dodge, M., & MacKian, S. (2012). Introduction: Placing touch within social theory and empirical study. In M. Paterson & M. Dodge (Eds.), *Touching space, placing touch* (pp. 1–28). Ashgate Publishing.

Pink, S. (2007). *Doing visual ethnography*. Sage.

Pink, S. (2009). *Doing sensory ethnography*. Sage.

Pink, S. (2015). Approaching media through the senses: Between experience and representation. *Media International Australia, 154*(1), 5–14. https://doi.org/10.1177/1329878x1515400103

Pink, S., & Leder Mackley, K. (2013). Saturated and situated: Expanding the meaning of media in the routines of everyday life. *Media, Culture & Society, 35*(6), 677–691. https://doi.org/10.1177/0163443713491298

Pink, S., Sinanan, J., Hjorth, L., & Horst, H. (2016). Tactile digital ethnography: Researching mobile media through the hand. *Mobile Media & Communication, 4*(2), 237–251. https://doi.org/10.1177/2050157915619958

Powers, D., & Parisi, D. (2020, July 29). The hype, haplessness and hope of haptics in the COVID-19 era. *TechCrunch*. https://techcrunch.com/2020/07/28/the-hype-haplessness-and-hope-of-haptics-in-the-covid-19-era

Richardson, I., & Hjorth, L. (2017). Mobile media, domestic play and haptic ethnography. *New Media & Society, 19*(10), 1653–1667. https://doi.org/10.1177/1461444817717516

Richardson, I., & Wilken, R. (2012). Parerga of the third screen: Mobile media, place and presence. In R. Wilken & G. Goggin (Eds.), *Mobile technology and place* (pp. 181–197). Routledge.

Richardson, I., & Wilken, R. (2017). Mobile media and mediation: The relational ontology of Google Glass. In T. Markham & S. Rodgers (Eds.), *Conditions of mediation: Phenomenological approaches to media, technology and communication* (pp. 113–123). Peter Lang.

Richardson, I., & Wilken, R. (2023). *Bodies and mobile media*. Polity Press.

Vagle, M. D. (2014). *Crafting phenomenological research*. Left Coast Press.

van Manen, M. (2014). *Phenomenology of practice: Meaning-giving methods in phenomenological research and writing*. Routledge.

Weiss, G. (2008). *Refiguring the ordinary*. Indiana University Press.

Wiley, S. B. C., Becerra, T. M., & Sutko, D. M. (2012). Subjects, networks, assemblages: A materialist approach to the production of social space. In J. Packer & S. B. C. Wiley (Eds.), *Communication matters: Materialist approaches to media, mobility, and networks* (pp. 183–195). Routledge.

Wilson, F. R. (1998). *The hand: How its use shapes the brain, language and human culture*. Vintage Books.

Young, I. M. (1990). *On female body experience: "Throwing like a girl" and other essays*. Oxford University Press.

Chapter 8

Re-engaging With Excess Data: Newbie Researchers, Tumblr and the Evolving Research Event

Navid Sabet

University of Canberra, Australia

Abstract

This chapter reflects on a media studies project exploring Sylvia Plath poetry on Tumblr. The project ultimately resulted in excess digital data, with no conventional publications or research outputs. Now writing 10 years after data collection, I take a storying approach to explore the original research concerns and the research process, thereby locating a reconfigured 'research event' that draws together various biographical, social, political and historical factors. I reflect on my evolving understanding of 'research', discussing early teaching experiences and postgraduate pathways that partly structured a particular relationship to research. This serves to bridge a discussion about the challenges of the initial process over a decade ago, including the uncomfortable pairing of inexperience among aspiring researchers and institutional pressures to publish. I then discuss the theoretical perspectives that inspire and, in retrospect, offer clarity for the project, given the amount of time passed since data collection and the synergistic relationship between the storying approach, poststructuralist thought and story-focused methodologies. I argue that Tumblr provides unique opportunities for identity negotiation, aesthetic appreciation, data extraction and commodification, which highlights both the creative agency of digital aesthetic curation and self-work, as well as the importance of algorithmic transparency. I also contend that engaging with excess data led to methodologically and theoretically useful insights, challenging assumptions about the temporality of usable data and the ever-changing relationship between art, technology and freedom.

Keywords: Poetry; Tumblr; epistemology; confession; algorithms; Syliva Plath

Introduction

This chapter reflects on a media studies project exploring Sylvia Plath poetry on Tumblr. The project ultimately resulted in excess digital data, with no conventional publications or research outputs. Now writing 10 years after data collection, I take a storying approach (Gravett, 2019) to explore the original research concerns and the research process, thereby locating a reconfigured 'research event' (Michael, 2021) that draws together various biographical, social, political and historical factors.

First, I reflect on my evolving understanding of 'research'. I discuss early teaching experiences and postgraduate pathways that partly structured a particular relationship to research. This serves to bridge a discussion about the challenges of the initial process over a decade ago, including the uncomfortable pairing of inexperience among aspiring researchers and institutional pressures to publish. I then discuss the theoretical perspectives that inspire and, in retrospect, offer clarity for the project, given the amount of time passed since data collection and the synergistic relationship between the storying approach, poststructuralist thought and story-focused methodologies (Gloviczki, 2021; Gravett & Winstone, 2019).

Drawing on research in media studies and literary studies, I also take a quasi-Foucauldian perspective on the politics of Tumblr posting and argue that over the last decade, forms, sites and practices of confession have emerged and evolved with developments in digital technology. Read against trends towards chatbots in clinical psychology, 'data selfies' (Robards et al., 2020) and the intertextual posting of confessionalist poetry on Tumblr in 2014, I raise concerns about the limits of confession, self-fashioning and care of the self (Foucault, 1978, 1990) in contemporary algorithmic societies. Posting poetry under these conditions, I suggest, provides unique opportunities for identity negotiation, aesthetic appreciation, data extraction and commodification. This chapter concludes with reflections on how excess data led to methodologically and theoretically useful insights, challenging assumptions about the temporality of usable data and the ever-changing relationship between art, technology and freedom.

Temporality and the Research Event: What Is Research?

> "A far sea moves in my ear." – *Morning Song* by Sylvia Plath, reposted on my personal Tumblr page in the early 2010s.

Data tells a story. Data has a story. But which one do we tell? How do we tell it? When does the story begin and end? Storying data sees research not so much as a linear procession from question to conclusion, but rather as an 'event' featuring assorted components – imperfect research questions, unpredictable participant engagement, heterogeneous writing and dissemination practices as well as the ambiguities of life (Gloviczki, 2021; Gravett & Winstone, 2019; Michael, 2021).

This approach also recognises that these ingredients are difficult to capture. As Michael notes:

> ...in the retelling of the anecdote, there is a refreshing (and altering) of the affects associated with the original event that is now caught up in a reconfiguration of times and places: and all these too feed into the research event. (2021, p. 1)

Storying data also involves recognising the researcher as a character with aspirations, anxieties, faults and motivations of their own. Discussing autoethnography, Chang (2008, p. 15) describes culture as 'a web of self and others'. Literary figures such as Sylvia Plath *created* complex and highly influential webs that captured the attention and passion of a global readership. Their works became subject to endless research and commentary that generated new knowledge, anecdotes, conspiracies, theories, practices and images. Digital spaces such as Tumblr have also been the site of substantial academic critique. While the 2014 project that inspired this article may have begun as something like Sylvia Plath + Tumblr = ? the 'research event' is now entirely different; the 'web of self and others' has been reconfigured and necessitates, I believe, a storying approach that reimagines what data can be (Hardy et al., 2023).

When starting this project, I began teaching undergraduate students for the first time. Our lesson on research fundamentals began with a simple question: *what is research?* The answer seemed clear enough; 'research' was defined relative to its antithesis – magazines, newspapers, blogs and industry publications, all of which had observable political, economic and social agendas and selective data collection practices that made them worthy of criticism but forbidden as scholarly references. Ten years later, without the challenge of ensuring first-year university students have a clear and coherent answer about what research is, the question feels more complicated. It's also a little more *exciting*. Perhaps that's a symptom of the postmodern condition. Maybe it's just plain old nostalgia.

This chapter is a reflexive muddle, but I'm leaning into that. Since the so-called 'reflexive turn' in the social sciences (Foley, 2002; Lumsden et al., 2019; Venkatesh, 2013), reflexivity is both a valued research principle and a legitimate ethnographic research practice. Methodologies based on concepts such as 'bricolage' (Schmidt & Kloet, 2017), performativity (Leeker et al., 2017), affect (Hillis et al., 2015), non-representational theories (Moores, 2018) and assemblage theory (Salovaara, 2015), when deployed towards diverse media, serve as inspiration for using diverse practices and theories to enrich research, without necessarily seeking a definitive conclusion. However, alongside the complexity embraced by these approaches lies the question of *what to do* with data. The 'sorting' of data (Mills, 1959, p. 12) can be perplexing in a postmodern world with rigid project timelines and the epistemological challenges of researching digital worlds that often presuppose an evolving object of study, as well as navigating the ever-growing dominance and complexity of platforms in datafied societies (Møller Hartley et al., 2021; Poell, 2020).

Moreover, as we develop as researchers, we gain new understandings of what research is, why it's important and why we do it. Perhaps the story of this project and its data begins with simple *curiosity*, which has been linked to a Freudian thirst for knowledge (Loewenstein, 1994), a motivation to diminish novelty and ambiguity (Silva, 2012) and something that drives our 'deepest and most persistent inquiries' (Watson, 2018, p. 1). We research because we want to question; we indulge our yearning to explore. We want to solve problems – and create new ones. Methodology is what we do to pursue our curiosity – it's a toolbox and a map. But sometimes, the tools don't work properly; sometimes, the map is wrong. Occasionally, we aren't ready or able to use them. Sometimes, we need more help. When I remember the beginning of this project – exploring Sylvia Plath quotes posted on Tumblr – I can picture myself holding a map upside down and scrambling for lost keys to the toolbox. I was in my early 20s, fresh out of my Honours year, and in the words of a former lecturer – I 'wouldn't know my arse from my elbow' (he wasn't being mean – he was criticising what he deemed to be unreasonable requirements for PhD scholarships).

But I was determined – driven by a passion developed through hours perusing the vibrant digital world of Tumblr, a microblogging and social networking platform founded in 2007. Tumblr was supposed to be, according to David Karp, its founder and former CEO, a space of 'limitless creative expression' (Dixon, 2011, p. 4:10) and unusually free from the ugliness of advertising. Karp's unorthodox yet hardnosed principles were fundamental to its maverick cultural identity (McCracken et al., 2020). Tumblr was a space for creative self-cultivation through the sharing of ideas and interests via text, photos, quotes, links, music and videos. Media could be original, such as digital artworks, or (more commonly) posts could be the work of others, usually reposted from other Tumblr pages. In the case of Sylvia Plath, posts were frequently fragments of her poetry or journals, sometimes accompanied by an image or occasional commentary. I was (and still am) a fan of Plath and poetry more generally, so my passion for the topic gave me a reason to want to know more about it – to reduce uncertainty, even if it left me with more questions than answers.

Especially in its first few years, Tumblr signalled an alternative to the social networking culture that centred on Facebook. Tumblr meant creative expression, dynamic fandoms and communities of practice and shared interest – it wasn't about stringing together networks of personal connections and sharing news articles. If Facebook and Twitter were the town square, Tumblr was the colourful bustling market and community arts centre – the rumble of music from the pub. Tumblr was *affect*. And Tumblr's alternative space and affective charge made it perfect for sharing and appreciating poetry and other art forms. Images hung in evolving galleries fuelled by millions of posts, reposts and likes. Songs were shared, and text circulated between accounts from around the world, many of which were anonymous. In fact, Tumblr's enabling of anonymity (or pseudonymity) further solidified its potential for creative self-cultivation.

A serendipitous encounter with a more experienced academic, who shared my interest in Tumblr and Plath, led to a collaborative project about the posting of her poetry. We met a few times to discuss the project, developed an online survey and posted it from a new account with the hashtags that were frequently associated with Plath. We also got in contact with a popular Plath fan page, who generously reposted our survey to their audience. We quickly received hundreds of responses. I was confident this would mean that we could write something, perhaps publish it (an imperative I was becoming acutely aware of), and ultimately share new insights about what Plath meant to Tumblr users, and how they were using her words. Perhaps our own understanding of Plath would change; maybe we would grow as readers of her work. Perhaps we would see something new in this extraordinarily talented and equally misunderstood literary figure (Van Duyne, 2023), defined as often (if not more) by her death than her life.

But in the end, the data we collected became 'excess' – all of it. No papers were written. I was too inexperienced to know what the next steps in the research process would or should be, and my colleague was going through a crisis about whether she wanted to be a researcher at all. And now, a decade later, I am unable to dig up the data from old laptops to inform any analysis of participants' specific responses. Perhaps most people would consider this data to be exceptionally outdated anyway. But I write this chapter from the present. Because while the research grew from an idea to design, eventually inspiring many survey responses before meeting an abrupt end, the data in a sense has become something else now – a reconfigured web. As a reflective exercise, it whispers something about Tumblr culture and my own journey as a researcher. It reminds me that cultural objects, like data and research events, are dynamic and evolving. It also likely reaffirms that nostalgia is hard to shake.

I have thought about Tumblr and the Plath posters project countless times over the years. I don't recall any verbatim responses from the survey respondents, but I do remember the culture of Tumblr in 2013. I remember how it felt to be part of it: the electric current that Sylvia Plath's words sent through its ecosystem and onto my dashboard. The generosity of Plath posters' responses in our survey, I believe, mirrored something about that culture. But engaging with outdated, 'excess' data from the present necessitates changing perspective – perhaps a new set of assumptions about what data can be. Was I better equipped to address the research topic 10 years ago, as an untested researcher with full access to the survey results? Or now, restricted in methodological 'precision' but more experienced, and hopefully slightly wiser? And what might that say about the data and my ongoing curiosity about it? If memory is 'a performance rooted in lived contexts' (Keightley, 2020, p. 58), perhaps memory *of* data can have broader utility than more rigid validity criteria suggest.

Why Research?

> My supervisor: *brags about the number of citations he has*
>
> My supervisor: *cites himself five times in my paper*
>
> My supervisor: *brags about the number of citations he has*

[repeat above for infinity]

Me:
Source: Tumblr.

They call me 007....0 publications, 0 conference presentations, 7 years of bullshitting my way through academia. Hang in there friend.
Source: Reddit.

I needed publications. It seems like a truism now, but the precise reasons didn't seem clear back then – that's just what I was told, and I didn't think too deeply about why. I just accepted it; it was unavoidable. PhD programmes and scholarships were competitive. My publication portfolio was light, but it *felt* heavy – full of vaguely defined and unfinished projects soaking in the noise of my inner critic. Little did I know that that was just the start. Indeed, whether they're plagued by publish or perish culture (Becker & Lukka, 2023), anxieties about career advancement or imposter syndrome, most PhD students won't tell you a story about a stress-free lifestyle consisting of interest-based reading and writing productivity in an air-conditioned office. In fact, the risk of developing psychiatric conditions, especially depression, is significantly higher among PhD students than comparison groups (Levecque et al., 2017).

I recently logged back onto several social networking websites including Tumblr and Reddit, recalling their utility during the most difficult moments of my PhD candidature. On the one hand, many PhD candidates express hope, humour and generosity – sharing advice and titbits on everything from the importance of choosing good supervisors to the state of their desks. However, postgraduate-related hashtags and forums also yield countless frustrations from students about the conditions of their journey. The stories shared on the subreddit r/PhD/ are fraught with toxic supervisors, abuse, gaslighting and deteriorated personal lives, as well as worries about career trajectories and a lack of publications. *Write what? Publish where?* The threads of anxiety, dread and self-doubt are endless.

Moosa (2018) contends that the pressure for academics to 'publish or persish' can be attributed to the forces of globalisation and the neoliberal perspective that advocates treating higher education as a commodity. While the term 'publish or perish' predates neoliberal globalisation, neoliberal social and economic restructuring has increased pressure on academic workers to publish to remain competitive in a tight employment market and continuously improve their portfolios. These pressures are especially troublesome for non-English speaking academics whose research remains marginalised due to the effects of cultural imperialism, linguicide, epistemicide and poor funding (Lee & Lee, 2013; Vurayai & Ndofirepi, 2020). Overarchingly, arguments for research publications for societal good are undermined in favour of those that seek to maximise human capital.

I share these thoughts because they are part of the reason the data *became* 'excess' in the first place. My interest in Sylvia Plath and Tumblr was drawn into the pressured environment of academic publishing; I was proving myself as a viable scholarship candidate and employable researcher. Evidence suggests that students who receive scholarships generate significantly more publications and citations and are less likely to withdraw from their PhD (Belavy et al., 2020). Scholarship assessment procedures, while not solely based on publications, still incentivise students to produce outputs before they are trained to be postgraduate researchers. It is common knowledge that exceptional performance in Honours or MA programmes is not sufficient to secure a scholarship or even entry to a PhD programme. This contributes to a culture where students are primed for the neoliberal 'publish or perish' culture before they receive proper research training. This is not only a research vulnerability but also a personal one, whereby postgraduate students may pursue doctoral studies and engage in potentially unhealthy and unpaid employability skills development in hope of future academic work (Cooksey & McDonald, 2019; McPherson et al., 2017).

Creative writers in academia experience additional challenges, finding their creative practice out of sync with the normative criteria of 'publish or perish' culture (Moore, 2017). The measure of productivity for creative writers who work outside academia typically includes the spectre of publishing, made complicated by a saturated cultural economy and an ontological crisis regarding the possibility of poetry's authenticity in modern society (Aguasaco, 2014). Plath had her share of publishing pressures and anxieties; she faced rejection from magazines and cited a fear of poverty and loss of inspiration as among her key concerns (Plath et al., 2017). Yet since her passing, poetry's visibility has reached new heights and levels of popularity. This, alongside the rise of digital culture, has changed the significance and shape of cultural objects once considered 'literary' in the conventional sense; we are experiencing authors and their work in new ways. Consumers have become prosumers. Attention has become scarce. This was the kernel of the idea that I wanted to explore over a decade ago, although a lot has changed since then in the digital media landscape, and I'm still curious.

Reading the Confessional Cultural Object

> Reblogs, Likes, and Replies are a matter of public record, so if you're truly ashamed of your desires it's best to keep them to yourself. But why? Be proud of who you are. You're beautiful. We're looking you in the eyes and telling you how beautiful you are. (Tumblr European Privacy Policy, last Modified 2023-06-07, accessed 5 Jan 2024; Tumblr, 2024a)

From a Foucauldian perspective, culture is assembled through networks of power, knowledge and governmental technologies, creating diverse opportunities for exclusion, agency and aesthetic governance (Bennett, 2000). The first way in which Foucault's ideas are relevant to the present chapter relates to the politics of confession and the broader topic of Sylvia Plath posters on Tumblr. We can divide this confessional connection into two threads. The first relates to the literary movement which Plath formed part of – the confessional poets that rose to prominence in the 1950s and 1960 and is generally associated with postmodernism. This group includes poets and writers such as Sylvia Plath, Anne Sexton, Robert Lowell and W. D. Snodgrass, who went on to influence well-known poets in future decades including Sharon Olds, Franz Wright and Marie Howe. The work of these authors was called 'confessional' (Rosenthal, 1969) because unlike other forms of poetry, their work was frequently personal and explored ideas related to identity, mental health and social expectations, among others.

Several years after the term 'confessional poetry' was coined, Michel Foucault published his volumes on the topic of confession – examinations of its more general social and historical significance (Foucault, 1978, 1990, 1992). Foucault contended that confession consistently formed part of modern power structures, popularised initially by Christianity and later by secular psychological disciplines and institutions. Yet confessional power, other scholars have since argued, also found a home in the field of literary studies and the secular English classroom, anchored in the moral infrastructure of close reading that was, prior to the development of popular schooling, the privilege of Sunday school bible study (Hunter, 1988). Indeed, the relationship between Christian confessionalism and the term 'confessional' poetry was not lost on poets, some of whom despised the term (Stitt & Berryman, 1972).

The second way in which a Foucauldian lens is useful relates to the reconfirmation of confessional power in digital societies. The confession has been reconfigured and redeployed as part of the expansion of online worlds, where social networking, blogging and microblogging websites encourage ongoing self-disclosure in ways that invite community surveillance and commentary. Tumblr and other social media websites have a history of popular pages for posting anonymous confessions about past misdeeds and feelings (Barari, 2015; Chianese, 2016; Sacks et al., 2021). In this context and given the significance of literary engagement as a practice of ethical self-fashioning more generally, it is possible that 'confessional' poetry can take on a new significance, not simply in form and medium but at times in *purpose*. As part of curating and displaying one's individuality and *beauty*, itself an ethical project, perhaps confessional poetry on Tumblr allows users to engage in a kind of second-hand, reconfigured confession – a kind of unburdening. To do otherwise would be, as Tumblr's Privacy Policy reminds us, a sign that one is 'truly ashamed' of their desires.

To be clear, this is not a claim I make about our survey respondents, but rather about what Tumblr felt like to me at the time, when Plath's words seemed to perform something 'extra' to other acts of aesthetic appreciation. The direct language of confessional poetry, which reduces the distance between speaker and reader, almost mirrors the emotional candour of Tumblr culture. Indeed, As Eler and Durbin note (2013, n.p): 'Sylvia Plath would have thrived on Tumblr'. Scrolling through Tumblr in 2024 evokes some of the same energy that I recall in 2013; countless quotes are tattooed on forearms and legs: *I am. I am. I am.* While more generic descriptions such as #quote frequently sat under the posts, lines and stanzas were also paired with more varied hashtags – #poetryislife, #femalerage and #mentalhealthmatters, all of which contextualised the work in different ways. I clicked on an account at random which was, according to the pinned post at the top of the page, explicitly intended to 'vent feelings and opinions' through the posting of artworks that resonated with how the user felt.

It is important, however, to avoid repeating past analytical mistakes that have marginalised and essentialised Plath and her readers since her death. This evokes Foucault's conception of the 'author function' – the discourse that surrounds an author or body of work. Badia (2002) asserts that 'confessional poetry' is not simply a mode of writing; rather, autobiographical *reading* practices are just as significant as any authorial intent. Badia also critiques the cultural anxiety about the reader that Plath's critics and commentators have constructed; the collective portrait of Plath's readership not only reinforces patriarchal ideology but also permeates engagement with her work. Indeed, how we engage with Plath is inseparable from the broader ways in which Plath has been represented and defined. Badia cites the main characters in movies such as '10 Things I Hate About You' and 'Natural Born Killers' as examples, which are not only Plath readers but also depict parallel qualities of depression and rebellion. These themes are reiterated in various television series ranging from *The Fresh Prince of Bel-Air* and *Law & Order: Special Victims Unit* to the animated series *Family Guy* (Badia, 2011). Popular culture has often drawn Plath and her peers into a game of bullying and meanspirited representation that has derided female writers and readers, as well as trivialised mental health and suicide (Badia, 2008, 2011; Urmila, 2022; Whelan-Stewart, 2008).

Self-Fashioning and Poetry in a Digital Age

On the other hand, Tumblr users are not necessarily literary critics. They are arguably not necessarily *readers* in the conventional sense; they are choice-making curators, situating Plath and her work in unique intertextual assemblages of content. It is arguable that Tumblr creates a new space for literary engagement and identity negotiation, one that is more fragmented and dynamic than the historical literary field. What Plath's words and image might mean at any given time can be fluid given the very nature of assembling and reassembling a user's page. Much like Nardone argues that each digital repository is 'an argument for a specific poetics' (2020, p. 249), there is arguably no particular poetics at stake in a Tumblr user's deployment of the cultural object. Indeed, the post's meaning can be as much the construction of the digital 'confessional' reader, myself included, as the user who posts or reposts it. In this light, we can appreciate that Plath posts may reflect agentic engagements with poetry in a dynamic digital world, one that allows them to curate their image through ethical or aesthetical self-fashioning (Foucault et al., 1988).

Criticisms of this reading might include assessments of the simulated and hyperreal environments underpinning the digital media era (Gordon, 2007; Morris, 2021; Nunes, 1995). From this perspective, the Tumblr profile erases the actual individual and those they engage with, causing stress and uncertainty when understanding and defining themselves and others. Plath's image and works are also reshaped under postmodern media-saturated conditions. Ferretter points to several books published about Plath or consisting of Plath-inspired characters, 'in which Plath features as one of the simulacra of postmodern hyper-reality' (2009, p. 278). This networked reconfiguration of Plath's image includes, of course, academic discourse that comments on her work and legacy. Whether the fragmentation and evolution of Plath's poetry (and poetry in general) under postmodernity is wholly undesirable is a matter of debate. While the democratisation of a historically restrictive cultural field (Bourdieu, 1996) would likely be welcomed and the loss of authorial intent forgiven – especially given the complexity of literary intent in general (Farrell, 2017) – the potential reappropriation and remixing for exploitative purposes and endless commodification would not.[1] We will return to this topic in the following section.

Despite the challenges that neoliberal postmodernity brings, it is worth noting that digital environments are also being recognised for *extending* possibilities and opportunities for poetic practice and engagement. For example, some scholars argue that the interaction between literary, visual and digital aesthetics that underpins movements such as 'Instapoetry' produces a distinct form of immersive ambience (Khilnani, 2023), while also expanding possibilities for the digital self-expression and self-representation of racial, ethnic and gender identities (Evans, 2023; Manning, 2020). Moreover, critical lenses regarding popular culture's misrepresentation of Plath and other poets are emerging in popular culture itself. For example, Leyda and Sulimma (2023) highlight the television series *Dickinson*, which subverts problematic representations of Emily Dickinson and Sylvia Plath, among others.

Moreover, in contrast to other social networking sites, Tumblr's facilitation of pseudonymity and low searchability is worth noting, especially insofar as they provide unique social and political affordances (Tiidenberg et al., 2021). In the case of Plath posters, this includes unsettling the relationship between viewer/reader and producer/author. Drawing Foucault's concerns into the digital realm, an author's name establishes intertextual relationships (Foucault, 1969). While *curator* is perhaps a more appropriate term than author, it seems likely that under conditions of relative anonymity (or pseudonymity), reblogging Plath quotes as part of an intertextual collage of digital content escapes clear classification and meticulous surveillance. Tiidenberg et al. (2021) use the term 'silosociality' to describe Tumblr's distinct form of sociality; the site is:

> ...experienced through silos – experiential tumblrs imagined and enacted by users as somewhat apart from each other. Silos emerge out of and are defined by people's shared interests, but sustained through shared practices, vernacular, and sensibility [...] it's] the cultural and experiential dynamic that relies on tumblr's features and governance. (p. 13)

---

[1]Farrell (2017) tries to strike a balance between the postmodern erasure of the author and the excesses of biographical reading.

Indeed, as Plath posters share and reblog the same quotes for different reasons, they engage in a localised and communal form of cultural engagement where Plath and her work can be felt and imagined in diverse ways. A quick scroll through Tumblr demonstrates this diversity – users are deconstructing Plath's poetry, noting that they share her Myer's Briggs Personality Type, remixing quotes with anime to form memes, exploring intersections between Plath and contemporary artists (such as Taylor Swift), highlighting sections of her journals – the examples are numerous and reflect a heterogeneous and dynamic cultural mix that has endured, in various formations, through the various stages of Tumblr's corporate restructuring.[2]

Of course, since I first began this project, the rapid expansion of data capitalism and surveillance society has raised new questions about what sharing content means. Long gone is Tumblr's unorthodox CEO and targeted advertising is now well established on the platform, although the road towards corporatisation has not been an easy one. Yahoo acquired Tumblr for $1.1 billion, with Yahoo CEO Marissa Mayer promising to not 'screw up' the platform (McCracken et al., 2020, p. 7). In 2019, WordPress owner Automattic acquired Tumblr $3 million, and today, the company continues to find ways to generate profit. Moreover, as digital self-disclosure and self-fashioning continue, data collection accelerates and becomes increasingly sophisticated, fuelling an even more complex interplay between the structuring power of digital platforms and the agency of individual users.

Microblogging in Algorithmic Societies of Control

In contemporary societies, microblogging and social media websites deploy flexible mechanisms that adapt to user behaviours and preferences, with continuous algorithmic refinement allowing the constant capturing and recapturing of attention. The collection of vast amounts of data, algorithmic curation and personalised advertising are commonplace in today's digital world. Users are not only self-curated – they are subjects of relentless data extraction. The current digital landscape mirrors many of the concerns that Deleuze articulated regarding the shift to 'societies of control' (Deleuze, 1992). In such a society, individual autonomy and self-expression pair seamlessly with invisible and increasingly sophisticated webs of power. This stands in contrast to the demarcated and rigid strategies and spaces of disciplinary societies. As Brusseau (2020) writes:

> ...if organising happens as control, and if the central mechanisms are the tracking technologies and luring encouragements of

---

[2]Such comparisons are now evident in academic research. Reinholdsson (2023), for example, uses concepts and theories including biographical performativity and mad studies to explore the works and personas of Sylvia Plath and Taylor Swift, including the tendency for their work to be interpreted autobiographically and marketed towards similar audiences.

predictive analytics, then those exercising control need to learn particular hungers, capabilities, vulnerabilities, aspirations, fears, and hopes. (n.p.)

As such, Plath's cultural image and even poetry's affective charge become potential resources for predictive analytics. Metaphor and allegory lend themselves to advanced and invisible metrics of consumer psychology. With Plath as its unwitting icon (Manavis, 2023), 'sad girl' cultures offer digital spaces for support and solidarity, but they are also accompanied by attempts to profit from vulnerability (Thelandersson, 2022). While their accuracy within scientific circles is debatable, a user declaring that they share the same Myer's Briggs Personality Type as Sylvia Plath, equipped with introverted, intuitive, feeling and prospecting traits, is likely useful data for advertising. Moreover, as Proferes and Morrissey (2020) argue, the Tumblr Dashboard structure, data structures, algorithms and protocols 'suggests that users are channelled toward constantly producing and consuming different media...through a homogenizing funnel' (p. 30) while experiencing 'community in fragmented and intensive bursts' (p. 32).

Underscoring these issues is the lack of transparency about algorithmic culture, as well as other digital intermediation processes and actors (Hutchinson, 2023), which affects not only our use of digital platforms but also our established ideas about cultural production and aesthetic appreciation (Naji, 2021; Rockmore, 2020). On the other hand, Tumblr's roots as an alternative and relatively unregulated cultural space may still underpin its economic vulnerability in an algorithmic society. It has proved to be an extraordinarily difficult product to monetise, while controversies about unsafe content and subsequent policy changes have added additional challenges. Outright bans on adult content, which has long been part of its ecology, have significantly impacted its userbase and profitability, while still failing to weed out bots through content filtering algorithms (Tiidenberg et al., 2021).

Perhaps a good measure of the workings of structuring power and agency on Tumblr is a simple analogy of cultural objects. While other social media platforms such as TikTok analyse user preferences, engagement, and interactions, as well as the individualised 'For You Page', to promote non-stop and highly personalised video feeds, Tumblr arguably relies more on the conscious action of its users and operates within a more sluggish and less monetisable temporality. Perhaps in years to come, we will see TikTok more obviously as the television to Tumblr's innocuous book, and the poetry and Sylvia Plath of the future will be something unrecognisable. Or as we have seen on other social networking websites, Tumblr may simply take on similar features to TikTok to maximise engagement and profit. A recent company memo describes a new algorithmically intensified era of Tumblr with guiding principles such as providing 'high-quality content with every app launch' and creating 'patterns that encourage users to keep returning to Tumblr' (Tumblr, 2024b). How these changes will impact interactions with Plath, poetry and literary culture, as well as Plath's place in the digital landscape, is yet to be fully seen.

Conclusion

It was a strange exercise to revisit a project from so long ago. Since 2013, when the excess data was laid to rest, I continued to read and write. I made more mistakes and learned lessons. Ideas resonated with me in ways that rekindled my appreciation of confessionalist poetry and Tumblr culture and helped me understand my journey into this project in new ways. The 'excess' data, in a sense, reawakened. I now appreciate Plath, Tumblr and Plath posters in ways that I couldn't a decade ago. Revisiting the 'excess data' from the Sylvia Plath posters project was made possible using diverse theoretical lenses and a broad 'storying' approach to analysis – drawing together a mix of ideas about research, cultural objects and researcher journeys. Thinking about my own experience *now* helped me expand the 'research event' beyond the original object of study into something new – including my path into the project and my own motivations and drives.

Predictably, we are left with more questions than answers. However, a common thread filters through this reflective exercise: the relationship between art, technology and freedom. The practice of digital confessional that is commonplace on Tumblr is, unfortunately, a gold mine for personalised advertising, especially as algorithms become more sophisticated. In response, perhaps our ethical imperative as researchers and educators is a more general one – to help ensure education about algorithms keeps pace with personal disclosure, including in unique digital spaces like Tumblr that have historically been associated with freedom and authenticity. Indeed, while calls for algorithmic transparency have largely centred on social media platforms like Facebook and Twitter, it is important to recognise that there can be no one-size-fits-all approach to best practice (Watson & Nations, 2019).

For poetry, the juncture of technology and freedom poses unique challenges given the rise of language processing tools. The idea that artificial intelligence can replace human poetic creations is still somewhat unconvincing; most non-commercial literary production is irreducible to simple prompts. Its *processes* are not entirely reproducible even if its outputs are (Elam, 2023). At the same time, it is worth acknowledging that aesthetic production and engagement have always been technologically mediated, whether it be a pre-modern epic written on clay tablet or post-humanist 'cyborg subjectivities' articulated at the interface of human and computer (Beals, 2018).

In terms of poetry *reading* practices, researchers have placed an emphasis on whether human beings can differentiate between AI and human-written texts. This speaks to the politics and ethics of freedom and aesthetics. For those appreciating Plath's work and persona, the challenge of differentiation is a legitimate concern given that poetic styles can be successfully emulated instantaneously (Köbis & Mossink, 2021), falsely attributed and widely circulated, introducing a new set of ethical challenges for digital platforms which are unlikely to be prioritised in their policing of content. Perhaps even more troubling is that stylistic emulations could be deployed at an unprecedented rate as marketing collateral towards the constant capturing of attention. Such futures seem a more likely pursuit for profit-seeking corporations than simply using data as a means of understanding art (Greenwald & Oosterlinck, 2022).

Publish or perish culture, part of my reconfigured research story, is still a persistent problem. More emphasis needs to be placed on other activities that support students in their research and professional development, as well as their ability to support each other. Jolley et al. (2015) highlight the importance of seeking out others for advice, guidance and friendship, especially in the final stages of their journey. McPhail-Bell and Redman-MacLaren's (2019) informal peer support model also proved successful in helping them complete their PhDs. Yet competitive and intimidating cultures undermine the ability for supportive peer networks. Moreover, challenges such as financial pressures, isolation and a lack of institutional support are even more pronounced among marginalised group (Mattocks & Briscoe-Palmer, 2016), and initiations into research culture need to be sensitive to the strengths and vulnerabilities of graduate students as well as meet the needs of diverse students.

Using the 'research event' as an entry point into this chapter has several benefits. Firstly, 'excess data' was not wasted but rather reintroduced into an experiential record of diverse and intersecting encounters with research, digital platforms and culture. Secondly, it allowed for examining the initial research concerns through a broader lens than would have been possible 10 years ago. I consider this a result of having more experience, more literature to draw on, and an extended view of the platform's journey. Thirdly, the pleasure of reigniting my curiosity about the topic – to be surprised. I recommend that others revisit projects they might feel like they've 'lost' or 'outgrown'. For some, the word 'excess' conjures up the image of overabundance – *surplus* data, but my preferred synonym is *reserve*. Like a 'reserve' basketball player waiting on the bench, season after season, data is sometimes not ready to go immediately, but you never know when you might need to draw up a new play – to explore a novel possibility.

Acknowledgements

Thank you to my colleague for her enthusiasm, encouragement, insight and invaluable contribution to this research story.

References

Aguasaco, C. (2014). On the origin and future of poetry: Notes towards an investigation investigation. https://academicworks.cuny.edu/cgi/viewcontent.cgi?article=1879&context=cc_pubs

Badia, J. (2002). Viewing poems as "bloodstains": Sylvia Plath's confessional poetics and the autobiographical reader. *A/B: Auto/Biography Studies*, *17*(2), 180–203. https://doi.org/10.1080/08989575.2002.10815291

Badia, J. (2008). "Dissatisfied, family-hating shrews": Women readers and Sylvia Plath's literary reception. *Lit: Literature Interpretation Theory*, *19*(2), 187–213. https://doi.org/10.1080/10436920802107633

Badia, J. (2011). *Sylvia Plath and the mythology of women readers*. University of Massachusetts Press.

Barari, S. (2015). Anxiety, alcohol, and academics: A textual analysis of student Facebook confessions pages. ArXiv (Cornell University). https://arxiv.org/abs/1506.05193

Beals, K. (2018). "Do the new poets think? It's possible": Computer poetry and cyborg subjectivity. *Configurations, 26*(2), 149–177. https://doi.org/10.1353/con.2018.0010

Becker, A., & Lukka, K. (2023). Instrumentalism and the publish-or-perish regime. *Critical Perspectives on Accounting, 94*(August), 102436. https://doi.org/10.1016/j.cpa.2022.102436

Belavy, D. L., Owen, P. J., & Livingston, P. M. (2020). Do successful PhD outcomes reflect the research environment rather than academic ability? *PLoS One, 15*(8), e0236327. https://doi.org/10.1371/journal.pone.0236327

Bennett, T. (2000). Acting on the social: Art, culture, and government. *American Behavioral Scientist, 43*(9), 1412–1428. https://doi.org/10.1177/000276400219559

Bourdieu, P. (1996). *The rules of art: Genesis and structure of the literary field*. Stanford University Press.

Brusseau, J. (2020). Deleuze's postscript on the societies of control: Updated for big data and predictive analytics. *Theoria, 67*(164), 1–25. https://doi.org/10.3167/th.2020.6716401

Chang, H. (2008). *Autoethnography as method*. Routledge.

Chianese, R. (2016). The tales we all must tell. *American Scientist, 104*(4), 212. https://doi.org/10.1511/2016.121.212

Cooksey, R., & McDonald, R. (2019). *Surviving and thriving in postgraduate research*. Springer.

Deleuze, G. (1992). Postscript on the societies of control. *October, 59*(Winter), 3–7. https://www.jstor.org/stable/778828

Dixon, C. (2011, March 2). Tumblr's jaw-dropping growth [video]. YouTube. https://www.youtube.com/watch?v=0SWjqKvTosk

Elam, M. (2023). Poetry will not optimize; or, what is literature to AI? *American Literature, 95*(2), 281–303. https://doi.org/10.1215/00029831-10575077

Eler, A., & Durbin, K. (2013). *The teen-girl tumblr aesthetic*. https://www.annkakultys.com/wp-content/uploads/2015/11/press_molly_soda_2013.03.01_hyperallergic.pdf

Evans, L. (2023). Lo vamos a conseguir": *Instapoetry* as a vehicle for feminist movements in the contemporary Spanish context. *European Journal of English Studies, 27*(1), 101–121. https://doi.org/10.1080/13825577.2023.2200415

Farrell, J. (2017). *The varieties of authorial intention*. Springer.

Ferretter, L. (2009). A fine white flying myth of one's own: Sylvia Plath in fiction – A review essay. *Plath Profiles, 2*, 278–298.

Foley, D. E. (2002). Critical ethnography: The reflexive turn. *International Journal of Qualitative Studies in Education, 15*(4), 469–490. https://doi.org/10.1080/09518390210145534

Foucault, M. (1969). Authorship: What is an author? *Screen, 20*(1), 13–34. https://doi.org/10.1093/screen/20.1.13

Foucault, M. (1978). *The history of sexuality. Volume I: An introduction*. Vintage Books.

Foucault, M. (1990). *The care of the self: The history of sexuality* (Vol. 3). Penguin Books.

Foucault, M. (1992). *The use of pleasure: The history of sexuality* (Vol. 2). Penguin Books.

Foucault, M., Martin, L. H., Gutman, H., & Hutton, P. H. (1988). *Technologies of the self.* University of Massachusetts Press.

Gloviczki, P. J. (2021). *Mediated narration in the digital age.* University of Nebraska Press.

Gordon, E. (2007). Mapping digital networks: From cyberspace to Google. *Information, Communication & Society, 10*(6), 885–901. https://doi.org/10.1080/13691180701751080

Gravett, K. (2019). Story completion: Storying as a method of meaning-making and discursive discovery. *International Journal of Qualitative Methods, 18.* https://doi.org/10.1177/1609406919893155

Gravett, K., & Winstone, N. E. (2019). Storying students' becomings into and through higher education. *Studies in Higher Education, 46*(8), 1–12. https://doi.org/10.1080/03075079.2019.1695112

Greenwald, D. S., & Oosterlinck, K. (2022). The changing faces of the Paris salon: Using a new dataset to analyze portraiture, 1740 –1881. *Poetics, 92*(Part B), 101649. https://doi.org/10.1016/j.poetic.2022.101649

Hardy, I., Phillips, L., Reyes, V., & Obaidul Hamid, M. (2023). Reimagining and demystifying data: A storytelling approach. *Comparative Education, 4,* 1–18. https://doi.org/10.1080/03050068.2023.2189677

Hillis, K., Paasonen, S., & Petit, M. (Eds.). (2015). *Networked affect.* MIT Press.

Hunter, I. (1988). *Culture and government.* Palgrave Macmillan.

Hutchinson, J. (2023). *Digital intermediation: Unseen infrastructure for cultural production.* Routledge.

Jolley, D., Griffiths, A. W., Friel, N., Ali, J. B., & Rix, K. (2015). The importance of peer support during the final stages of a PhD. In E. Norris (Ed.), *A guide for psychology postgraduates: Surviving postgraduate study* (pp. 36–41). British Psychological Society.

Keightley, E. (2020). Remembering research: Memory and methodology. *International Journal of Social Research Methodology, 13*(1), 55–70. https://doi.org/10.1080/13645570802605440

Khilnani, S. (2023). #Instapoetry in India: The aesthetic of the digital vernacular. *European Journal of English Studies, 27*(1), 14–32. https://doi.org/10.1080/13825577.2023.2200416

Köbis, N., & Mossink, L. D. (2021). Artificial intelligence versus Maya Angelou: Experimental evidence that people cannot differentiate AI-generated from human-written poetry. *Computers in Human Behavior, 114.* https://doi.org/10.1016/j.chb.2020.106553

Lee, H., & Lee, K. (2013). Publish (in international indexed journals) or perish: Neoliberal ideology in a Korean university. *Language Policy, 12*(3), 215–230. https://doi.org/10.1007/s10993-012-9267-2

Leeker, M., Schipper, I., & Beyes, T. (Eds.). (2017). *Performing the digital: Performativity and performance studies in digital cultures.* Transcript.

Levecque, K., Anseel, F., De Beuckelaer, A., Van der Heyden, J., & Gisle, L. (2017). Work organization and mental health problems in PhD students. *Research Policy, 46*(4), 868–879. https://doi.org/10.1016/j.respol.2017.02.008

Leyda, J., & Sulimma, M. (2023). Pop/poetry: Dickinson as remix. *Arts, 12*(2), 62. https://doi.org/10.3390/arts12020062

Loewenstein, G. (1994). The psychology of curiosity: A review and reinterpretation. *Psychological Bulletin*, *116*(1), 75–98. https://doi.org/10.1037/0033-2909.116.1.75

Lumsden, K., Bradford, J., & Goode, J. (2019). *Reflexivity: Theory, method and practice*. Routledge.

Manavis, S. (2023, August 8). "A smorgasbord of unlikability": The authors helping "sad girl lit" grow up. *The Guardian*. https://www.theguardian.com/books/2023/aug/08/a-smorgasbord-of-unlikability-the-authors-helping-sad-girl-lit-grow-up

Manning, M. (2020). Crafting authenticity: Reality, storytelling, and female self-representation through Instapoetry. *Storytelling, Self, Society*, *16*(2), 263. https://doi.org/10.13110/storselfsoci.16.2.0263

Mattocks, K., & Briscoe-Palmer, S. (2016). Diversity, inclusion, and doctoral study: Challenges facing minority PhD students in the United Kingdom. *European Political Science*, *15*(4), 476–492. https://doi.org/10.1057/s41304-016-0071-x

McCracken, A., Cho, A., Stein, L., & Hoch, I. N. (2020). You must be new here: An introduction. In A. McCracken, A. Cho, L. Stein, & I. N. Hoch (Eds.), *A Tumblr book: Platforms and cultures* (pp. 1–22). University of Michigan Press.

McPhail-Bell, K., & Redman-MacLaren, M. L. (2019). A co/autoethnography of peer support and PhDs: Being, doing, and sharing in academia. *Qualitative Report*, *24*(5), 1087–1105. https://doi.org/10.46743/2160-3715/2019.3155

McPherson, C., Punch, S., & Graham, E. (2017). Postgraduate transitions from masters to doctoral study: Managing independence, emotions and support. *Stirling International Journal of Postgraduate Research*, *5*(2), 42–50. https://doi.org/10.14297/jpaap.v5i2.265

Michael, M. (2021). *The research event*. Routledge.

Mills, C. W. (1959). *The sociological imagination*. Oxford University Press.

Møller Hartley, J., Bengtsson, M., Schjøtt Hansen, A., & Sivertsen, M. F. (2021). Researching publics in datafied societies: Insights from four approaches to the concept of "publics" and a (hybrid) research agenda. *New Media & Society*, *25*(7). https://doi.org/10.1177/14614448211021045

Moore, M. (2017). Articulate walls: Writer's block and the academic creative. *New Writing*, *15*(3), 348–359. https://doi.org/10.1080/14790726.2017.1384025

Moores, S. (2018). *Digital orientations: Non-media-centric media studies and non-representational theories of practice*. Peter Lang.

Moosa, I. A. (2018). *Publish or perish: Perceived benefits versus unintended consequences*. Edward Elgar Publishing.

Morris, J. (2021). Simulacra in the age of social media: Baudrillard as the prophet of fake news. *Journal of Communication Inquiry*, *45*(4), 299–410. https://doi.org/10.1177/0196859920977154

Naji, J. (2021). *Digital poetry*. Springer.

Nardone, M. (2020). Poetics in a networked digital milieu. *College Literature*, *47*(1), 248–258. https://doi.org/10.1353/lit.2020.0010

Nunes, M. (1995). Jean Baudrillard in cyberspace: Internet, virtuality, and postmodernity. From possible worlds to virtual realities: Approaches to postmodernism. *Style*, *29*(2), 314–327.

Plath, S., Steinberg, P. K., Kukil, K. V., & Hughes, F. (2017). *The letters of Sylvia Plath*. Harper.

Poell, T. (2020). Three challenges for media studies in the age of platforms. *Television & New Media*, *21*(6), 650–657. https://doi.org/10.1177/1527476420918833

Proferes, N., & Morrissey, K. (2020). Lost in the "dash": How Tumblr fosters virtuous cycles of content and community. In A. McCracken, A. Cho, L. Stein, & I. N. Hoch (Eds.), *A Tumblr book: Platforms and cultures* (pp. 23–36). University of Michigan Press.

Reinholdsson, K. (2023). *Sylvia Plath, Taylor Swift, and confessional performances*. Master's thesis, Lund University. https://lup.lub.lu.se/lupStat/record/9140026

Robards, B., Lyall, B., & Moran, C. (2020). Confessional data selfies and intimate digital traces. *New Media & Society*, *23*(9), 2616–2633. https://doi.org/10.1177/1461444820934032

Rockmore, D. (2020, January 7). What happens when machines learn to write poetry. *The New Yorker*. https://www.newyorker.com/culture/annals-of-inquiry/the-mechanical-muse

Rosenthal, M. L. (1969). *The modern poets*. Oxford University Press.

Sacks, B., Gressier, C., & Maldon, J. (2021). #REALTALK: Facebook confessions pages as a data resource for academic and student support services at universities. *Learning, Media and Technology*, *46*(4), 1–14. https://doi.org/10.1080/17439884.2021.1946559

Salovaara, I. (2015). #Je suis Charlie: Networks, affects and distributed agency of media assemblage. *Conjunctions. Transdisciplinary Journal of Cultural Participation*, *2*(1), 100–115. https://doi.org/10.7146/tjcp.v2i1.22272

Schmidt, L., & Kloet, J. (2017). Bricolage: Role of media. *The International Encyclopedia of Media Effects*, 1–9. https://doi.org/10.1002/9781118783764.wbieme0116

Silva, P. J. (2012). Curiosity and motivation. In R. M. Ryan (Ed.), *The Oxford handbook of human motivation* (pp. 157–166). Oxford University Press.

Stitt, P., & Berryman, J. (1972). The art of poetry. *The Paris Review*, *53*(Winter).

Thelandersson, F. (2022). *21st century media and female mental health*. Springer Nature.

Tiidenberg, K., Hendry, N., & Abidin, C. (2021). *Tumblr*. Polity.

Tumblr. (2024a). *Tumblr*. Tumblr. https://www.tumblr.com/privacy/en

Tumblr. (2024b). *Tumblr's core product strategy*. Tumblr. https://staff.tumblr.com/post/722477242948747264/tumblrs-core-product-strategy

Urmila, G. (2022). A writer's suicide: On creativity, mental health, gender and ethics. *Indian Journal of Medical Ethics*, *7*(2), 133–137. https://doi.org/10.20529/ijme.2021.066

Van Duyne, E. (2023). *Loving Sylvia Plath: A reclamation*. W. W. Norton & Company.

Venkatesh, S. A. (2013). The reflexive turn: The rise of first-person ethnography. *The Sociological Quarterly*, *54*(1), 3–8. https://doi.org/10.1111/tsq.12004

Vurayai, S., & Ndofirepi, A. P. (2020). "Publish or perish": Implications for novice African university scholars in the neoliberal era. *African Identities*, *20*(2), 1–14. https://doi.org/10.1080/14725843.2020.1813084

Watson, L. (2018). Introduction: The moral psychology of curiosity. In I. Inan, L. Watson, D. Whitcomb, & S. Yigit (Eds.), *The moral psychology of curiosity*. Rowman & Littlefield.

Watson, H. J., & Nations, C. (2019). Addressing the growing need for algorithmic transparency. *Communications of the Association for Information Systems*, *45*, 488–510. https://doi.org/10.17705/1CAIS.04526

Whelan-Stewart, W. (2008). Role-playing the "feminine" in letters home. *Intertexts*, *12*(1–2), 129–143. https://doi.org/10.1353/itx.2008.0011

Chapter 9

Museums, Smart Cities and Big Data: How Can We Transform Data Excess Into Data Intelligence?

Natalia Grincheva

LASALLE, University of the Arts, Singapore
The University of Melbourne, Australia

Abstract

This chapter discusses the challenges and opportunities of integrating big data generated by contemporary museums into data ecology and data fabrics of smart cities. First, it exposes that smart cities could enhance their global reputation, visibility and image by building on closer collaborations with museums. Second, it demonstrates that museums in the 21st century have transformed into hyper-connected cultural hubs, spreading their reach and impact beyond their immediate urban locations. Finally, this chapter discusses creative approaches to data-curation mechanisms that stress the role of museums and cultural heritage sites in supplying data for a more strategic and proactive smart city co-design and management. Specifically, this chapter offers a three-dimensional framework for integrating heritage data in the design of smart city data ecosystems, which includes such components as *Data Resources, Data Republics* and *Data Impacts. Data Resources* stresses museum collections' data and meta-data as a strategic resource to empower creative public data-curation practices to tell meaningful stories about the city and enhance place-making. *Data Republics* focuses on big data generated by visitors online or on-site as a foundation for evidence-based urban research, design and management, empowering more sustainable, safe and enjoyable tourism. *Data Impacts* details data-driven methodologies that museums could employ to measure public sentiment and opinion to offer new human-centred indicators to understand the performance of smart cities. This chapter shares a conceptual framework for repurposing museum data within a smart city data ecology to translate the current data excess into data intelligence.

Keywords: Big data; museums; heritage; smart city; urban data; cultural analytics; data ecosystem

Introduction

Museums as major cultural hubs and powerful social actors operate and produce large amounts of data that digitally capture their activities locally and globally, on-site and online. Museum collections, spread across physical and virtual realities, accumulate vast digital records. Museum visitors generate complex geospatial data that transcends the geographic boundaries of museums as single-location entities. Finally, user-centric interactions across museum communities, objects and exhibitions produce new digital content and facilitate online engagements. While some smaller museums still suffer from underbudgeting and understaffing to sustain their digital operations and improve their digital assets, the processes of digitalisation and datafication of museums are unstoppable. Worldwide, museums are transforming into powerful 'information centres', not only generating big data but also rapidly improving their capacity to collect, organise, process and analyse exponential volumes of data aggregated from different sources (de Vasconcellos Motta et al., 2019).

Strategic use of such big data allows museums to address many curatorial, management and development tasks. Data management helps museums preserve and share their collections and archives with larger audiences, generating new knowledge and linking historical artefacts with contemporary audiences (Scott et al., 2019). Indeed, efficient data capture and strategic analysis also enable museums to create new cultural and spatial experiences, catering to audiences' expectations, interests and demands (Alexander, 2014). Developing data intelligence moves museums to new capacities for understanding their audience, significantly enhancing the museum-visit experience and creating stronger educational engagements with collections and exhibitions (Schreiber & Pekarik, 2014).

In 2018, for instance, researchers from the University of Melbourne collaborated with the Australian Centre for the Moving Image to produce an experimental web application, Museum Soft Power Map that could measure and map the soft power of museums.[1] The research was instrumental in unlocking the power of big data generated by contemporary museums on-site and online to tell meaningful stories about their local, regional and global audiences, connections, engagements and implications for international cultural relations and diplomacy (Grincheva, 2019; 2022a). Some museums go beyond these traditional management data-intensive tasks and already offer their audiences new ways to play and interact with big data, enhancing visitors' data literacy through interactive visualisations and dynamic installations (Borner et al., 2016; Letourneau et al., 2020). In another example, the signature Future City Lab developed by the Museum of

---

[1] Museum Soft Power Map web application: https://victoriasoftware.com/demo/. Watch a 2 min video demo: https://www.youtube.com/watch?v=vIbSSiukcLk.

the City of New York in 2017 delivered creative design games, animated maps and dynamic data visualisations tools to play with big data accumulated in the city to offer new solutions to re-imagine New York possible and impossible urban futures (Grincheva, 2022b).

However, the increased datafication of museums produces unwelcome effects as well. Harari (2015) argues that reducing all agencies and social structures to digital data processing systems decreases the value and meaning they produce. A new ideology of *dataism* – interpreting all phenomena and interactions primarily through data processing – puts pressure on cultural institutions and urges them to maximise their dataflows by connecting to more and more media (Harari, 2015). As a result, many museums are involved in a constant race for data collection. This results in data excess, which in many cases could neither be meaningfully used to inform institutional development nor serve their audiences and stakeholders well. Pile Pruulmann-Vengerfeldt (2022), a media scholar who devoted her academic career to consulting with Malmö museums, stresses that 'Museums often have more data than they give themselves credit to and oftentimes museums have much more data than they know what to do with'.

Acknowledging the problematic consequences of museum datafication processes, this chapter argues that such overwhelming data excess could provide a crucial foundation for more intelligent, integrative and meaningful sharing and enjoyment of heritage within the urban context of a smart city. The smart city is a conceptual technology-and-innovation-driven urban development model. It employs digital technology to accumulate, organise and manage big data defined as a vast amount of information generated by and accessible to an increasing number of people. The smart city model aims to improve economic and political efficiency to facilitate a more proactive and strategic urban development (Caird, 2018). The rise of smart cities requires developing new tools and expertise to properly manage and understand big data generated by various stakeholders, including museums and heritage institutions, in the urban context. Specifically, strategically incorporating heritage in both urban policies *and* data frameworks can make smart cities more human- and culture-centred.

For instance, Siountri and Vergados (2018, p. 30) stress that 'the fact that cultural heritage must be preserved and protected in any context of Smart Cities is not negotiable. A city needs an appreciation of its past before moving to a digital future'. However, they point out that while most smart city frameworks rely on more than 120 city service indicators across 20 theme areas ranging from education and finance to health and safety, cultural heritage data is not included (Siountri & Vergados, 2018). Heritage integration in a smart city, as A. Georgescu Paquin (2020) explains, should be based on strategic flow management and sustainable heritage protection in a unified urban model of the smart city, leveraging resources across economic infrastructure, energy flows, transportation and environment protection. Such data platforms can enhance urban design and planning, especially if they are able to analyse insights from smart tourism recommendation engines to customise cultural places, services and offerings, manage safe and environmentally friendly human traffic and facilitate co-existence among urban communities (Glasmeiera & Christopherson, 2015).

However, even though arts and culture play one of the most important roles in the liveability and economic vitality of contemporary cities, they are typically not systematically exploited and formally incorporated into smart city initiatives (Angelidoua et al., 2017; Iyer, 2017; Leorke et al., 2018). While the smart city model stresses managing data efficiently for more proactive strategic urban development (Malik et al., 2018; Okwechime et al., 2018), data generated by museums is not meaningfully integrated into strategic smart city planning and implementation (Borda & Bowen, 2017; Grincheva, 2022b). There is no dedicated research yet that would connect all issues together in relation to heritage and big data generated by key creative city actors such as museums. In this chapter, I address this gap by outlining new integrative frameworks and methodologies to transform rapidly accelerating museum data excess into more intelligent systems that can benefit the social and urban development of smart cities.

The research I draw on in this chapter includes interviews and focus groups conducted via a series of global webinars within the research project 'GLAM and Digital Soft Power in the Post-pandemic World' (Data to Power, 2022). The focus groups brought together 25 museum professionals from Europe and Asia-Pacific to explore the potential for technologies to translate museum collection metadata and audience analytics into meaningful narratives. These focus groups were instrumental in revealing how museums in different city contexts grapple with the challenges of meaningful data collection, analysis and public sharing. They helped identify new avenues for more productive data use beyond museum walls to benefit a wide spectrum of stakeholders, including smart city governments. I summarise these insights by presenting different examples supported by conceptual observations and rationale within a three-dimensional framework. In the following sections, I explore each in turn: *Data Resources, Data Republics* and *Data Impacts*.

In the opening section, *Data Resources,* I demonstrate that museum collections' data and metadata can be effectively employed to empower public data curation to enhance place-making. The second section, *Data Republics*, reveals that smart cultural heritage spaces can generate massive data on visitors' experiences to enable safe, sustainable and more enjoyable tourism. Finally, this chapter concludes with *Data Impacts,* where I focus on data-driven methodologies that museums could employ to measure public sentiment and opinion to offer new human-centred indicators to understand the performance of smart cities. This chapter offers my conceptual framework for repurposing museum data within a smart city data ecology to translate the current data excess into data intelligence.

Data Resources: 'Smart' Place-Making

Place-making – the strategic efforts of multiple stakeholders to market a city for the purposes of attracting investments, customers and tourists (Clarke et al., 2017) – draws on spreading and popularising cultural ideals, values and identities to create a positive image of place. It engages local myths and symbols to articulate aspirations for wealth, power and enhanced visibility (Anholt, 2007). Place-making is a crucial task for cities, helping them retain residents' loyalty, facilitate urban growth and sustain long-term development (van Ham, 2008). Historically, museums have earned their reputation as key urban heritage repositories that create the symbolic image of a place and play a leading role in urban place-making (Olivares, 2015). For Anholt (2011), the presence of a museum in a place signifies a community sense of self-respect.

Considering that place-making 'is seldom under the control of one central authority' (van Ham, 2008, p. 133), strategic heritage data curation could distribute this labour among multiple actors and potentially transform place-making into a more democratic and open endeavour that engages with locals and travellers and shares cultural resources with larger audiences (Angelidoua et al., 2017; Clarke et al., 2017). In the past decades, museums have invested considerable resources and efforts to digitalise their collections to open them to wider and more diverse audiences and expand their reach far beyond physical walls. While these cultural resources acquire greater potential for circulating virtually, thus enhancing local and international discoverability and visibility of cities, more effort is required to transform such collection data and meta-data into digital storytelling, as one example of place-making.

Digital museum resources achieve high levels of global circulation, consumption and meaningful reuse through their Application Programming Interfaces (APIs). An API is a set of instructions that specify how two or more software programs communicate with each other, allowing users to request data from museums and have it delivered to them in a useable digital form. By releasing free and useable data, APIs provide a digital platform for discovery and innovation. They allow users to 'creatively re-envision and re-engineer museum collections' (Winesmith & Carey, 2014). Specifically, creative commons copyright access to the content enables wider public use of museum digital assets. Using heritage collections' API, smart citizens can develop new digital environments, dynamic mobile applications and games that can tell a more appealing story about the city. Employing an API as a new data-sharing and data-curation platform enhances how museums and smart cities are able to construct their human-centred narratives.

In the past several years, many museums have followed the Open Access movement and created APIs for their collections, making them more interoperable and accessible to a wider community of stakeholders, from researchers and city planners to simply casual audiences. Yet, this has not necessarily facilitated meaningful use of the wealth of these resources. For example, Seb Chan (2022), former Chief Experience Office at ACMI, stressed, 'I think I've learned over the past decade and a half, that sometimes an API is not the best way of releasing your collection data if it is going to be used in the broadest possible way'. Morgan Strong (2022), Digital Transformation Lead at Queensland Art Gallery, concurred, sharing that 'what comes out of a collection system is not necessarily that interesting to a lot of people'; it could remain an abandoned data excess completely unattended and unclaimed for a long time.

Transforming this digital data excess into a meaningful narrative that can tell stories about the culture and history of the city requires focused actions and collaborations with communities of creatives, academics and engaged citizens. Illustrating this, The Science Museum Group in the United Kingdom oversees a collection of 400,000 objects and approximately half a million archival records. They launched their collection API back in 2017 and, since then, have run several focused hackathons to explore different ways of employing the data to enhance their storytelling potential, resulting in a wide spectrum of illuminating ideas (Patten, 2022). These public-facing efforts were productive because they helped the museum connect with interested stakeholders and sparked collaborations that have led to many interesting projects. These included 'The Congruence Engine' and 'Random Object Generator', as well as the Lightship platform, the most recent collaboration with the world's first successful augmented reality (AR) urban context-based platform, Pokémon GO. The Lightship app aims to deliver an entire universe of AR activities that will connect people to science examples in the urban environment while they move around the city (Patten, 2022). In this way, the Science Museum Group's digital collections and metadata could really contribute to place-making in London. This could expose a completely new perspective of the city and showcase how science and technology are employed in different elements of urban infrastructure and design.

However, urban imaginaries mediated through digital collections could also inform, engage and inspire residents or travellers – but only if they can attract public attention. For example, the Never Been Seen app was developed to expose objects in the Science Museum Group (SMG) collections that have never been seen online (and probably in real life) before (SMG, 2021). This app showcases unseen objects from the collections, 'making you the very first person to see it' (SMG, 2021). This app genuinely attempts to address the problems that museums encounter with data excess. As this data comprises repositories of vast amounts of digital artefacts and objects, it often far exceeds the total capacity of physical exhibition spaces. Merely digitising these objects do not guarantee their online visibility and discoverability; without meaningful avenues to find their audiences, they remain a digital waste.

For instance, Kati Price (2022), Head of Digital Media at the Victoria and Albert Museum (VAM), raised concerns about mediating some of the biases of the API data as it could be 'swaying or steering digital activity around particular behaviours and interactions'. She questioned if it would be possible to overcome such biases and attract audiences to 'the areas that are under indexed' through increased transparency and exposure of the collections' most silenced areas. Yet the Never Been Seen app does seem to address some of these problems by providing a tool to explore objects that have never been exposed to a wider world in their digital manifestation. With hundreds of new photographs being added each month as the museum digitises its vast collection, this online project is an invaluable resource to give a virtual life to the objects, which 'can be quite addictive once you start looking at images and discovering new things' (Patten, 2022).

In the context of a rapidly growing 'app culture' that proliferates in data-driven smart cities and often transforms cities into an infrastructure for consumption (Zittrain, 2008), the cultural and heritage API-enabled apps developed by museums and heritage sites promise to return cultural rights back to citizens and help them define and express their cultural identities, thus potentially shaping a city image and positively contributing to digital place-making. Museum education narratives around urban communities can go beyond one-way communication or propaganda, or a mere 'gloss or spin or the placing of a territory on the map as an attractive tourist destination'. By contrast, API data translated into creative apps can offer 'the totality of the thoughts, feelings, associations and expectations' stemming from the unique culture, heritage and history of a city (van Ham, 2008).

Data Republics: Smart Urban Experiences

In tourism development, the power of urban attraction capitalises on participant motivations of cost, culture and curiosity (Kwek et al., 2014). Cultural heritage sites attract millions of tourists to museums and are known as the most popular and most visited places within urban environments (Iyer, 2017; Wu, 2019). However, strategic use of smart technologies is required to increase these 'attraction' powers of museums and heritage sites. A contemporary traveller demands smart capabilities that can facilitate a convenient and informative visit: 'Today's holidaymaker wants to have a fully connected experience from hotel check-in to GPS around town and immediate access to the things they want to see during their limited time in the area' (Iyer, 2017).

The attractiveness and sustainability of museums are enhanced when designers plan 'ubiquitous and pervasive solutions within cultural environments', such as parks, historical centres or exhibitions (Picciali & Chianese, 2014, p. 514). Smart city technologies developed in conjunction with these 'pervasive solutions' can enable more sustainable tourism. This could be achieved by monitoring transportation and economic patterns generated through museum visitors' data that might leverage city resources. For example, an analysis of tourists' and museum goers' walking patterns can help manage street lighting and police deployment, making the urban environment more safe, resilient and liveable (Rodríguez-Núñez & Periáñez-Cañadillas, 2016).

Museums could apply the Internet of Things (IoT) as smart technology that enables a more intelligent, immersive and educational experience. IoT is a system of interrelated computing devices, machines and objects that are connected through a network that facilitates an automatic and dynamic data exchange. It could enable visitors to have a more enjoyable and genuine exploration of cultural heritage sites and supplies a large amount of data to inform a more strategic and proactive design of cultural experiences within interconnected urban environments (Picciali & Chianese, 2014). Smart maps, wayfinding applications or journey planners can enhance urban experiences if they organically integrate museum information with other leisure attractions (Angelidoua et al., 2017).

For example, the damaging consequences of 'overtourism', or over-crowdedness, especially in the areas of famous landmarks, can lead to environmental damage and erosion through daily movement (Wu, 2019). Here, data generated by visitors of museums and heritage sites could inform more strategic and safe management of urban tourism flows. Addressing the problems posed by the unpredictable nature of tourist visitor patterns due to the non-linearity and seasonal fluctuations in tourism, Wu (2019) designed an application that could analyse big data for smart tourism by conducting a case study on museum visitor behaviour in Florence, Italy. His research employs machine learning to develop a system to forecast museum visit volume over time to make tourism safer and heritage sites more resilient (Wu, 2019). Iorio et al. (2020) also offer a model of a Digital Tourism System that employs big data for more effective management of the tourism sector. Specifically, they explore how big data generated by museums and heritage sites can inform and improve adequate tourist infrastructure to increase visitor satisfaction and protect the environment (Iorio et al., 2020).

However, user-generated content is the most important data that can provide meaningful insights into the visitors' experiences (Shoval & Ahas, 2016; Xiang et al., 2017). Data such as personal experience sharing, directions and wayfinding tips, or complaints or comments have strong social implications. For example, non-moderated self-generated geo-tagged data from popular social networks can provide valuable crowd-sourced semantic annotations that offer reliable tools to understand public experiences within urban locales (Chen et al., 2018). These new possibilities in dynamic and integrated data analysis of public contributions can enable grass-roots co-documentation of audience urban experiences that can pave the way for dynamic public usages of heritage spaces (Jethani, 2014).

For instance, the app Paisatge Urba, developed by the Barcelona City Council in collaboration with local museums, provides useful tools to save, share and bookmark travellers' trails and journeys, creating social communities and making smart cultural experiences more than a matter of personal journey. Such apps enable data to share and exchange preferences and personal insights that enhance urban design by customising places and offerings to make them more relevant and responsive. They can also generate recommendation engines, returning the value visitors collect back to them in the form of users' tips and rankings. Indeed, smart cities can become powerful 'data republics' that employ data sharing to create more secure, resilient and enjoyable urban spaces to enable sustainable tourism.

While these implications are especially appealing, it is striking that there are only a handful of cases where these smart systems have been installed to integrate museum data flows into the data ecology of smart cities. As Pruulmann-Vengerfeldt (2022) observes, museums accumulate substantial and otherwise excess data, such as website visitor analytics, social media profiling, ticket sales, sensors data, mobile phone tracking data or logged data 'that museums don't actually use or analyse that often'. David Batchelor (2022), who led Wellington Heritage and Urban Design Portfolio in the past years, also shares that he rarely – if ever – comes across smart heritage systems that are well integrated by municipal governments to inform urban management.

In contrast, Morgan Currie (2022), Principal Investigator of the Culture and Communities Mapping Project, has shared a more strategic and rewarding approach to involve citizens in creating heritage spaces. The project has been developing since 2018 and aims to demonstrate the value of public data sharing and mapping activities 'to produce collective knowledge that can inform community strategies, planning processes or other initiatives' to enhance city management of Edinburgh, Scotland, 'the world's leading festival city' (Edinburgh Festival City, 2023). The project collaborated with the City of Edinburgh Council to conduct seven cultural mapping workshops with local communities to collect public intelligence and produce spatial knowledge on 'classifying places and ranking them as places of value' (Currie, 2022).

Participants contributed a total of 211 cultural assets during workshops and added another 453 assets based on categories that participants suggested themselves, resulting in an increase in spaces from 95 to 759. As a result, they created the Edinburgh Cultural Map (ECM), which features 1,300 spaces annotated with several context layers provided by participants and shares socio-demographics and geographic data (ECM, 2019). In 2021, the project partnered with Festivals Edinburgh, an umbrella organisation for the 11 major festivals in the city, to conduct workshops around the city neighbourhoods.

These activities were instrumental in revealing that residents are highly 'invested in festival activities and positive about how the festivals could build stronger, more connected relationships with communities and the cultural hubs that serve them' (ECM, 2022). However, citizens also indicated that there are still economic, geographical, structural and sociocultural barriers to fully accessing the festival sites, and a lot of information that could be aggregated from residents remains poorly integrated in the design of the major festival activities. In light of the negative consequences associated with smart tourism that relies on the constant aggregation of human data, user-generated content is promising for addressing problems related to marginalised communities 'prone to technological invisibility' (Longo et al., 2017; O'Neil, 2016).

Popham et al. (2020) emphasise that pragmatic data aggregation should be subject to greater scrutiny and public consultation should involve citizens in co-designing and co-creating urban experiences. While museums become 'smarter' and more data savvy, there is a need to develop 'more socially relevant uses of new technology applications' of smart cities that go beyond a 'techno-fix' to re-imagine data curation as a collaborative endeavour across institutions and publics (Glasmeiera & Christopherson, 2015). This approach could bring more productive results in planning activities around smart heritage and smart tourism and even enhance the reputation of cities.

Data Impacts: Smart Reputation

Developing an urban global brand is an essential task for cities and rests on such factors as trust and perceptions. As van Ham (2008) indicates, the social power embedded in perceptions 'has become an important factor in contemporary politics, shaping expectations as well as policies' of cities (p. 240). This position is based on assumptions articulated by communication scholars (Castells, 2008; Ronfeldt & Arquilla, 1999), who argue that public opinion in the 21st century is a new superpower. Public perceptions serve as the culmination of urban performance, leading to distinct social and cultural impacts on audiences. However, a 'city's image is not a simple object isolated from society' but is the means through which residents and global visitors interpret and relate to the city (Castillo-Villar, 2018, p. 37). In this way, tracking and understanding public opinion can help us understand the impacts of urban spaces on audiences and assess the public value of their cultural offerings.

In the age of social media, people actively use their mobile devices to share emotions and engage in online conversations about places they visit and experience. Social media is a perfect tool to measure and monitor public perceptions and even track how opinions shift over time (Ji, 2017). Jiang (2017) proposed a 'web-ecological' analysis of social networks focusing on specific political or cultural ideas circulated through multimedia content by employing data mining and sentiment analysis. For example, academics from the University of Vermont estimated the happiness levels of states and cities in the United States by using data mining of a geo-tagged dataset of over 80 million words on the social network service Twitter (Mitchell et al., 2013). Their American research has revealed that Napa, California, is the happiest city in the United States, while Beaumont, Texas, is the least happy.

Since that time, data mining on popular social media has significantly progressed, offering new avenues for more contextual research of urban spaces. Publicly available geo-tagged sentiment and valence data aggregated from social networks could provide rich and valuable information to both cultural institutions and city designers to monitor the level of public engagement and assess audiences' perceptions of their urban experiences. This information can offer insights into how visitors encounter museums and cultural heritage sites and what is meaningful for residents and visitors (Budge, 2018). However, before using social media sentiment analysis to understand the value of urban experiences, museums need to make sure that their social media feeds and audience feedback do, in fact, adequately capture people's opinions, perceptions and views.

This underscores the rationale behind the redevelopment and planning of Stratford's former Olympic Park in East London, UK, aimed at opening a new branch of the VAM – Victoria and Albert East – in 2025, which started with research on social media habits, preferences and activities of local residents (Hobson, 2022). Marie Hobson, VAM Senior Manager of the Audience Research and Insight, explains that the project aims to embrace the communication and social media language of their primary target audiences, which predominately consist of people from Black, Asian or minority ethnic communities, as well as young Londoners under 35 years of age. The audience research aimed to answer the following questions: 'How does this audience use and interact with social media? What defines exciting and engaging social media content for them? Where do their online interests and our content areas overlap? And how can we use this to launch a new marketing strategy for the new site?' (Hobson, 2022).

Insights from the focus groups and interviews with residents revealed specific social media channel preferences and use at particular times of the day, which is helpful information for monitoring digital behaviour. VAM also learnt that to win the attention of their potential audiences, their social media feed needs to prioritise people before things and feature creators rather than makers (Hobson, 2022). Understanding these specifics could help set up more diverse social media feeds that represent a totality of museum audiences, not just a narrow segment of regular dedicated visitors. However, even being able to generate engagement does not necessarily lead to understanding the feelings and perceptions of audiences. Kati Price (2022), the Head of Digital Media at the VAM, points out:

> The challenge of social is that it doesn't necessarily say anything about the quality of that engagement, and I think the idea of sentiment and how one might use it for data analysis is very important. Instead of measuring just reach and volume, the quality of engagement, this is what matters.

Kidd (2011) notes that museums adopt social media to interact with their audiences in accordance with three 'organising frames': marketing, inclusivity and collaborative. These frames define key purposes of institutional social media usage, from merely broadcasting information to fostering communities and even co-producing cultural and community narratives (Kidd, 2011). However, for social media to be used productively in a 'collaborative frame', institutions must recognise the value of audience participation. Co-ownership of public discourses could be achieved only when museums, cultural organisations and even smart city authorities advance their openness and dynamism to adequately reflect and enact changes expressed through online deliberations.

While these 'deliberations' may not be so easy to arrange, Amanda Solomons (2022), Marketing Manager at the Museum of Contemporary Art Australia (MCA) in Sydney, shared a project called 'Your Feelings Welcome' that used simple emoji to help audiences feel that 'they're part of something bigger' by sharing their emotions and experiences. In 2021, for four weeks in between lockdowns in Sydney, 'Your Feelings Welcome' featured artworks depicting ordinary but unique to Australia objects, from oyster shells to bush tucker to dried corncobs, which accumulated a plethora of local meanings for residents (MCA, 2021). The project offered just 18 emoji on the app for visitors to express how specific artworks made them feel and then demonstrated how different people react to the same objects. With the help of the mobile app, audiences could collectively share their emotional reactions to artworks on display as well as provide more insights by posting their comments in response to different questions depending on the emotions they shared. The Museum published these responses on the digital screens at the building, 'so they went through our digital signage, they went through a marketing campaign as well, which went through the entire city', to expose 'what we were finding out about people and their experiences' (Solomons, 2022).

Reaching out to four million people, the campaign helped reveal what objects, places and locations excited visitors, 'making them feel inspired', what artefacts made 'them feel magical and deadly, or in, Aboriginal terms, awesome, fantastic', and what art pieces, by contrast, incited anxiety or depression (Solomons, 2022). While this project illustrates existing avenues for constructing and sharing narratives and stories created and told by visitors themselves through their emotions, there was no meaningful link back to the data ecology of the smart city. The accumulated data informed the future activities of the museum's 'curatorial team, public programming team, and leadership team' (Solomons, 2022), but it missed telling and circulating important urban stories in global media spaces. Understanding, interpreting and sensing these digital conversations of residents and travellers through a timely aggregation and analysis of social media data could significantly improve smart city performance and contribute to effective strategic assessment of a city's attractiveness in both local and international contexts.

Conclusion

A contemporary smart city that aims for innovative urban management needs dynamic access and power to effectively manage up-to-date information on several critical urban domains, including its cultural capital. It should incorporate a wide variety of big datasets ranging from the geographic distribution of cultural amenities to the use and crowdedness of public/heritage spaces and landmarks in the city to understand a profile of its cultural visitors (Kourtit, 2019). Nevertheless, these capacities of contemporary museums to supply reliable data are currently overlooked by municipal governments and, moreover, are disintegrated across all stages of data curation, from resources to outputs to outcomes. There are few cases when smart cities and museums come together to exchange and cross-pollinate data management literacy to address common challenges. However, there is no single example yet of a smart integrative digital data curation system that might capture 'excess' data and wire museums and cultural heritage sites with local city businesses for collaborative data sharing, analysis and strategic use. There is a need to develop such systems that can transform the abundance and even excess of disintegrated big data into platforms of data intelligence to enhance smart city work and inform urban design strategies (Caird, 2018).

Without effective data evaluation, reporting and management processes, smart cities are poorly equipped to identify and assess the value, outcomes and impacts of their efforts to serve residents and visitors. While numerous challenges are ahead, and substantial work has to be done to develop meaningful data curation tools to enable smart cities to capitalise on big data intelligence, this chapter starts an important conversation. First, it exposes that smart cities could enhance their global reputation, visibility and image by building on closer collaborations with museums. Second, this chapter demonstrates that museums in the 21st century have transformed into hyper-connected cultural hubs, spreading their reach and impact beyond their immediate urban locations. Finally, it offers a three-dimensional framework of data-curation mechanisms that stress the role of museums and cultural heritage sites in supplying data for more strategic and proactive smart city management. It illuminates that big data generated by contemporary museums can improve the efficiency of smart cities in their efforts in city branding and tourism development.

Future research can expand this three-dimensional model by adding important data on museum energy conservation or a carbon footprint that measures the environmental impacts on a smart city's liveability and resilience (Lambert & Henderson, 2010). This could significantly enhance environmentally friendly modern urban design, which sometimes favours expansive 'starchitecture' constructions at the cost of gentrification and increased energy use. Further explorations could also employ more critical approaches to analyse empirical attempts that combine efforts across museums, municipal governments and local creative industries to build effective data intelligence platforms that measure the attraction powers of smart cities. These efforts across emerging practices and academic reflection could help advance smart cities to more progressive urban models that are dynamic, mobile and responsive to urban challenges and public needs.

References

Alexander, J. (2014). Gallery One at the Cleveland Museum of Art. *Curator: The Museum Journal, 57*(3), 347–362. https://doi.org/10.1111/cura.12073

Angelidoua, M., Karachalioua, E., & Stylianidisa, E. (2017). Cultural heritage in smart city environments. *The International Archives of the Photogrammetry, Remote Sensing and Spatial Information Sciences, 42*, 27–32. https://doi.org/10.5194/isprs-archives-xlii-2-w5-27-2017

Anholt, S. (2007). *Competitive identity: The new brand management for nations, cities and regions*. Palgrave Macmillan.

Anholt, S. (2011). Competitive identity. In M. Nigel, A. Pritchard, & R. Pride (Eds.), *Destination branding: Creating the unique destination proposition* (pp. 21–32). Routledge.

Batchelor, D. (2022). Webinar: Urban data infrastructures and digital place-making. *Data to Power*. https://www.datatopower.net/session3

Borda, A., & Bowen, J. P. (2017). Smart cities and cultural heritage – A review of developments and future opportunities. *Electronic Visualisation and the Arts*, 9–18. https://doi.org/10.14236/ewic/EVA2017.2

Borner, K., Maltese, A., Balliet, R., & Heimlich, J. (2016). Investigating aspects of data visualization literacy using 20 information visualizations and 273 science museum visitors. *Information Visualization, 15*(3), 198–213. https://doi.org/10.1177/1473871615594652

Budge, K. (2018). Encountering people and place: Museums through the lens of Instagram. *Australasian Journal of Popular Culture, 7*(1), 107–121. https://doi.org/10.1386/ajpc.7.1.107_1

Caird, S. (2018). City approaches to smart city evaluation and reporting: Case studies in the United Kingdom. *Urban Research & Practice, 11*(2), 159–179. https://doi.org/10.1080/17535069.2017.1317828

Castells, M. (2008). The new public sphere: Global civil society, communication networks, and global governance. *The Annals of the American Academy of Political and Social Science, 616*(1), 78–93. https://doi.org/10.1177/0002716207311877

Castillo-Villar, F. (2018). City branding and the theory of social representation. *Bitacora, 28*(1), 33–38. https://doi.org/10.15446/bitacora.v28n1.52939

Chan, S. (2022). Datathon: Mapping potential appeal of heritage collections - From API to geo-visualization. *Data to Power*. https://www.datatopower.net/session1

Chen, X., Vo, H., Wang, Y., & Wang, F. (2018). A framework for annotating OpenStreetMap objects using geo-tagged tweets. *GeoInformatica, 22*, 589–613. https://doi.org/10.1007/s10707-018-0323-8

Clarke, D., Bull, A., & Deganutti, M. (2017). Soft power and dark heritage: Multiple potentialities. *International Journal of Cultural Policy*, *23*(6), 660–674. https://doi.org/10.1080/10286632.2017.1355365

Currie, M. (2022). Webinar: Urban data infrastructures and digital place-making. *Data to Power.* https://www.datatopower.net/session3

Data to Power (DTP). (2022). GLAM and digital soft power in the post-pandemic world. *Data to Power.* http://www.datatopower.net

de Vasconcellos Motta, F. M., Barbosa, C., & Barbosa, R. (2019). Big Data como fonte de inovação em museus: O estudo de caso do Museu Britânico. *Informação & Sociedade*, *29*(1), 83–100. https://doi.org/10.22478/ufpb.1809-4783.2019v29n1.44005

Edinburgh Cultural Map. (2019). Cultural mapping workshops. The Edinburgh culture and community mapping project. https://www.edinburghculturalmap.org/research/cultural-mapping-workshops/

Edinburgh Cultural Map (ECM). (2022). Mapping cultural dispersal. Festivals mapping report. https://www.edinburghculturalmap.org/wp-content/uploads/2022/02/Festivals-Mapping-Report-FINAL-070222.pdf

Edinburgh Festival City. (2023). About the city. https://www.edinburghfestivalcity.com/the-city

Glasmeiera, A., & Christopherson, S. (2015). Thinking about smart cities. *Cambridge Journal of Regions, Economy and Society*, *8*, 3–12. https://doi.org/10.1093/cjres/rsu034

Grincheva, N. (2019). The form and content of 'digital spatiality': Mapping soft power of DreamWorks animation in Asia. *Asiascape: Digital Asia*, *6*(1), 58–83. https://doi.org/10.1163/22142312-12340102

Grincheva, N. (2022a). Making museum global impacts visible: Advancing digital public humanities from data aggregation to data intelligence. In A. Schwan & T. Thomson (Eds.), *The Palgrave handbook of digital and public humanities* (pp. 397–419). Palgrave MacMillan.

Grincheva, N. (2022b). City museums in the age of datafication: Could museums be meaningful sites of data practice in smart cities? *Museum Management and Curatorship*, *38*(4), 367–393. https://doi.org/10.1080/09647775.2021.2023904

Harari, Y. N. (2015). *Homo Deus: A brief history of tomorrow.* Harper Perennial.

Hobson, M. (2022). Datathon: Understanding and mapping digital museum audiences. *Data to Power.* https://www.datatopower.net/session2

Iorio, C., Pandolfo, G., D'Ambrosio, A., & Siciliano, R. (2020). Mining big data in tourism. *Quality and Quantity*, *54*(5/6), 1655–1669. https://doi.org/10.1007/s11135-019-00927-0

Iyer, J. (2017). *The heart of smart cities: A case for the relevance of art in data driven cities.* Carnegie Melon University: Arts Management and Technology Lab.

Jethani, S. (2014). Can digital mapping re-politicize urban mediation in the Indian context? *Graduate Journal of Asia-Pacific Studies*, *9*(1), 13–30.

Ji, L. (2017). Measuring soft power. In N. Chitty, L. Ji, C. Rawnsley, & C. Hayden (Eds.), *Routledge handbook of soft power* (pp. 75–92). Routledge.

Jiang, Y. (2017). Social media and e-diplomacy: Scanning embassies on Weibo. In N. Chitty, L. Ji, C. Rawnsley, & C. Hayden (Eds.), *Routledge handbook of soft power* (pp. 122–134). Routledge.

Kidd, J. (2011). Enacting engagement online: Framing social media use for the museum. *Information Technology & People, 24*(1), 64–77. https://doi.org/10.1108/09593841111109422

Kourtit, K. (2019). Cultural heritage, smart cities and digital data analytics. *Eastern Journal of European Studies, 10*(1), 151–159.

Kwek, A., Wang, Y., & Weaver, D. (2014). Retail tours in China for overseas Chinese: Soft power or hard sell? *Annals of Tourism Research, 44*, 36–52. https://doi.org/10.1016/j.annals.2013.08.012

Lambert, S., & Henderson, J. (2010). The carbon footprint of museum loans: A pilot study at Amgueddfa Cymru – National Museum Wales. *Museum Management and Curatorship, 26*(3), 209–235. https://doi.org/10.1080/09647775.2011.568169

Leorke, D., Wyatt, D., & McQuire, S. (2018). "More than just a library": Public libraries in the 'smart city'. *City, Culture and Society, 15*(1), 37–44. https://doi.org/10.1016/j.ccs.2018.05.002

Letourneau, S., Liu, C., Donnelly, K., Meza, D., Uzzo, S., & Culp, K. (2020). Museum makers: Family explorations of data science through making and exhibit design. *Curator: The Museum Journal, 63*(1), 131–145. https://doi.org/10.1111/cura.12348

Longo, J., Kuras, E., Smith, H., Hondula, D. M., & Johnston, E. (2017). Technology use, exposure to natural hazards, and being digitally invisible: Implications for policy analytics. *Policy & Internet, 9*, 76–108. https://doi.org/10.1002/poi3.144

Malik, K. R., Sam, Y., Hussain, M., & Abuarqoub, A. (2018). A methodology for real-time data sustainability in smart city: Towards inferencing and analytics for big-data. *Sustainable Cities and Society, 39*(1), 548–556. https://doi.org/10.1016/j.scs.2017.11.031

Mitchell, L., Frank, M. R., Harris, K. D., Dodds, P. S., & Danforth, C. M. (2013). The geography of happiness: Connecting Twitter sentiment and expression, demographics, and objective characteristics of place. *PLoS One, 8*(5). https://doi.org/10.1371/journal.pone.0064417

Museum of Contemporary Art (MCA). (2021). The MCA invites you to share your feelings about contemporary art. https://www.mca.com.au/media/mca-invites-you-share-your-feelings-about-contemporary-art/

Okwechime, E., Duncan, P., & Edgar, D. (2018). Big data and smart cities: A public sector organizational learning perspective. *Information Systems and e-Business Management, 16*(3), 601–625. https://doi.org/10.1007/s10257-017-0344-0

Olivares, F. (2015). Museums in public diplomacy. In G. Lord & N. Blankenberg (Eds.), *Museums, cities and soft power* (pp. 49–56). Rowman & Littlefield Publishers.

O'Neil, C. (2016). *Weapons of math destruction*. Crown Publisher.

Paquin, A. G. (2020). The 'smart' heritage mediation. *The Smart City Journal*. https://www.thesmartcityjournal.com/en/articles/smart-heritage-mediation

Patten, D. (2022). Datathon: Mapping potential appeal of heritage collections: From API to geo-visualization. *Data to Power*. https://www.datatopower.net/session1

Piccialli, F., & Chianese, A. (2014). Designing a smart museum: When cultural heritage joins IoT. In *Third International Conference on Technologies and Applications for Smart Cities*, Oxford (UK). https://bit.ly/2H07ksL

Popham, J., Lavoie, J., & Coomber, N. (2020). Constructing a public narrative of regulations for big data and analytics: Results from a community-driven discussion.

Social Science Computer Review, *38*(1), 75–90. https://doi.org/10.1177/0894439318788619

Price, K. (2022). Datathon: Mapping potential appeal of heritage collections: From API to geo-visualization. *Data to Power*. https://www.datatopower.net/session1

Pruulmann-Vengerfeldt, P. (2022). Webinar: Global communications and audiences: Propaganda, fake news & AI censorship. *Data to Power*. https://www.datatopower.net/session2

Rodríguez-Núñez, E., & Periáñez-Cañadillas, I. (2016). Intellectual capital as the fostering factor for sustainable smart urban development in the Basque Autonomous community. In M. Peris-Ortiz, D. R. Bennett, & D. P. Yábar (Eds.), *Sustainable smart cities: Creating spaces for technological, social and business development* (pp. 31–47). Springer.

Ronfeldt, D., & Arquilla, J. (1999). *The emergence of noopolitik: Toward an American information strategy*. Rand Corporation.

Schreiber, J., & Pekarik, A. (2014). Technical note: Using latent class analysis versus k-means or hierarchical clustering to understand museum visitors. *Curator: The Museum Journal*, *57*(1), 45–59. https://doi.org/10.1111/cura.12050

Science Museum Group (SMG). (2021). Never been seen. https://www.sciencemuseumgroup.org.uk/blog/never-been-seen/

Scott, B., Baker, E., Woodburn, M., Vincent, S., Hardy, H., & Smith, V. (2019). The natural history museum data portal. *Database*, *3*, 1–14. https://doi.org/10.1093/database/baz038

Shoval, N., & Ahas, R. (2016). The use of tracking technologies in tourism research: The first decade. *Tourism Geographies*, *18*(5), 587–606. https://doi.org/10.1080/14616688.2016.1214977

Siountri, K., & Vergados, D. (2018). Smart cultural heritage in digital cities. *Journal of Sustainable Development, Culture, Traditions*, *15*, 25–32.

Solomons, A. (2022). Datathon: Understanding and mapping digital museum audiences. *Data to Power*. https://www.datatopower.net/session2

Strong, M. (2022). Datathon: Mapping potential appeal of heritage collections: From API to geo-visualization. *Data to Power*. https://www.datatopower.net/session1

van Ham, P. (2008). Place branding: The state of the art. *The Annals of the American Academy of Political and Social Science*, *616*, 126–149. https://doi.org/10.1177/0002716207312274

Winesmith, K., & Carey, A. (2014). *Why build an API for a museum collection?* San Francisco MoMA. https://bit.ly/2xQwir4

Wu, S. (2019). Forecasting museum visitor behaviors using deep learning. In *Proceedings of the 2019 International Conference on Machine Learning, Big Data and Business Intelligence*, pp. 186–190.

Xiang, Z., Du, Q., Ma, Y., & Fan, W. (2017). A comparative analysis of major online review platforms: Implications for social media analytics in hospitality and tourism. *Tourism Management*, *58*, 51–65. https://doi.org/10.1016/j.tourman.2016.10.001

Zittrain, J. (2008). *The future of the internet – And how to stop it*. Yale University Press.

Chapter 10

Evaluation, Digital Data and Excess(es) in Health Interventions

Benjamin Hanckel

Institute for Culture and Society, Western Sydney University, Australia

Abstract

Evaluation and evaluative design aim to assess the impact of programmes, services and interventions. Underpinned by programme logics and theories of change, evaluation aims to assess intervention effectiveness and to determine an intervention's capacity to produce the intended change and achieve 'success'. This chapter is focused on evaluative data and the stories that data and its production make (in)visible and the excess data that gets left behind. I document the ways that health interventions use evidence and the shifts in evaluation towards making sense of the complex contexts and systems where interventions are embedded. Taking digital health interventions as an example of a critical contemporary shift in health, I examine the ways digital data is used to offer 'evidence' of interventions and how data excess emerges in evaluative research where potentially useful data is not collected or is ignored as seemingly irrelevant. Here, I situate excess in two ways. The first is in relation to the broadening of data that emerges with new digital technologies and what it promises. The second form of excess is data about social life, complexity and practices, which can get left behind when there is a focus on the 'digital'. I argue that continuing to interrogate the use(s) of digital data is critical for situating health within complex contexts and social practices of everyday life. Excess offers a useful framing to make sense of data and its (non)uses and the implications of such actions in evaluative research.

Keywords: Evaluation; health; interventions; digital; data; evidence

Introduction

Health interventions aim to improve health. They can include interventions focused on obesity (Hanckel et al., 2019), smoking and vaping (Barnes et al., 2023), mental health and sexual health (Hanckel, 2023), air pollution (Varaden et al., 2021) and/or vaccine uptake (Odone et al., 2015). They are often framed towards changing behaviours (Baum & Fisher, 2014; Mair, 2011) in the here and now for future public health (Hanckel et al., 2024) and aim to effect change in dynamic health systems (Byrne, 2013). Determining whether an intervention delivered online and/or offline is effective (or not) is the task of evaluation; evaluative design involves research and the collection of data to determine intervention effectiveness and what works (and what does not work). Evaluation also asks 'why' questions, aiming to measure the anticipated and unexpected causal relationships that produce (un)intended effects. These provide decision-makers and practitioners with evidence of what works, as well as contributing to broader forms of knowledge (Green et al., 2015; Stern et al., 2015). Evaluative design and the data that is produced to make sense of health interventions are the focus of this chapter.

This chapter takes the present moment – the 'digital turn' – as a key contemporary shift in health, requiring interrogation as digital data becomes part of digital health evaluative practices. This emergence of digital technologies in health (Lupton, 2017; Petersen, 2018) is impacting almost all aspects of health, including health intervention delivery and, in turn, evaluation and the data health researchers have to work with. That is, this 'digital turn' has changed not only the mode of delivery for health interventions but also the data available for evaluative purposes (Hanckel, 2023). Much writing on digital health data has focused on privacy and the potential bio-surveillance that comes through health data storage and capture. However, there has been less written on the digital data that is collected and the promises that data holds in relation to evaluation. Interventions can be implemented across online and offline settings; this can range from digital interventions such as mental or sexual health programmes online (Hanckel, 2023; Hanckel & Collin, 2024), vaccine reminders via the use of digital technologies (Odone et al., 2015) and/or those that incorporate aspects of the 'digital', such that they might use digital devices that track and monitor health progress (Clark et al., 2022).

Of particular interest in this chapter is not the way digital technologies are deployed, but rather the ways these interventions with digital components produce new data, analytics or metrics and 'evidence' for evaluative research. This data emerges from devices, dashboards and digital technologies, which can offer new evidence to evaluate the effectiveness of interventions and in turn determine their value. Indeed, it is becoming difficult to imagine a health researcher and/or evaluator who is not engaging with digital data in their work, and such conversations are critical as such data becomes a common part of research workflows. While there is increasing use of this data, there remains limited work on how digital data has entered into health intervention research and evaluation and how the promises of digital data and their generalisability collide with shifts in evaluative research, which aim to locate interventions in the contexts and complexity of everyday life. The aim of this chapter is to provide an overview of these shifts and interrogate digital data – the digital data that is collected and processed in the evaluation of digital health. Specifically, I examine how digital data – mostly analytical metrics from digital platforms, which is the form of digital data that is most common in the field – is situated within evaluative practices, and how we might make sense of this new(er) data and its promises (Halford & Savage, 2017) and the excesses that it (re)produces.

This chapter is thus focused on evaluative data and the stories that data and its production make (in)visible. To this end, I situate excess in two ways. The first is in relation to the broadening of data that emerges with new digital technologies and what it promises. The second form of excess is data about social life, complexity and practices, often qualitative data, which can get left behind when there is a focus solely on the 'digital', and specifically when evaluators use digital data in limited ways. In what follows, I first examine the ways that health interventions and evaluative design are not only underpinned by programme logics but are also situated in evidence-based health that values certain forms of data as evidence. There has, arguably, been a paradigm shift towards 'complexity' in health intervention research, broadening the scope of evidence that informs evaluation (Byrne, 2013; Greenhalgh & Papoutsi, 2018). Further, work stemming from the social sciences, and particularly sociology, has started to shift the conversation towards locating interventions in everyday life and making sense of them in relation to the social practices that situate their (non)use (Blue et al., 2016; Cohn, 2014). These shifts have brought back in excess data. Interestingly (or perhaps paradoxically!), new digital data has provided new excess, in the form of digital data points that can inform and make sense of digital health interventions. The promises of this digital data can paradoxically work to obscure complexity and the everyday spaces interventions enter into making invisible certain data and its contextual emergence. I argue that reading shifts in evaluative research and emergent uses of digital technologies together provide a productive collision of sorts, offering a framework to think about the limits and excess of data and its use(s) as we turn towards the digital to inform and make sense of the world.

Evaluation and Programme Logics

Evaluation is commonly understood as the process by which a service or intervention is measured to assess its effectiveness. Evaluative research will generally ask whether a service or intervention works and/or what aspects need to be improved for the future. While there is not one agreed upon definition of evaluation (see Clarke, 1999), as Hall and Hall (2004) note, frequently:

> ...evaluation focuses on the aims of a program and investigates to what extent the intentions of the program providers are realized [...] Evaluation thus implies a judgement of the worth or value of a program. (Hall & Hall, 2004, pp. 6–7)

In this way, evaluation is focused on programme and services 'intentions' and whether such intentions are realised. Wark (2019), in discussing the evaluation of health interventions, offers a similar definition, emphasising the 'systematic' aspects of evaluation

> [Evaluation is] a systematic approach to assessing the implementation and outcomes of a public health intervention to identify problems and/or determine whether the program has met its nominated goals. (Wark, 2019, p. 260)

Both definitions offer similar themes: evaluation is purposeful, systematic and involves the intentional collection of data to assess the effects of programmes and interventions. Evaluation asks 'what works' (or what doesn't work), and 'why' it works (or not). This offers an assessment and judgement of the value of a programme, service or initiative, against predetermined goals or outcomes.

A key aspect of evaluative work is to determine why an intervention works, measuring a presumed causal relationship between intervention and outcomes. As McLaughlin and Jordan (2015, p. 63) highlight 'if a program is implemented as planned, then certain results are expected to follow, given the context within which it is implemented'. That is, interventions have a 'logic' embedded in them, such that the implementation of intervention 'x' (e.g. knowledge of vaping, distribution of sexual health materials) can result in intended health outcomes (e.g. reduced vaping, increased sexual health practices). This is often referred to as a theory of change, which is underpinned by an explicit (or implicit) 'programme logic'. The programme logic is often a diagrammatic explanation of the relationship and causal pathways between intervention implementation and outcomes. Interventions are usually the input in such a model, and outcomes are often divided into short-, medium- and long-term outcomes, whereby intervention effects are often theorised to occur at each stage, within the contexts of implementation (McLaughlin & Jordan, 2015). While evaluators are often asked to consider the intended and unintended consequences of programmes in their evaluative practice (Robson & McCartan, 2016, p. 191), the programme logic plays an important role: it orients evaluation, focusing data collection and guiding the interpretation of findings (Cooksy et al., 2001). That is, programme logics situate data collection around the outcomes and proposed causal pathways and relationships of interventions, which are being tested in evaluation.

The logic model was evident, for instance, when I was undertaking a research project for a multi-country digital health intervention. The intervention was a digital mental health and sexual health offering online for sexuality and gender diverse young people across Southeast Asia. The intervention was oriented by broad goals, which directed the intervention: to promote health-seeking behaviour and resilience among young people, to encourage the young users to take charge of their own health, and have greater participation in the community. Towards these goals, the designers of the programme had mapped out a logic: if young people engaged with the intervention (an input), then their participation would result in short- to medium-term outcomes: increased subcultural knowledge related to sexuality and gender diversity; they would be linked to relevant services and have a heightened sense of belonging from participating in the intervention. They also had longer term outcomes as well: young people would have greater confidence accessing services and be more positive in their outlook, resulting in greater confidence to advocate for other sexuality and gender diverse people, and have increased participation in social life. The programme logic was developed not only to inform service delivery but also to explain to the funder how the programme would do what it said it would do. This is an indication of the ways that applied research has varied stakeholders who are invested in the project and how often several stakeholders are interested in how interventions meet their aims and the causal pathways and relationships that effect change (Green et al., 2015; Stern et al., 2015). This logic informed and directed the evaluation, which meant compiling a data set: a combination of user data, user surveys, website analytics (from where the intervention was hosted) and social media analytics (where the intervention was being promoted and engaged with outside of the intervention website). We also drew on interview data with young people who had come into contact with the intervention. Given this digital health intervention was still in its early development, the evaluation was focused on the short-term goals, as well as examining if the intervention was having the short-term impact that was intended. This directed the types of questions asked of participants, which included demographic details, use(r) data, as well as intervention acceptability, and effectiveness, which included knowledge acquisition and sense of connection to others. Evaluative discussions circulated in the development of the intervention, with questions about how to measure causal relationships for this digital service using digital data points. For instance, discussions internally focused on building components into the platform to measure and monitor, such as a confirmation button for a user indicating if knowledge products on sexuality were 'useful'; or the use of 'clicks' and/or user confirmation that links to external sites provided safe health and legal resources and were used; and/or whether the 'chat' feature with a peer successfully linked them to the required resources.

Formulated in this way, evaluation met the criteria – it was intentional and systematic and aligned to the programme logic. The logic of success built into the programme gave priority to (and demanded) certain kinds of data. In so doing, 'success measures' guide and orient; however, they can also work to obscure excess data. By this, I mean 'success measures' are designed and quantified (often before the study starts), and often programmes are funded to produce such success measures, so it is in the interest of evaluators to look for and surface this information. Thus, such data uncovers data about the programme, specifically data that has (often pre-defined) programme value. In this way, data uncovers data relevant to the programme, excluding information that *could* be (and often is) collected, but might not be considered 'data' (or what we might call excess) because the logic does not consider it valuable.

In these circumstances, we might say that excess is not just the data that is captured and ignored but *also* the data that is never captured or even imagined as data. In the study above, I drew on qualitative techniques as well, which included interviews with young people that offered alternate critical information that situated the intervention and digital data in the lives of the participants. For example, the information resources, a component of the intervention, generated a series of data points as evidence of impact: including being clicked on and read (click and time on site), if a positive response was associated with the information (from an embedded analytics tool to indicate feeling or 'mood' following engagement with the resource) and/or whether the resource was shared. In the intervention logic these data points offered evidence of an anticipated causal logic embedded in the platform, where the digital data points indicated it was 'useful' if they enhanced a sexuality and gender-diverse young person's subcultural information. However, in the interviews, a repeated concern was the limitations of the resources. While the young people did report finding them useful, they wanted more information that provided *contextually specific* health resources, information about gender diversity and transitioning as well as narratives of similar relatable others to help them make sense of their own diverse identities, which they saw as important. The interviews in this way brought in 'excess data' to surface and illuminate experiences more broadly and the needs of intervention users, which digital data or digital evidence (the clicks, shares and digital user journeys from the digital analytic data) could not illuminate.

Evidence

One of the key aspects of evaluative research as noted above are the data points or evidence used to determine 'effectiveness'. That is, a health researcher needs to be able to evidence the effects of an intervention. To understand the role of 'evidence' in health interventions, we need to locate this within a wider shift and turn towards the role of evidence in health more broadly. In the late 20th century, the paradigm of 'evidence-based medicine' emerged and was formally introduced as a term in the early 90s (Brownson et al., 2010; Guyatt et al., 1992). Evidence-based medicine emphasises the need to evidence or visibly show the effects of medicine on people, privileging random control trials (where individuals are randomly assigned to one group that receives an intervention or another group that receives no intervention or a placebo). This was seen to provide sufficient evidence of the effects of the medical intervention, where a change in one variable (i.e. intervention or not) would evidence the effects and support investment in an intervention to improve health. This paradigm shift impacted health more broadly, including public health and health promotion, where 'evidence-based public health' emerged, as:

> ...the development, implementation, and evaluation of effective programs and policies in public health through application of principles of scientific reasoning. (Brownson et al., 1999, p. 87)

Important here is an assessment of effectiveness through applying 'scientific reasoning' through all stages of programmes and interventions, including during the process of evaluation. 'Scientific reasoning' required methods that could assess an intervention's capacity to produce the outcomes via the intended and presumed causal relationships. As Stern and colleagues note, this relied on certain methods designed to scientifically measure outcomes and show causality, which imagined the researcher in a particular way:

> Historically evaluation has depended on a remarkably limited repertoire of methods and tools: interviews, surveys, statistical analyses of administrative records mostly enacted within a traditional view of the objective scientist, who observes and remains disengaged. (Stern et al., 2015, p. 384)

There are two key aspects to note. The first is the absence of digital data in the form of, for example, digital analytics or digital data points in the researcher's toolkit, given its more recent emergence, which is a point I will return to. The second, important for now, is the ways the tools of evaluative science stem from positivist research traditions. Olson et al. (2015) note how evaluative design is situated within broader hierarchies of knowledge production, which stem from positivist traditions that value experimental studies and quantitative data as 'gold standard' evidence. As Green and Thorogood (2018, pp. 322–323) note, experimental designs are often considered the strongest study designs for questions of programme and intervention effectiveness, as they measure the effects of an intervention on specified outcomes. This often (but not always) has prompted the use of quantitative data to establish causation, validity and (seemingly) avoid bias. Historically, qualitative data is brought in to simply triangulate data. Experimental designs are however limited in that they are not able to illuminate the differing ways causal conditions operate, and how they operate across differing contexts. That is, by focusing on causal relationships, such research designs *remove contextual complexity as excess data*. For example, consider random control trials. They are considered a 'gold standard' for evaluating intervention effectiveness (Green et al., 2015); however, they are often not effective for evaluating complex interventions (Woolcock, 2013), and as Byrne (2013, p. 221) points out, they are unable to account for individuals' 'past history, present context, and the inter-relationship of the individuals considered as complex systems with other complex systems'. Where research requires discrete variables, such histories might be considered as excess, removed from evidence programmes and their causal mechanisms. There are shifts that are occurring in what constitutes evidence, as I discuss shortly; however, 'gold standard' approaches continue to influence and orient programme evaluation and expectations in public health.

In my own work, I recall conversations with a digital mental health organisation for whom I was undertaking an evaluation with colleagues. They wanted to be able to show the effectiveness of their programme, seeking to identify the mechanisms in their programme that had causal impacts on young people's mental health who had started using their digital service. That is, they wanted an early indication that their digital programme was having effects and producing the outcomes intended. These outcomes included increased knowledge, improved awareness of mental health services, strategies for self-care and increased feelings of belonging. Showing 'proof of concept' early is particularly important for digital services when they may have had early funding to develop a prototype or model to be implemented. For this service, they wanted data and evidence during this early stage of intervention delivery, to not only identify if the programme was working and that the intended causal relationships were in place as expected, but also they wanted this evidence to be seen as legitimate within the broader mental health sector. Evaluation, in this way, as noted earlier, is often subject to competing demands and expectations from multiple stakeholders (Green et al., 2015; Stern et al., 2015), which includes hopes of digital and non-digital data to evidence effects in particular ways.

In early conversations with the team, they referred to random control trials and/or quasi-experimental studies as a 'gold standard', which they felt would legitimatise and validate the service. While they appreciated approaches that might surface other evidence, which we later incorporated, they also wanted to convince the mental health sector and future funders that this was a legitimate intervention, and 'gold standard' evaluative research and quantitative data could (seemingly) do this work. In the first instance, there were hopes for digital data points to do much of this work – the quantitative measurement of data points such as sign-ups, completion of a validated survey on the digital platform, digital user data, including platform engagement, user time on platform and the digitally generated content of the intervention. These offered a substantive number of digital data points – excess – that had to be made sense of for the evaluation. In conversations with the service, we also discussed potential interviews with young users, which as we progressed, they were receptive to including to contextualise the digital data and broaden the scope of the evaluation. That is, we included interviews with users, as we wanted to make sense of not only the intervention and its impact on young people's lives but also the ways that the intervention was being engaged with, how they understood their digital practices and the histories and practices of the young people who participated and engaged – the 'past history, present context' that Byrne (2013, p. 221) refers to. Important here was not only the use of mixed-methods research but also how interview data offered a tool to make sense of these data points. Digital data had to be selected that would offer meaningful data as it related to the logic and also offered data that could be read with the interviews. This allowed us to contextualise the data with interviews, to show how the intervention was fitting (or not) into the lives of young people who were engaging with the intervention.

The work and the tensions of methods and what was being surfaced speak to broader concerns in evaluative research. Specifically, evaluative work has increasingly asked researchers to account for the varied contexts of implementation and the complexity inherent in systems where interventions are deployed. There has been much written on this with authors arguing for shifting the focus of evaluation towards complexity and its emergence (Byrne, 2013). This has also included bringing qualitative research into evaluative design, not just to triangulate data but as a measure for enhancing causal credibility and validity of findings (for instance see Green et al., 2015). Increasingly, research in this area has argued for case-based methods that are able to investigate in-depth interventions in the contexts they are deployed, which also allows for comparative work across cases that can account for the differing conditions that might produce the outcome of interest across differing contexts (Green et al., 2022; Hanckel et al., 2021; Paparini et al., 2020). These changes in the measurement and evidencing of health and health interventions are often referred to as part of a broader turn or 'paradigm shift' towards complexity (Greenhalgh & Papoutsi, 2018). While still focused on health outcomes, complexity has arguably created space for conversations about the use(s) of, and engagement with, excess data – data that helps to make better sense of intervention use, adoption and impact across and within the complex contexts within which health interventions are embedded. Intentionally, or not, complexity expands the intended *and* unintended scope of data that must be used to make sense of and evidence health interventions and has brought in data, excess data, that was either previously not collected or was seemingly not relevant or simply ignored in datasets.

Further work in the social sciences, and particularly sociology, has sought to further extend the scope of data collected, for making sense of evaluations in the everyday spaces they are deployed. Specifically, authors have argued for shifting the unit of evidential analysis away from the individual and behavioural change, towards the social practices which produce (in)action (Blue et al., 2016; Cohn, 2014; Guise, 2024; Nettleton & Green, 2014). Behavioural change, as discussed, is often the focus of interventions (Baum & Fisher, 2014; Mair, 2011), whereby there is often a focus on individual barriers to change (Blue et al., 2016; Cohn, 2014). In this context, evidence is focused on behaviours, which are viewed as 'outcomes of the individual and determined only by such things as motives, intentions and the subjective reception of norms and cues' (Cohn, 2014, p. 159). Even when there is a focus on structural conditions, the 'focus [is often] on the material and social environments that limit opportunities for taking up healthier habits' (Nettleton & Green, 2014, p. 240). Such a focus on behaviours has been criticised for being removed from everyday social life; by treating behavioural change as a variable in health, it is often 'conceived of as discrete, stable, homogeneous, observable and, crucially, measurable' (Cohn, 2014, p. 159), removed from the social settings where practices take place.

Emergent work in this field has argued instead for a focus on social practices: a focus on practices as embedded and embodied social actions, that occur within specific social and material environments (Blue et al., 2016; Cohn, 2014; Guise, 2024; Nettleton & Green, 2014). Consider vaping from a social practices perspective; it might examine when vaping is taking place, where, why (e.g. socialising, to relieve stress), with whom (e.g. friends, colleagues, family members, alone), what social norms are being adhered to by those participating (or not). An intervention and subsequent evaluation focused on vaping as behaviour would largely focus on the choice to vape or not as an individual behaviour rather than examine the social practices that (re)produce the action and the variance to those practices. Or put another way, we might say that a behaviour change intervention might obscure the embedded and embodied relational assemblage of practices, the materials, conditions and circumstances, which together produce social action. It would exclude or obscure the ways vaping as a practice is socially produced, situated and embedded; it would be excess data. Shifting the evidential unit to social practices (rather than behaviour) has been argued to better situate interventions and their logics in the social milieu in which they are deployed. As interventions are focused on change, this means, as Nettleton and Green (2014, p. 248) argue, moving 'beyond merely noting that practice is contingent and complex, and start building new more theoretical models of where, how, and when change is more or less likely to happen'. This requires engaging with the data that was initially not considered important – the excess data that can get left behind if the interventions are not situated in the social lives of those engaging with them.

Consider an example from the digital mental health intervention. It offered young people the opportunity to share their digital stories of mental health with peers on the platform. Digital data points showed how many people had shared their stories as a proportion of platform users, and analytics and user data indicated how many young people watched these stories and platform engagement as analytic data points, and digital surveys offered information about user health and wellbeing. These data points told a story of behaviours – a user engages, they see or produce a story, and in turn there is an impact (or not) on a user. However, such a framing tells an individual story and excludes the variable practices associated with participation. In undertaking interviews with young people, we were able to complicate this simple story and explore the social practices that situated their use(s) and engagement with the intervention. They spoke about feeling a sense of trust and security with the platform and the organisation facilitating the intervention because of its reputation in the field of mental health. They spoke about the importance of finding similar others and sense of community on the platform, given the stigmas associated with mental health, as well as the varied reasons for engaging on the platform – as advocates in broader stigma reduction through their participation, as beneficiaries of the existing stories, and to support their peers. They also spoke about why they did not engage at times, for both their mental health and for concerns about privacy and stigma. They also spoke about the design limitations, such as no captions, which had impacts on accessibility, particularly for those with a dis/ability, though also impacted its usability in public spaces. They also spoke about the ways they kept their use/s (in)visible from other on/offline spaces due to stigma concerns. Making sense of social practices in this way was critical to surface the ways the intervention was (mis)aligning with lives lived across online and offline spaces. Interviews and contextualising the existing digital data were critical to exploring these practices in the evaluation.

Digital Interventions, Data and Complexity

In this final section, I want to reflect on digital data as evidence. Perhaps most notable are the types of digital data that have emerged for evaluation, which have been evident in the vignettes I have described throughout. Digital data offers information about intervention engagement, use and impact, which is sourced from platform specific dashboards (both user-facing and back-end dashboards), analytical data outputs, platform-embedded surveys and data collection tools, as well as digital data from other sources such as social media, where an intervention might be implemented (in full or part) or promoted. In this way, digital data and its analysis – and the excess it produces – are part of the new(er) tools in the 'toolbox' to measure impact and make sense of an intervention as it unfolds.

There are two key points here about excess. The first is the expansive dataset that digital data offers and the promises embedded in this dataset. Digital data is of course not just health data but has become an important part of contemporary life, promising to illuminate everyday practices through bringing together digital data points. Perhaps most evident in discourses of big data, digital data promises to track, measure and evidence social life as it unfolds as an unquestioned generalisable truth (Halford & Savage, 2017). Digital data as it emerges on dashboards and in analytics offers neat frameworks and seemingly shows what people are doing, generating new ways to track and monitor impact. However, this often does not provide a nuanced or contextual picture. In my own work, I have shown the limits of relying on this data to 'know' engagement, whereby analytics situate and place people in categories, such as according to binary gender, which do not reflect people's lived experience (Hanckel, 2023). As others (Clark et al., 2022) have shown, digital intervention participation can be haphazard, which is often not reflected in data points. Use(s) (including who are using intervention platforms) are not always evident in digital data, and the reasons 'why' are often obscured. That is, interventions are not necessarily uniformly engaged with and can be affected by a variety of contextual conditions, such as device access, literacy and temporal/spatial demands, and how they intersect across on/offline lives and are used with other interventions. Decontextualised digital data, while producing an expansive (and often excessive) dataset, struggles to attend to the complexities of social life and the social practices which situate use. Simple, positivist or quantitative interpretations of digital data, which often promise the truths of social life, often obscure aspects of social life and by extension the claims that can be made about the effects of an intervention.

Understanding digital data (and what it possibly obscures) is perhaps critical to a meaningful assessment of digital health interventions. This requires acknowledging the ways that digital health interventions are situated in existing social practices, where the online and offline entangle. As authors such as Hine (2015, p. 192) have proposed, in new reconfigured environments, online and offline spaces converge, where the internet is a culturally embedded phenomenon and 'online activities acquire meaning and significance insofar as they are interpreted within other online and offline contexts'. This requires, as digital researchers have argued for some time, making sense of and understanding digital health technologies and interventions in this context, with and through people's lived experiences and practices, as they use, make sense of and come into contact with these technologies (Baym, 2006; Hine, 2015). In short, assumptions that are made about this data must take this into account and be reflexive of the ways that digital data (and its promises) are situated in existing social practices, which limit, constrain and enable change to happen within the social and material environments where social action occurs. This data needs to be considered alongside the complexity of other social life data.

This is also particularly pertinent to consider as services reflect on what evaluative data can do. In my discussions with digital health organisations, there are always concerns about how best to advocate for the people they are targeting. Digital data, which is now a feature of these programs, often gets framed as potential 'insights' that can be used for advocacy. As I have noted elsewhere, interventions:

> ...demand some data from users to be used for internal and/or external purposes. This in itself is not negative per se: however how data is collected and also how it is analysed and the types of claims made of such data on a single platform need scrutiny. These back-end data points are interesting, but perhaps not the whole story. [...] capturing back-end data points of the use of such initiatives provides some insight, but is unlikely to provide a clear picture of how an initiative is used in the 'real world'. Such insights also struggle to determine the degree of impact of those using it, particularly if this is one amongst a number of initiatives and interventions engaged with (which is likely). (Hanckel, 2023, p. 70)

As organisations employ varied technologies and utilise dashboards for analytics, we need to ask questions about the ways such data comes about and how it is used. This includes asking about what the digital data is doing, how it is showing change in everyday social life and questioning the generalisability of such findings. It also requires asking, perhaps more broadly, who owns the technologies and what logics are already embedded in the design of dashboards and analytics, which are being relied on to make claims and advocate. The impact of evaluations is difficult to ascertain from data points on a website, without understanding how the digital intervention is made sense of in its contextual use(s).

If excess comes from too much digital data, I have also argued throughout that excess is also the data that is never collected or is discarded as potential evidence for interventions. The recent shifts towards complexity and shifting of the evidential unit (or at least advocacy for it) create spaces to surface the relational assemblages that can emerge through contextualising digital data points in the environmental and material conditions of everyday life.

Take, for example, a component of one of the digital health interventions that I was researching. This component supported young people to develop and upload YouTube videos about their experiences of being sexuality and/or gender diverse. A reading of the YouTube analytics told one story; certain people from the 'target countries' of the intervention were watching the videos on and off the intervention platform. The analytics data included approximate age ranges of these participants and gender (skewed to the binary model – data about women and men only). In contrast however, in interviews with the young people producing the videos, they spoke about the careful negotiations of sharing their videos both on- and offline across their networks, how they considered the contexts in which their video could circulate and based on their own practices, decided how 'public' their videos were and how they would share them, as part of their own practices. Further, the interviews also surfaced the ways that a 'watch' on YouTube meant many things to the people involved, as the videos travelled across dinner tables, advocacy and organisational seminars and settings and into university spaces. In each, they generated discussions about the videos. They not only perpetuated existing experiences of discrimination and stigma but also created opportunities for peer support across online and offline settings, fostering what I have called elsewhere 'spaces of disclosure' (Hanckel, 2023, p. 131). The young users of the platform also spoke about the benefits of the videos and seeing representations of themselves. If we were to just rely solely on digital data in the form of analytics, such nuanced engagements would become invisible or obscured as excess. This excess would not be included in the evaluative data set, impacting the possibilities of determining the effect of the intervention, and how and when change happens. Here, we see the value of surfacing the practices of participants, their histories and the relational assemblages that situate their use(s), alongside digital data points and the limitations they come with.

Concluding Comments

This chapter has broadly asked about the shifts in health intervention research and how interventions are evaluated, and specifically the data that is used to evidence their effectiveness. Recent shifts in evaluative research in relation to complexity and social practices offer new tools and types of data to respond to the promises of digital data (and the excesses it produces). These shifts in evaluative research and emergent uses of digital technologies together provide a productive collision to think about the limits and use of excess data. Future research would do well to interrogate further how such decisions are made in evaluative research and the ways that social life and the digital are brought together. Such work is critical as evaluation informs and provides evidence towards the development of interventions that we are all likely to encounter in everyday life.

References

Barnes, C., Turon, H., McCrabb, S., Hodder, R. K., Yoong, S. L., Stockings, E., Hall, A. E., Bialek, C., Morrison, J. L., & Wolfenden, L. (2023). Interventions to prevent or cease electronic cigarette use in children and adolescents. *The Cochrane Database of Systematic Reviews*, *11*(11), CD015511. https://doi.org/10.1002/14651858.CD015511.pub2

Baum, F., & Fisher, M. (2014). Why behavioural health promotion endures despite its failure to reduce health inequities. *Sociology of Health & Illness*, *36*(2), 213–225. https://doi.org/10.1111/1467-9566.12112

Baym, N. (2006). Finding the quality in qualitative research. In D. Silver & A. Massanari (Eds.), *Critical cyberculture studies* (pp. 79–87). New York University Press.

Blue, S., Shove, E., Carmona, C., & Kelly, M. P. (2016). Theories of practice and public health: Understanding (un)healthy practices. *Critical Public Health*, 26(1), 36–50. https://doi.org/10.1080/09581596.2014.980396

Brownson, R. C., Baker, E. A., Left, T. L., Gillespie, K. N., & True, W. R. (2010). *Evidence-based public health*. Oxford University Press.

Brownson, R. C., Gurney, J. G., & Land, G. H. (1999). Evidence-based decision making in public health. *Journal of Public Health Management and Practice*, 5(5), 86–97. https://doi.org/10.1097/00124784-199909000-00012

Byrne, D. (2013). Evaluating complex social interventions in a complex world. *Evaluation*, 19(3), Article 3. https://doi.org/10.1177/1356389013495617

Clark, M., Southerton, C., & Driller, M. (2022). Digital self-tracking, habits and the myth of discontinuance: It doesn't just 'stop'. *New Media & Society*. https://doi.org/10.1177/14614448221083992

Clarke, A. (1999). *Evaluation research: An introduction to principles, methods and practice*. Sage Publishing.

Cohn, S. (2014). From health behaviours to health practices: An introduction. *Sociology of Health & Illness*, 36(2), 157–162. https://doi.org/10.1111/1467-9566.12140

Cooksy, L. J., Gill, P., & Kelly, P. A. (2001). The program logic model as an integrative framework for a multimethod evaluation. *Evaluation and Program Planning*, 24(2), 119–128. https://doi.org/10.1016/S0149-7189(01)00003-9

Green, J., Hanckel, B., Petticrew, M., Paparini, S., & Shaw, S. (2022). Case study research and causal inference. *BMC Medical Research Methodology*, 22(1), 307. https://doi.org/10.1186/s12874-022-01790-8

Green, J., Roberts, H., Petticrew, M., Steinbach, R., Goodman, A., Jones, A., & Edwards, P. (2015). Integrating quasi-experimental and inductive designs in evaluation: A case study of the impact of free bus travel on public health. *Evaluation*, 21(4), 391–406. https://doi.org/10.1177/1356389015605205

Green, J., & Thorogood, N. (2018). *Qualitative methods for health research*. Sage Publishing.

Greenhalgh, T., & Papoutsi, C. (2018). Studying complexity in health services research: Desperately seeking an overdue paradigm shift. *BMC Medicine*, 16(1), 95. https://doi.org/10.1186/s12916-018-1089-4

Guise, A. (2024). Stigma power in practice: Exploring the contribution of Bourdieu's theory to stigma, discrimination and health research. *Social Science & Medicine*, 347, 116774. https://doi.org/10.1016/j.socscimed.2024.116774

Guyatt, G., Cairns, J., Churchill, D., Cook, D., Haynes, B., Hirsh, J., Irvine, J., Levine, M., Levine, M., Nishikawa, J., Sackett, D., Brill-Edwards, P., Gerstein, H., Gibson, J., Jaeschke, R., Kerigan, A., Neville, A., Panju, A., Detsky, A., ..., Tugwell, P. (1992). Evidence-based medicine: A new approach to teaching the practice of medicine. *JAMA*, 268(17), 2420–2425. https://doi.org/10.1001/jama.1992.03490170092032

Halford, S., & Savage, M. (2017). Speaking sociologically with big data: Symphonic social science and the future for big data research. *Sociology*, 51(6), 1132–1148. https://doi.org/10.1177/0038038517698639

Hall, D., & Hall, I. (2004). *Evaluation and social research: Introducing small-scale practice* (1st ed.). Red Globe Press.

Hanckel, B. (2023). *LGBT+ youth and emerging technologies in Southeast Asia: Designing for wellbeing* (Vol. 14). Springer Nature.

Hanckel, B., & Collin, P. (2024). Youth, health and the digital. In J. Bessant, P. Collin, & P. O'Keeffe (Eds.), *Research handbook on the sociology of youth*. Edward Elgar Publishing. https://doi.org/10.4337/9781803921808.00038

Hanckel, B., Garnett, E., & Green, J. (2024). Risk ambassadors and saviours: Children and futuring public health interventions. *Sociology of Health & Illness*. https://doi.org/10.1111/1467-9566.13802

Hanckel, B., Petticrew, M., Thomas, J., & Green, J. (2021). The use of qualitative comparative analysis (QCA) to address causality in complex systems: A systematic review of research on public health interventions. *BMC Public Health, 21*(1), Article 1. https://doi.org/10.1186/s12889-021-10926-2

Hanckel, B., Ruta, D., Scott, G., Peacock, J. L., & Green, J. (2019). The Daily Mile as a public health intervention: A rapid ethnographic assessment of uptake and implementation in South London, UK. *BMC Public Health, 19*(1), 1167. https://doi.org/10.1186/s12889-019-7511-9

Hine, C. (2015). *Ethnography for the internet: Embedded, embodied and everyday*. Bloomsbury Academic.

Lupton, D. (2017). *Digital health: Critical and cross-disciplinary perspectives*. Routledge.

Mair, M. (2011). Deconstructing behavioural classifications: Tobacco control, 'professional vision' and the tobacco user as a site of governmental intervention. *Critical Public Health, 21*(2), 129–140. https://doi.org/10.1080/09581596.2010.529423

McLaughlin, J. A., & Jordan, G. B. (2015). Using logic models. In K. E. Newcomer, H. P. Hatry, & J. S. Wholey (Eds.), *Handbook of practical program evaluation* (pp. 62–87). John Wiley & Sons.

Nettleton, S., & Green, J. (2014). Thinking about changing mobility practices: How a social practice approach can help. *Sociology of Health & Illness, 36*(2), 239–251. https://doi.org/10.1111/1467-9566.12101

Odone, A., Ferrari, A., Spagnoli, F., Visciarelli, S., Shefer, A., Pasquarella, C., & Signorelli, C. (2015). Effectiveness of interventions that apply new media to improve vaccine uptake and vaccine coverage: A systematic review. *Human Vaccines & Immunotherapeutics, 11*(1), 72–82. https://doi.org/10.4161/hv.34313

Olson, K., Young, R. A., & Schultz, I. Z. (Eds.). (2015). *Handbook of qualitative health research for evidence-based practice* (1st ed.). Springer.

Paparini, S., Green, J., Papoutsi, C., Murdoch, J., Petticrew, M., Greenhalgh, T., Hanckel, B., & Shaw, S. (2020). Case study research for better evaluations of complex interventions: Rationale and challenges. *BMC Medicine, 18*(1), 301. https://doi.org/10.1186/s12916-020-01777-6

Petersen, A. (2018). *Digital health and technological promise: A sociological inquiry*. Routledge.

Robson, C., & McCartan, K. (2016). *Real world research*. John Wiley & Sons.

Stern, E., Saunders, M., & Stame, N. (2015). Standing back and looking forward: Editors' reflections on the 20th anniversary of evaluation. *Evaluation, 21*(4), 380–390. https://doi.org/10.1177/1356389015608757

Varaden, D., Leidland, E., Lim, S., & Barratt, B. (2021). "I am an air quality scientist"– Using citizen science to characterise school children's exposure to air pollution. *Environmental Research, 201*, 111536. https://doi.org/10.1016/j.envres.2021.111536

Wark, S. (2019). *Public health: Planning and evaluation.* Cambridge University Press.

Woolcock, M. (2013). Using case studies to explore the external validity of 'complex' development interventions. *Evaluation, 19*(3), 229–248. https://doi.org/10.1177/1356389013495210

Index

Academic publishing, 110–111
Actual practice, 90
Affective atmosphere, 40–41
  of offcuts, 44–49
Affects, 89
African Australian youth on social media, 30–33
Algorithmic mediation on YouTube, 71–73
Algorithmic societies of control, microblogging in, 115–116
Algorithms, 70–71, 116–117
Ambient touch, 90
'App culture', 128–129
Application Programming Interfaces (APIs), 61, 77, 127
Assemblages, 6
Augmented reality (AR), 127–128

Barbie social media, 45
Big data, 5, 16–17, 124
  data impacts, 131–134
  data republics, 129–131
  data resources, 126–129
#BlackLivesMatter (BLM), 26, 30
Blogging, 112
Boundaries of field, 6–7, 41, 43
'Bricolage', 107
'Burrell's approach, 64
'By-products' of research, 3–4

Care, 29
  case-based methods, 146–147
  ethics of, 27
Complexity, 148–151
Computational research techniques, 71
Confession, 106
Confessional cultural object, reading, 111–113

Confessional poetry, 112–113
Contemporary cities, 126
Contemporary media culture, 2
Contextual integrity, 29–30
Corporeal feminism, 92
COVID-19
  in Australia, 45
  health information, 48
  pandemic, 26, 30–31, 40
'Crafting method', 21
Crafting phenomenological research, 95
Creative data, 8
Creative writers, 111
Crisis, wellness discourses in, 48–49
Criticisms, 113–114
Cultural chronology, 91
'Cultural Economy of Locative Media', 17
Curiosity, 108

Data, 15, 106, 130, 140, 148, 151
  analysis, 28–29, 133
  assemblage, 77
  collection, 17, 19, 43–44, 61, 76–78, 126
  ecology, 130, 133–134
  ghosts, 9–10
  holds memories, 58–59
  impacts, 126, 131, 134
  management, 124
  republics, 126, 129, 131
  resources, 126
  saturation, 6–7, 15
  sets, 76–78, 142–143
  volume and quantity, 63
Data excess, 3, 6, 17–18, 56, 88, 125
  collecting data, generating excess data, 17–19

Index

inevitability of data excess in research, 59–63
method assemblage, 21–22
parergon, 19–21
qualitative data, 14–16
reframing, 19–22
Data minimalism, epistemic culture of algorithmic mediation on YouTube, 71–73
classifying tourism destinations on YouTube, 78–83
locating place images on YouTube, 76–78
observing production of place images, 73–76
Datafication of museums, 124
Dataism, 125
Derrida, Jacques, 14
Digital 'confessional' reader, 113
Digital age, self-fashioning and poetry in, 113–115
Digital archives, 60–62
Digital artworks, 108
Digital atmospheres, 40–41
Digital context, 58
Digital cultures, 3, 64, 111
digital ethnography, relations as fields and ethnographic sensibility, 63–66
hoarding possessions and personal digital archiving, 57–59
inevitability of data excess and digital hoarding in research, 59–63
Digital data, 2–4, 57–59, 63, 71, 140–141, 145–146, 148–150
collection tools, 78
excess, 56–57, 127–128
processing systems, 125
produce, 4
Digital disorganisation and excess, 65
Digital ethnographers, 26, 60–61
Digital ethnographic field site, 30–31
Digital ethnography, 3–4, 40, 42, 56, 63–66, 70–71

affective atmospheres of offcuts, 44–49
messy boundaries of field, 41–43
remixed methods for pandemic atmospheres, 43–44
of travel influencers, 70–71
Digital Ethnography Research Centre, 2
Digital excess, 2, 9
Digital fieldwork, 56–57, 60
Digital formats, 4
Digital health interventions, 150–151
Digital hoarder, 58
Digital hoarding, 58–59, 65–66
inevitability of digital hoarding in research, 59–63
Digital intermediation processes and actors, 116
Digital interventions, 148–151
Digital media, 27
affect, haunting and unexpected discovery, 8–10
ethics, visibility and waste, 5–8
towards excessive thinking and writing, 10
head of, 128
methodologies of excess in, 3–5
research, 2, 56
Digital museum resources, 127
"Digital pack-rattery", 59
Digital platforms, 64, 70–71, 140–141
Digital politics, 3
Digital practices, 3
Digital research(ers), 5, 8, 26, 64–65, 149–150
Digital scholars, 60–61
Digital self-tracking, 9
Digital spaces, 107
Digital technologies, 7, 64
in health, 140
Digital touch communication, 90
Digital tourism system, 129–130
Digital tracking practices, traces of self in, 33–35
Digital Transformation Lead at Queensland Art, 127

Index   157

Digital turn, 140
Digitalisation of museums, 124
Digitally mediated interactions, 40
Discovery Early Career Researcher
    Award (DECRA), 17, 20–21
Doctoral research projects, 9
'Doomscrolling', 48

Edinburgh Cultural Map (ECM), 131
Embodiment, 45, 92
Ergon, 19–20
Ethics, 5–8
    of care, 27
Ethnographic collection of data, 92–93
Ethnographic data, 99–100
Ethnographic research into vlogging,
    70–71
Ethnographic sensibility, 63–66
Ethnographic tactics, 75
Ethnography, 63–64, 75–76, 88, 91,
    94
Evaluation of health interventions,
    141–144
Evaluative research, 144
Evidence-based medicine, 144
Excess data, 2, 5–9, 14, 16–19, 59–60,
    117, 143–147
    generation, 17–19
    microblogging in algorithmic
        societies of control,
        115–116
    reading confessional cultural object,
        111–113
    research, 109–111
    reserve data, 117–118
    self-fashioning and poetry in digital
        age, 113–115
    temporality and research event,
        106–109
Excess digital data, 106
Exercise, 47–48

Fabrication, 98–101
Facebook, 18, 27, 31, 40, 71–72, 108,
    117
#femalerage, 112–113

Feminist phenomenology, 88
Fields, relations as, 63–66
Fieldwork, 40, 42, 63–64
'Fitspo', 26
    fitness inspiration, 26
    on Instagram, young women's
        relations with, 27–30
Foucault, Michel, 112

Galleries, 8
Global tourism, 70–71
Grounded theory, 14, 19

Haptic(s), 89
    fabrication and partial translation,
        98–101
    haptic experiments, 96–98
    haptic methods, 94–98
    haptic turn, 89–91
    interviews and observations in situ,
        94–95
    media, 95
    methods, 88, 94, 98
    mobile media, 89–91
    phenomenology,
        post-phenomenology and
        ethnography, 91–94
    turn, 89–91
Hashtag practices, 62–63
Health
    diet, 47–48
    digital interventions, data and
        complexity, 148–151
    digital technologies in,
        140
    evaluation and programme logics,
        141–144
    evidence, 144–148
    interventions, 140
    research, 56
    researcher, 144
    workers, 3–4
Heritage
    institutions, 125
    integration, 125
    sites, 129–130

158   Index

Hoarding, 57
  possessions, 57–59

Images, 56, 108
Individual practice, 90
'Industry stakeholder' group, 7
Information centres, 124
Information saturation, 46–48
Instagram, 4, 18, 26–27, 31, 40, 70–71, 78–79
  story post, 45
  young women's relations with 'fitspo' on, 27–30
Instagrammable moments, 21–22
'Instapoetry', 114
Intercorporeality, 91–92
Interdisciplinary insights for digital touch communication, 90
Internet, 2–3, 149–150
  ethnography, 65
  internet-mediated social contexts, 99–100
Internet of Things (IoT), 129
Interventions, 140
  acceptability, 142–143
Interviews, 94–95
Intimacy, 89, 91, 96

Key performance indicators (KPIs), 9

Law, John, 14
Law proposes method, 21
Law's response, 21
Literary studies, drawing on research in, 106
Locative media industries, 17
Logic model, 142–143
Lyall draws, 26–27

Malaysian travel influencer, 70
Market research firm, 18
Markham, Annette, 4
Media, 2–3
  drawing on research media studies in, 106
  ethnography, 97–98
  produce, 7
  researchers, 80–83
  studies, 106
Mediated social touch, 90
Memories, 9, 58–59
Mental health, 60
  programmes, 140
  services, 145–146
#mentalhealthmatters, 112–113
Messaging, instant, 40
Messiness, 40–41, 61
Meta (company), 40
Metadata, 61
Method assemblage, 21–22
Metrics, 140–141
Microblogging in algorithmic societies of control, 115–116
Mobile apps, 97
Mobile device, 88
Mobile media, 88–89, 91
  research, 91
  usage, 88
Mobile phone, 89, 97, 101
Mobile touchscreens, 89, 91
Moran reflects, 26
MRT station, 70
Multistability, 91–92
Museum of Contemporary Art Australia (MCA), 133
Museums, 124, 129–130
  data impacts, 131–134
  data republics, 129–131
  data resources, 126–129
  datafication processes, 125

Netflix's recommender system, 71–72
Network(s), 64
  analysis, 78–79
  data, 78
  nodes, 78–79

visualisation software, 78–79
NodeXL Pro, 78
Non-linear methods of data collection, 78

Observations in situ, 94–95
Offcuts, affective atmospheres of, 44–49
  information saturation and responsibilisation, 46–48
  unprecedented times, 45
  wellness discourses in crisis, 48–49
Opaque production processes, 77
Open-ended methods of data collection, 78
'Orthosomnia', 35
Overtourism, 129–130

Pandemic atmospheres, remixed methods for, 43–44
Parergon, 19–21
Partial translation, 98–101
Participant observation, 27–28
PayPal (company), 72
'Perish' culture, 110–111
Personal digital archiving, 57–59
Phenomenology, 88, 91, 94
Photo elicitation techniques, 17–18
Physical hoarding, 58–59
Place images, observing production of, 73–76
Place images on YouTube, 76–78
Place-bound fieldwork, 76
Place-making, 126–127
Platform content, 75–76
Plath, Sylvia, 10, 106
  created complex, 107
  poetry, 106
Plath's poetry, 113–114
Poetry
  in digital age, 113–115
  reading practices, 117
#poetryislife, 112–113
Popular culture, 113

Post-phenomenological approach, 95
Post-phenomenology, 88, 91, 94
Postgraduate research, 110–111
Printing visual data, 61–62
Productive data, 8
Programme logics of health interventions, 141–144
Project combined phenomenology, 88
Pseudonymity, 108, 114
Publish culture, 110–111
Published data, 16–17

Qualitative data, 14, 16, 141, 145
  published and unpublished data, 16–17
Qualitative digital researchers, 40
Qualitative methods, 94
Qualitative research, 15
  in digital spaces, 41
  methods, 14
  methods, 16
Qualitative researchers, 41
Qualitative techniques, 143–144
Query design, 76–77

Racism, 32
Random control trials, 146
Reade draws, 26
Reading confessional cultural object, 111–113
Reddit, 110
'Reflexive turn', 107
Relational ethnography, 63–64
Remix method, 43
Research, 109–111
  data, 14
  event, 106–109
  inevitability of data excess and digital hoarding in, 59–63
  management software, 3
  practice, 59–60
  process, 2, 25–26
  questions, 6, 15–16, 63

'Reserve' data, 117–118
Responsibilisation, 46–48
Retelling insights from studies, 58–59

'Saturation', 15
Science Museum Group (SMG), 128
'Scientific reasoning' required methods, 144–145
Screen recording, 28–29
Screenshots, 28–29, 44–47
Search-as-research approach, 76–77
Self-fashioning in digital age, 113–115
Self-reflexivity, 93
Self–tracking, 33–35
"Sensorium", 91
Sensory ethnography, 89–90
Sensory perception, 91–92
Sexual health programmes, 140
'Show-and-tell' approach, 33
'Silosociality', 114
Single videos, 80
Situatedness, 92
Sleepy tourist, 70
Smart cities, 8, 125, 131
　data impacts, 131–134
　data republics, 129–131
　data resources, 126–129
　technologies, 129
Smart maps, 129
Smart reputation, 131–134
Smart technologies, 129
Smart tourism, 125
Smart urban experiences, 129–131
'Smart' place-making, 126–129
Snapchat, 31
Social media, 56, 64, 132
　African Australian youth on, 30–33
　platforms, 40–41, 116
　research, 60
　websites, 115–116
Social networking sites, 114
Social networking websites, 106
Social practices, 147–148
Social proprioception, 100–101
Social science methods, 21
Social space, 90

'Sort-of' friendship, 31–32
Specificity, 92
Spotify, 73–74
Stakeholders, 127
Storying
　approach, 117
　data, 106–107
Success measures, 143
'Surplus' screenshots, 41

Tactile digital ethnography, 90
Technologies, 89
　researchers, 2–3
Temporality, 106–109
Thematic coding, 65
Theory of change, 142
Three-dimensional framework, 8
TikTok, 3–4, 40, 43–44, 60, 116
TMI, 2–3
Touch
　experience of, 91
　figures of, 90
　senses of, 89
Tourism, 80
　destinations on YouTube, 78–83
　development, 129
Touristic content, 70–71
Travel vloggers, 76
Travel vlogs, 73–75
Tumblr
　culture, 109, 117
　demonstrates, 115
　facilitation of pseudonymity, 114
　meant creative expression, 108
TV series, 71–72
Twitter, 5, 18, 48, 108, 117, 132

Unanticipated excess
　African Australian youth on social media, 30–33
　anticipating excess, 27
　contextualising our excess, 26–27
　traces of self in digital tracking practices, 33–35
　young women's relations with 'fitspo' on Instagram, 27–30

Uncertainty, 29, 64–65
Unpublished data, 16–17
Urban areas, 70–71
Urban locations, 76–77

Victoria and Albert East, 132
Victoria and Albert Museum (VAM), 128
Video calling, 40
Video clusters, 80
Video footage, 18
Videomaking, 76
Vignettes, 26, 99–101
Virtual ethnography, 65
Visibility, 5–8
Vlog, 80
  portraying tourist places, 70–71
Vloggers, 72

Waste, 5–8
Wellness discourses in crisis, 48–49

WhatsApp, 40
Work on Zoom, 40
World Health Organization (WHO), 47
Writing, 5, 58, 65–66, 113

Yelp, 18
Your Feelings Welcome project, 133
YouTube, 4, 70–74, 77–79, 150–151
  algorithmic mediation on, 71–73
  classifying tourism destinations on, 78–83
  locating place images on, 76–78
  techno-social recommender system, 80–83

Zoom
  drinks, 40
  work on, 40

Printed and bound by CPI Group (UK) Ltd, Croydon, CR0 4YY
18/12/2024

14614139-0003